Rethinking Chronic Absenteeism

Rethinking Chronic Absenteeism

Why Schools Can't Solve It Alone

SARAH WINCHELL LENHOFF
JEREMY SINGER

HARVARD EDUCATION PRESS
CAMBRIDGE, MASSACHUSETTS

Paperback ISBN 9781682539613

Library of Congress Cataloging-in-Publication Data

Names: Lenhoff, Sarah Winchell, author. | Singer, Jeremy (Professor), author.
Title: Rethinking chronic absenteeism : why schools can't solve it alone /
Sarah Winchell Lenhoff, Jeremy Singer.
Description: Cambridge, Massachusetts : Harvard Education Press, [2025] |
Includes bibliographical references and index.
Identifiers: LCCN 2024052964 | ISBN 9781682539613 (paperback)
Subjects: LCSH: School attendance—United States. | Education—Social aspects—United States.
Classification: LCC LB3081 .L46 2025 | DDC 371.2/940973—dc23/eng/20250108
LC record available at https://lccn.loc.gov/2024052964

Published by Harvard Education Press,
an imprint of the Harvard Education Publishing Group

Harvard Education Press
8 Story Street
Cambridge, MA 02138

Cover Design: Patrick Ciano
Cover Image: Imgorthand via iStock

The typefaces in this book are Adobe Garamond Pro and Myriad Pro.

To Frances and Hazel, who wish pizza parties were enough. To Greg, for writing, "Believe!!!" And to Detroit's families, for never giving up on what our children deserve.

—Sarah

To my parents, Marcie and David; my sisters, Cara and Julie; and my wife, Jenn, for a lifetime of love and support. And to Detroit's educators, for your hard work and commitment to our students.

—Jeremy

Contents

Introduction

It's fall 2018, and Aretha Johnson's first task when she gets to her job as an attendance agent at a Detroit elementary school is to run her data.[1] She looks for how many students were absent the day before, the percentage of students who have missed 10 percent of school days so far, and which students she needs to contact. On many days, this process takes several hours, as she works across different data-tracking systems, requests permission from her principal to access certain data, and looks up the contact logs for students on her caseload, which will number more than five hundred students by the end of the year. As Aretha shared with us, "I was looking at data. I was looking at a lot of data. Not really understanding. This equals this, this person has this many absences, and so this is why they're qualified in this. That's why they're labeled as this. That's not helping me get to know the student, the parent, the situation, or figure out what that parent needs, what words they need to hear, what message needs to be brought to them."

Aretha was not alone. At the end of the 2017–18 school year, 70 percent of the Detroit public school district's students were chronically absent. Nearly forty thousand students were missing at least 10 percent of the school year, or about eighteen days, and many were missing far more. School attendance in Detroit had been poor for many years, with more than half of students considered chronically absent and average daily attendance hovering around 85 percent since the early 2010s.[2] But attendance now had even bigger stakes, as the state had recently incorporated chronic absenteeism into its school accountability system.

The district decided to try something new. They hired an attendance agent and organized attendance teams in each of the one hundred K–12 schools in the district. They worked closely with a community-based coalition [the Coalition] to adopt a set of strategies that the agents would implement. And they committed to the idea that, by addressing chronic absence like other school improvement issues (analyzing data, grouping students, incentivizing behavior), they could reduce their chronic absence rate and get many more students back in school. By the end of that first year of implementation, the district saw a meaningful decrease in chronic absenteeism, from 70 percent in 2017–18 to 62 percent in 2018–19. Yet attendance agents were still struggling with the mismatch between school improvement strategies and the reality of chronic absenteeism in Detroit. As Aretha shared in April 2019,

> I just proactively got a phone call today about two students whose mom called me because the water's off. She's living in between places, so I asked her if she felt comfortable enrolling her kids on the east side, where she happens to be staying right now. She said, "Yeah, I don't know how long I'll be here." That kind of situation, it's not healthy for our numbers, but these are people, and their experience, and their life. It's my job to not give her a hard time, to be there for whatever needs she has. I recommended, perhaps, seeing if there's a shelter, and she wasn't very receptive. She's like, "In Detroit? I don't think so." But I'm still going to look, I'm still going to ask around and see if there's space for a single mom and her five kids because kids need to be in school. She needs to have a stable place for the kids, and she needs one for herself. As much as I can do, that's: enrolling families into the McKinney-Vento Program, which is a homeless program, picking up bus tickets for them, alerting the department that transportation is needed, trying to find them clothes . . . school supplies, any other services that might [help the family with] regular school attendance.

Aretha, with the support of coaches hired by the Coalition and an emerging district infrastructure to address absenteeism, was going to great lengths to learn what students and their families needed, and her efforts contributed to a decline in chronic absenteeism in her school from around 90 percent in 2017–18 to 70 percent in 2019–20. But by then Aretha was already burning out, coming up against the limits of what she or her school could do. And although 70 percent was a dramatic improvement, it still represented one of the highest rates of chronic absence in the country. How were Aretha and her fellow attendance agents meant to approach the problem going forward? What could they and their schools do?

OUR PURPOSE

This book is about the role of schools in solving chronic absenteeism, a problem that, although measured in schools, is not only or even mostly an educational issue. Chronic absenteeism is a problem *for* schools that gets in the way of improving teaching and learning, mutes progress in academic growth and graduation rates, and creates instability in the relationships between students and educators. Yet it is not a problem *of* schools, or at least not only of schools. Chronic absenteeism has both educational and noneducational causes (e.g., poor school climate; housing instability) and consequences (e.g., dropout; mental health) and is best understood as a symptom of a larger set of factors affecting the child, family, or neighborhood rather than an accountability metric for educators, schools, or districts.

Despite the significant complexity in the causes and consequences of absenteeism, schools have been tasked with solving the problem of chronic absenteeism largely on their own. This assignment of responsibility has consequences for whether and how the problem is addressed. As we will document, schools are organized to solve problems in common ways—with certain dispositions, assumptions, tools, and measures. These approaches are often well suited to address instructional or classroom management issues that are within the direct influence of schools and educators. Therefore, it made sense that, given what education and community leaders understood in the mid-2010s, they would adopt these approaches to address chronic absenteeism. Our research on how school leaders, educators, and community members designed and implemented plans to reduce chronic absenteeism over the last decade shows the inadequacy of these methods in the face of extreme social inequality.

The setting for this book is Detroit, a city with a rich cultural and industrial history that has been devastated by racism, deindustrialization, and political upheaval. As documented by historian Thomas Sugrue, while Detroit flourished as a center of industrial progress in the early twentieth century, the city fell into a state of "urban crisis" in the late twentieth century. White residents fled to resist the racial integration of their schools and neighborhoods, and automakers and related industries moved jobs and capital investment out of the city.[3] Detroit's economic and population decline persisted well into the 2010s, exacerbated by the 2008 recession and to an extent culminating with the city's municipal bankruptcy in 2013.[4] The Detroit public school system endured hardships throughout this time as well, with enrollment declines, multiple waves of school closures, and a financial crisis that nearly resulted in bankruptcy due to years of mismanagement under state takeover.[5] State policy changes in the 1990s also contributed to the creation of a "wild west" of school choice, resulting in a system in which 40 percent of Detroit students now attend the Detroit Public Schools Community District, a quarter attend around eighty different charter schools in the city, and another quarter attend school outside Detroit.[6] Detroiters have demonstrated their resilience and commitment to the city time and time again, despite the decades of divestment and discrimination they have experienced.

In some ways, Detroit has a uniquely challenging context for school attendance. A combination of traditional public school closures and the rapid growth of charter schools has meant that most students have to travel farther to school, public transportation infrastructure is weak, and the poverty rate is among the highest in the nation. Not to mention it's one of the coldest major US cities. Getting to school is tougher in Detroit than in many other places.[7]

In other ways, though, Detroit reflects—perhaps in more vivid detail—the challenging conditions for school attendance that many students face nationwide. Over the last three decades, school has been increasingly difficult to access. Families have seen an explosion of school choice options without an expansion of school bus offerings.[8] They have also seen persistent economic segregation and concentrated poverty in schools, especially in districts with similar histories of racial inequality and postindustrial decline.[9]

During the COVID-19 pandemic, chronic absenteeism rose dramatically, from 15 percent in 2018–19 to 28 percent in the 2021–22 school year.[10] Across the country, policy makers introduced new laws to crack down on absenteeism, sometimes punishing parents with jail time.[11] And educators nationwide threw everything at the wall to see what stuck—parties and prizes to make school more enticing, contracts with private companies to visit absent students' homes, and new policies to hold students and parents accountable for missing days.[12]

Yet Detroit educators, policy makers, and community members have been wrestling with this issue for far longer than most school districts. Since 2012, they have tried citywide messaging campaigns and community pledges; phone calls, home visits, and parent contracts; church buses and afterschool programming; data-driven tiered support systems; and court-run diversion programs. Some of these efforts paid off in success stories for individual students, schools, and programs, and while the rest of the country was still reeling with postpandemic absenteeism highs, Detroit got more or less back to normal in 2022–23. Yet systemwide, chronic absenteeism persisted and was still among the highest in the nation at 66 percent.[13]

This isn't a silver-bullet story. Instead, it's a story, documented in dozens of research studies, meetings, conversations, and observations, about how schools came to be held responsible for a problem largely outside their traditional purview and how that responsibility inevitably manifested in practices and policies that did not work at the scale and magnitude required to ensure most students in Detroit could get to school regularly. This book will show how, despite significant effort, dedication, and resources, schools were not designed to solve a problem like chronic absenteeism. Educational solutions are executed within schools and within school improvement frameworks that are ill-equipped to manage the complexity and extreme variation in the circumstances that lead students to be absent. By applying educational solutions to the problem of absenteeism, schools can further push families from school, reinforcing the social inequality that makes accessing school so hard for many families.

This is also a story of intense, deliberate, often uncomfortable learning—learning among committed, hardworking community members and educators who bravely took on a problem no one knew how to solve. In doing so, they got firsthand experience on what sorts of strategies and ideas about chronic absenteeism might be helpful, and they learned just as much about what did not work. Often, their disappointments were the most fruitful sources of new ideas and advice for others set to embark on this challenging work. We have learned alongside them through an intentional, community-engaged research partnership characterized by a continuous improvement orientation. Our goal is to share what we have learned in the hope that educators, community leaders, and policy makers within and beyond Detroit can come to understand what we have: chronic absenteeism is more than just an educational problem, and it needs more than just an educational solution to solve it.

HOW "CHRONIC ABSENTEEISM" BECAME A THING

How and why have schools become responsible for chronic absenteeism, and what does it mean to treat attendance as an educational issue? The answer lies in the long history of education and inequality in the United States, as well as the more recent history of education reform. Schools are our most ubiquitous and well-established social institutions. They're found in every community, and almost every school-age American attends them. As a result, we turn to schools as a solution to many of our social problems.[14] This is especially true for issues of racial and socioeconomic inequality. For decades, reformers in the United States have elevated schools as a solution to inequality—a mix of our meritocratic ideals and resistance to other forms of social welfare and public service provision.[15]

In the modern education reform era, accountability policies have formalized the notion that schools are responsible for overcoming inequality. Prior periods of education reform emphasized universal access to education, with a focus on establishing consistency in the form of education (e.g., age-graded classes, core subjects, teacher credentials) and providing adequate and equitable inputs (e.g., funding, teachers, materials, facilities). From the 1980s to the present, however, reformers have placed a greater emphasis on student outcomes, including new standards for student learning, centralized efforts to monitor and improve instruction, and test-based accountability to measure student outcomes.[16] The underlying logic is that poor school performance is the result of poor teaching and school organization rather than pervasive social and economic inequalities, and thus a combination of accountability pressure and effective management will spur innovation and improvement among teachers and school and district leaders.[17]

That modern emphasis on educational accountability and improvement is at the heart of the way educators and policy makers think about attendance today, and the way they are trying to improve it. Attendance issues date back to the early days of public schools in the United States, when districts first employed truancy officers to enforce compulsory school attendance laws. Now, however, the emphasis is on "chronic absenteeism" rather than truancy, and that represents more than just a change in language. We expect schools to develop the expertise and capabilities necessary to improve attendance, and we hold them accountable for doing so. The evolution of attendance policies and practices in the United

States provides important context for the rest of our book—and our argument that schools alone cannot solve the problem of absenteeism.

Compulsory School Attendance and Truancy Officers

The first initiatives to promote school attendance in the United States were part of the creation and expansion of public education more broadly. Massachusetts—the birthplace of American public education—passed the first state compulsory school attendance law in 1852. More states adopted compulsory attendance laws throughout the late nineteenth century, with all states requiring school attendance by 1918. The specifics varied, but generally the laws defined truancy based on a certain number of "unexcused" absences and called for criminal punishments of truant children or their parents.[18]

The prosecution of truancy stemmed from both educational and public safety concerns. States viewed compulsory school attendance as a vehicle for expanding participation in public schools.[19] Indeed, these laws played a role in advancing universal public schooling in the United States by increasing school attendance as well as decreasing gaps in attendance by class, race, and immigrant status.[20] However, truancy was also viewed as a safety issue, and prosecuting it was a way to deal with potentially delinquent youth. Even before children were required to attend school, cities like Boston and New York used "reform schools" or "truant homes" as early forms of juvenile detention. This was a form of punishment and rehabilitation for children who committed crimes, but also in many cases for those who were neither participating in school nor working as child laborers.[21] The introduction of compulsory school attendance laws thus married the imperative of universal education with the punitive means of the legal system.

Compulsory school attendance laws were adjudicated by courts but implemented by truancy officers. The role initially mimicked that of a police officer: they sought out students who were absent from school or followed up on referrals from teachers, and they relied on intimidation and ultimately punishment under the law to get students to school. As historians David Tyack and Michael Berkowitz write, "Communities thought of truant officers primarily as quasi-police who dealt with quasi-delinquents."[22] In the early to mid-twentieth century, as districts developed into more sophisticated educational bureaucracies, they institutionalized and professionalized the role of the truancy officer. Districts created "pupil accounting" departments with systematic attendance data tracking, supervisors and training for truancy officers, and a more complex set of rules and processes for issuing truancy charges.[23] With this new professionalization came some reimagining of the truancy officer's role. As Tyack and Berkowitz write, truancy officers "sought to escape the decrepit policeman image by comparing their work with that of ministers, social workers, salesmen, school administrators, psychologists, and a number of other groups."[24]

Truancy officers remain active across the country, and state compulsory attendance laws are still in place, now covering both primary and secondary school. These laws involve sanctions for students and their parents or guardians—from monetary fines and suspended social services to court referrals and possibly even jail time—though some states have reduced the severity of truancy-related punishments in recent years.[25] In fact, stricter truancy policies are associated with increased absenteeism.[26] In addition, low-income and racially minoritized students are more likely to be identified and prosecuted for truancy, not only because they are more likely to be absent but also because their absences are more likely to be marked as "unexcused" and their schools are more likely to take more punitive approaches.[27]

In sum, the history of truancy laws and truancy officers tracks with the development of universal public education.[28] Districts appointed truancy officers to implement state compulsory attendance laws in a fledgling American education system, with the goal of establishing universal access to and participation in education. As school systems expanded their administrative capacities, they professionalized and formalized the truancy officer role. Although students and their families are still penalized and (in some cases) prosecuted under existing truancy laws across the country, in the past decade or so, educators and policy makers have adopted a new lens on attendance issues, rooted in a new way of defining and understanding them: chronic absenteeism.

The Shift from Truancy to Chronic Absenteeism

The term *chronic absenteeism*, which has become synonymous with the issue of school attendance in the United States, is defined and measured differently from truancy. Generally, students are considered chronically absent when they miss 10 percent or more of school days (e.g., 18 days in a 180-day school year), and this includes all absences, whether they are "excused" or "unexcused" by schools.[29] In contrast, truancy is determined based on unexcused absences only (and the specific number of absences varies among states). These differences between chronic absenteeism and truancy go beyond semantics and statistics; they reflect two entirely different ways of thinking about the issue of school attendance. Truancy is based on unexcused absences only, in part because the original purpose of truancy laws was to increase participation in public education.

Chronic absenteeism, however, includes both unexcused and excused absences because the underlying concern is about more than participation: it is about the educational consequences of missing school. The term *chronic absenteeism* was first adopted in educational research in the mid-2000s, with a compelling set of findings on the breadth and consequences of chronic absenteeism. By accounting for both excused and unexcused absences, researchers showed that far more students are chronically absent than educators and policy makers had realized. In addition, they showed that chronic absenteeism is associated with lower test scores, weaker social skills, and increased likelihood of dropout.[30] This research sent a clear message: attendance is a key factor in student development and educational success, and it is a problem for more students than schools and districts tend to recognize. This way of looking at attendance contrasts with the truancy approach, which is more focused on enforcing the legal requirement for school participation.

Indeed, as early research on chronic absenteeism gained traction in the late 2000s and early 2010s, educators and policy makers around the country started to use the term and pay attention to chronic absence rates in their own contexts. Advocacy organizations such as Attendance Works encouraged districts to track chronic absenteeism and develop new practices to improve attendance, and some early adopting districts garnered attention for initiatives that helped improve attendance. States also had systematic attendance data in the longitudinal education databases they developed as part of the No Child Left Behind Act (NCLB), and some began to use those data to analyze state and district chronic absenteeism rates.[31] Researchers also used these large-scale and longitudinal state data to produce even more evidence on the negative consequences of absenteeism for student achievement.[32]

In the mid-2010s, the federal government bolstered the profile of chronic absenteeism in education policy. First, Congress allowed chronic absenteeism to be used as a component of state education accountability systems under the Every Student Succeeds Act (ESSA). One criticism of NCLB, which preceded ESSA, was that it did not call for nonacademic measures of school quality in state accountability systems. Under ESSA, lawmakers required states to include at least one nonacademic indicator of school quality or student success in their accountability systems. Even before the end of NCLB, a handful of states had added chronic absenteeism into their accountability systems. This requirement for a nonacademic measure under ESSA, however, provided a new opportunity for advocacy organizations calling for formal efforts to track and respond to chronic absenteeism. ESSA was signed into law in 2015, and states were required to submit their plans (including the accountability measures they would use) to the federal government in 2017.[33]

In that time, the federal government gave chronic absenteeism another boost, through the release of national chronic absenteeism data. The Office of Civil Rights (OCR) conducts the Civil Rights Data Collection on a biennial basis, requiring all public school districts that receive federal funds to report information on topics such as discipline and access to advanced coursework. In the 2013–14 wave, OCR included chronic absenteeism.[34] In June 2016, shortly after Congress passed ESSA, the Department of Education released the results of the 2013–14 OCR data collection, including a report and interactive data map highlighting chronic absenteeism rates across the country. The report showed that over seven million students—about one out of every six public school students—were chronically absent.[35] These nationwide data helped place chronic absenteeism firmly into the education reform zeitgeist and strengthened the case that states should use chronic absenteeism as a nonacademic indicator in their educational accountability systems.[36]

As states implemented their new accountability systems under ESSA, they cemented chronic absenteeism's place in American education. Most states used chronic absenteeism as a nonacademic measure, meaning that tens of thousands of schools would now be formally accountable for student attendance.[37] This points to yet another important contrast between chronic absenteeism and truancy. Under truancy laws, children and parents are held responsible for attendance; with chronic absenteeism in accountability systems, however, schools are held responsible. Thus, the emergence of "chronic absenteeism" as a concept represents a new way of thinking about student attendance, and a new requirement for schools to address it.

THE NEED TO RETHINK CHRONIC ABSENTEEISM

The shift from truancy to chronic absenteeism has been helpful for reframing attendance *problems*, but it has also narrowed the way we think about attendance *solutions*. Policy makers and educators understand that absenteeism is not just an issue of educational participation. Instead, there is now broad recognition of the importance of attendance for student well-being, academic achievement, and school quality. Holding schools accountable for attendance, however, means that we expect schools to solve the problem of absenteeism through organizational effectiveness and innovative practices. In other words, we have prescribed an educational solution, even though absenteeism is much more than an educational problem.

The fact is that chronic absenteeism is the product of social and economic inequality, and it must be seen as and dealt with as a societal problem rather than only an educational problem. By expecting schools to solve the problem of chronic absenteeism alone, we make it harder for them to accomplish their primary goals of supporting student learning, cognitive and emotional development, and civic consciousness. If schools devote an increasing share of their time, resources, and staff to attendance in the absence of policies that substantively address social inequality, they risk straining their organizational coherence and weakening school-family relationships, in essence pushing them further away from an even better version of what they could be.[38] Further, if attendance issues are only dealt with by educational tools and strategies, then the root inequalities that drive high absenteeism rates will not be reduced. In fact, if policy makers continue to apply accountability pressure and impose sanctions on schools with high absenteeism rates, schools may even end up making these underlying social problems worse—for example, through the widespread use of punitive measures.[39] Schools will be central to any effort to improve attendance, but as we show in this book, they can't do it alone.

OVERVIEW OF THE BOOK

In *Rethinking Chronic Absenteeism*, we argue that the problem of chronic absenteeism cannot be addressed until we fundamentally reconceptualize it and, in turn, adjust our policies and interventions to reflect this new understanding. We develop this argument across the following six chapters by discussing the "ecological" nature of chronic absenteeism and the many factors that contribute to whether and how students get to school (chapter 1); illustrating how current conceptualizations of the problem and the tools available within schools structure current interventions (chapters 2–3); demonstrating the limits of these efforts in Detroit (chapter 4); and developing an alternative view of the problem (chapters 5–6).

This book is largely based on the community-engaged research we conducted from 2016 to 2023 as part of a research-practice partnership with Detroit school systems and a coalition of community-based organizations working to reduce absenteeism in Detroit. Supported by grants from the Skillman Foundation, Spencer Foundation, and Midwest Mobility from Poverty Network, this partnership was established to inform evidence-based improvements in district and community efforts around attendance and grew into what is now a college center at Wayne State University called the Detroit Partnership for Education Equity & Research.

Our research included four formal developmental evaluations of district and community efforts designed to improve attendance, including an afterschool program led by a community-based organization, a new attendance strategy and attendance agent role in the Detroit Public Schools Community District, a principals' learning community, and a networked improvement community. We also conducted three related studies with Detroit parents and students focused on barriers to attendance, experiences with attendance during the pandemic, and housing instability and attendance. Together with our research teams, we conducted 177 interviews with community leaders and district staff, 113 interviews with parents and students, and 198 hours of observation of professional learning and meetings across these projects. We also analyzed student-level attendance data from the State of Michigan's Center for Educational Performance and Information and about 150 traditional public and charter schools operating in the city of Detroit. Finally, we administered two surveys of Detroit parents and two surveys of Detroit Public Schools Community District staff working on attendance, along with two additional staff surveys in case study schools. Details on the methods and data used can be found in the appendix.

Chapter 1 centers on the experiences of parents, woven throughout an evidence-rich portrayal of the barriers that families face in getting their children to school. Using neighborhood, school, and student data, we show how the challenging conditions for school attendance in Detroit collide with the logics of school reform. While Detroit is a uniquely challenging context, our analysis demonstrates how its characteristics of white flight, deindustrialization, broad poverty, and political upheaval echo throughout many US cities and rural communities.

In chapter 2, we explain how local and national players influenced plans to improve attendance in Detroit, and we follow community leaders as they come to understand the consequences of chronic absenteeism and the limits of schools in solving it. Chapter 3 describes the central component of school and community plans to address chronic absence—a multitiered system of support implemented by attendance agents and school-based teams. Then, in chapter 4, we trace how the district and community organizations implemented their plans and how their efforts were undermined by the highly unequal context they faced. We focus here on attendance agents like Aretha and their experiences as school staff dedicated to combatting absenteeism. We finally describe how, in the wake of the COVID-19 pandemic, the district and the Coalition began to imagine alternative ways to improve student attendance and highlight the challenges of a more holistic approach (chapter 5).

In chapter 6, we return to our core argument: policy makers and practitioners have misdiagnosed chronic absenteeism as an educational problem and have struggled to address it using the tools available to schools. We provide recommendations for how policy makers and practitioners can take a fundamentally different approach to school reform, including engaging in advocacy for reducing social inequality, aligning school-based tools with the limited scope of attendance barriers within their control, and partnering with community agencies to remove other barriers to attendance.

CHAPTER 1

Chronic Absenteeism as an "Ecological" Problem in Detroit

Gladys is a Detroit mom of four boys, all of whom attended the Detroit Public Schools Community District (DPSCD) in 2019–20. In February of that year, they had missed twelve days of school, or about 15 percent of the school year so far. At first, the reasons why her kids missed school might seem straightforward. First, there were a few days when they stayed home sick: "They had a virus. . . . If one gets sick, all of them get sick." Second, Gladys worked seven nights a week on a manufacturing line for an auto parts plant, from ten at night until six in the morning, and her children sometimes missed school if she was too tired to drive them: "Sometimes I will be so drained. . . . But when I come in after working ten or twelve hours for seven days . . . I'm tired and my eyes is burning, do you want to get in that car with me if my eyes is burning? That's kind of risky." These were the only two reasons Gladys's children missed school: "If I'm not tired or they're not sick, they don't miss school."

The immediate reason why Gladys's children were chronically absent was her work schedule. Digging a bit deeper into Gladys's experiences, however, reveals a more complex story. Her current situation was related to a recent history of housing instability and financial precarity. Gladys originally lived across the street from her children's school, which is why she chose to enroll them there. During the 2018–19 school year, however, she fell on hard times and could not afford the apartment. For most of that year, she and her children lived in a hotel several miles away, and later they moved in with one of her cousins. Her children were absent even more often during this period. She could only afford to move them into their own apartment—one located fifteen minutes away from the school by car—after getting the manufacturing job. Gladys also did not have family or friends who could help with transportation to and from school: "It's just me. . . . I don't have no help. I pick them up, I take them to school. . . . I wish I had somebody to take them to school when I get off work."

While Gladys's specific circumstances are unique, the types of barriers to attendance that her children faced are typical for families in Detroit. Many families deal with financial precarity, housing instability, transportation challenges, and lack of backup options for getting to and from school, among other issues. These are the reasons why Detroit has among the highest levels of chronic absenteeism in the country. In the 2015–16 school year, the US Department of Education released national data on attendance. At that time, about 48 percent of all Detroit students were chronically absent; in the Detroit public school system, the chronic absenteeism rate was even higher.[1] No other major city had a chronic absenteeism rate above 40 percent (table 1.1).[2] In the city's public school system specifically, more than half of students have been chronically absent each school year for the past decade.[3]

In this chapter, we elaborate on why so many children in Detroit are chronically absent from school, drawing on quantitative analyses and interviews with parents and students conducted during the 2018–19 and 2019–20 school years. In many places, we discuss the issue citywide (i.e., for students in DPSCD and Detroit charter schools). We start by describing how high levels of social and economic inequality create a uniquely challenging context for attendance. Then we discuss the many factors associated with chronic absenteeism in Detroit, such as student health and well-being, family socioeconomic circumstances, school characteristics, and neighborhood conditions. We end by framing attendance as an "ecological" issue resulting from a complex set of overlapping factors. Throughout the chapter, we present additional examples from the DPSCD families we interviewed, which show how these broad inequalities and specific circumstances create barriers to regular attendance for children throughout the city. Attendance may be a problem for schools, but the reasons for absenteeism extend far beyond the school walls.

DETROIT'S UNIQUELY CHALLENGING CONTEXT FOR ATTENDANCE

Why does Detroit have such a high rate of chronic absenteeism? And why is it so much higher than those of other major US cities? Later in this chapter, we will

TABLE 1.1 Chronic absenteeism rates in major US cities, 2015–16

City	*Population*	*Chronic absenteeism rate (%)*
Detroit	**672,795**	**47.8**
Milwaukee	595,047	38.2
Philadelphia	1,567,872	31.8
Washington	681,170	30.8
Baltimore	614,664	29.5
Columbus	860,090	28.8
Louisville	616,261	27.2
Tucson	530,706	26.4
Denver	693,060	25.9
Chicago	2,704,958	24.5
Portland	639,863	23.1
Albuquerque	559,277	21.8
Seattle	704,352	21.2
Las Vegas	632,912	20.5
Jacksonville	880,619	20.5
Nashville	660,388	19.2
New York	8,537,673	18.5
Phoenix	1,615,017	18.5
Boston	673,184	17.3
Oklahoma City	638,367	15.8
Fort Worth	854,113	15.6
Indianapolis	855,164	15.0
Los Angeles	3,976,322	14.4
San Antonio	1,492,510	12.9
San Diego	1,406,630	12.4
Houston	2,303,482	11.6

Continued

TABLE 1.1 *continued*

City	*Population*	*Chronic absenteeism rate (%)*
El Paso	683,080	11.2
San Jose	1,025,350	11.1
Austin	947,890	10.9
Dallas	1,317,929	10.8
Charlotte	842,051	10.2
Fresno	522,053	7.5
San Francisco	870,887	6.2

Source: United States Department of Education Civil Rights Data Collection.

discuss specific student, family, school, and neighborhood factors that explain why some Detroit students miss more school than others. But if we only focus on individual students, we might miss the forest for the trees. So, as part of our research, we compared Detroit with other major cities. This helped us see the impact of the broader socioeconomic context on student attendance.

We started with national attendance data from the US Department of Education (shown in table 1.1). Then we collected publicly available data on a variety of structural and environmental factors that could be theoretically related to chronic absenteeism: from population change to segregation to health, housing, safety, poverty, employment, and even weather patterns. We identified eight citywide statistics that were correlated with citywide chronic absenteeism rates, and on every one of these measures, Detroit ranked among cities with the most challenging conditions for student attendance (table 1.2).[4] Detroit had the highest asthma rate (14 percent), unemployment rate (about 20 percent), poverty rate (about 38 percent), violent crime rate (about twenty per one thousand people), residential vacancy rate (27 percent), and the third-lowest average monthly temperature (about 49°F). In addition, the city had the greatest population loss since 1970 (about 52 percent decline) and had the second most segregated metropolitan area. These macro-level challenges provide important context for understanding why so many students are chronically absent in Detroit. Students and their families face more adverse conditions citywide in Detroit than in any other major US city.

TABLE 1.2 Ranking of major US cities on structural issues associated with chronic absenteeism

Percentage of adults with asthma (%)	
1. Detroit	**14.0**
2. Baltimore	12.3
3. Louisville	12.3
4. Philadelphia	11.6
5. Boston	11.4

Violent crime per 1,000 people	
1. Detroit	**19.9**
2. Milwaukee	14.9
3. Baltimore	13.4
4. Indianapolis	12.6
5. Washington, DC	11.9

Unemployment rate (%)	
1. Detroit	**19.8**
2. Philadelphia	11.3
3. Fresno	11.1
4. Baltimore	10.0
5. Chicago	9.9

Poverty rate (%)	
1. Detroit	**37.9**
2. Fresno	28.4
3. Milwaukee	27.4
4. Philadelphia	25.8
5. Tucson	24.1

Continued

TABLE 1.2 *continued*

Racial segregation index for greater metro area	
1. Milwaukee	69.4
2. Detroit	**68.4**
3. New York	63.7
4. Chicago	62.6
5. Philadelphia	61.6

Average monthly temperature (°F)	
1. Denver	46.5
2. Milwaukee	46.7
3. Detroit	**49.0**
4. Chicago	49.6
5. Boston	50.4

Residential vacancy rate (%)	
1. Detroit	**27.0**
2. Baltimore	18.0
3. Chicago	14.0
4. Houston	13.0
5. Indianapolis	13.0

Population change (%), 1970–2010	
1. Detroit	**–52.9**
2. Baltimore	–31.5
3. Philadelphia	–21.7
4. Washington, DC	–20.5
5. Chicago	–19.9

Sources: Census Bureau's American Community Survey, Center for Disease Control and Prevention, FBI Uniform Crime Reporting Program, Population Studies Center at the Institute for Social Research, National Oceanic and Atmospheric Administration's Climate Divisional Database.

FIGURE 1.1 Structural and environmental challenges index and citywide chronic absenteeism, 2015–16

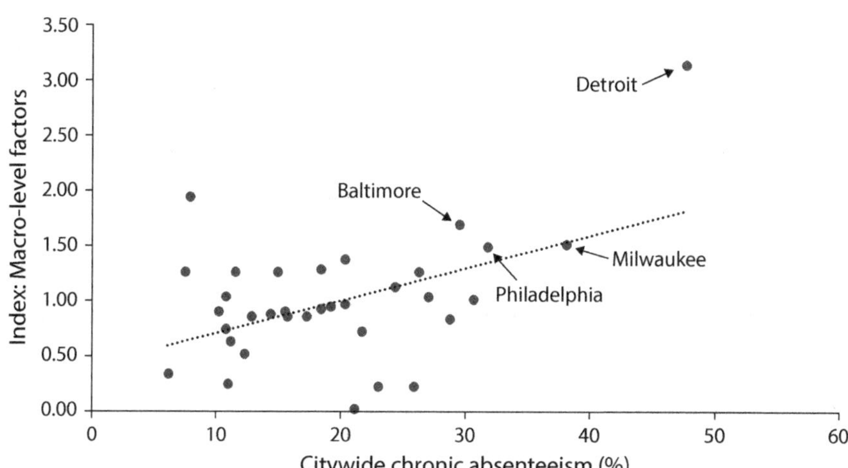

Recognizing the uniquely challenging context in Detroit, however, also reveals something more universal about chronic absenteeism. We combined all these different macro-level measures into one standardized "structural and environmental challenges" index and analyzed the correlation between the index and citywide chronic absenteeism rates.[5] Cities with higher overall scores on that index tended to have higher chronic absenteeism rates (figure 1.1). There are plenty of structural factors that we couldn't include due to a lack of data, such as differences in the education policy context or the quality and availability of public transportation. And these citywide statistics certainly do not fully account for the complex combination of individual, family, school, and neighborhood factors that we will discuss in the next section. But these findings provide clear evidence that, when it comes to attendance, the broader context matters. In districts with more challenging structural and environmental conditions—conditions that are the result of similar histories of racial inequality and postindustrial decline—families will have a harder time ensuring their children attend school every day.[6] And Detroit is among the most challenging contexts nationwide.

FACTORS ASSOCIATED WITH CHRONIC ABSENTEEISM IN DETROIT

Even with these challenging circumstances, the fact is that not every student in Detroit is chronically absent. And some students are only moderately chronically absent (missing 10–20 percent of days), while others are severely chronically absent (missing 20 percent or more of days). To identify the specific factors associated with chronic absenteeism in Detroit, we analyzed student attendance data and interviewed parents and students. We did so from an "ecological" perspective, paying attention not only to the characteristics of individual students but also to their families, schools, and neighborhoods. The barriers to attendance that we discuss here—socioeconomic inequalities, transportation issues, health and well-being, and school-based issues such as relationships and school climate—are not unique to Detroit. They may be especially difficult or widespread for Detroit, given the deep social and economic inequalities, but they are common drivers of chronic absenteeism in districts across the country.[7]

Family Socioeconomic Circumstances

Detroit students with more difficult socioeconomic circumstances are more likely to be chronically absent. Chronically absent students in Detroit have lower household incomes on average, their parents are less likely to be employed full-time, and they are more likely to experience homelessness or housing instability. Students who are severely chronically absent have household incomes far below the poverty line and much lower parental employment rates. For example, in one survey, we found that only 35 percent of severely chronically absent students had a parent or guardian who worked full-time, compared with 55 percent for moderately chronically absent students and 63 percent for not chronically absent students. In addition, households with severely chronically absent children had an average income of $18,500, compared with about $36,000 for households with children who were not chronically absent. These socioeconomic disadvantages are associated with persistent chronic absenteeism—in other words, they seem to explain why students who are chronically absent in one school year are very likely to be chronically absent again in the following school year.[8]

This relationship between socioeconomic status and chronic absenteeism is not much of a surprise: researchers and educators have been documenting this connection for over a century. For example, a 1917 study of truancy in Chicago found that 80 percent of truant students were from poor households, and most absences were related to illness, the need to assist with childcare, a lack of adequate clothing, or a duty to work to contribute to the household financially.[9] Records from truancy officers across the country at that time reinforced those findings.[10] The large body of research on attendance confirms that socioeconomically disadvantaged students are more likely to be chronically absent.[11]

What we found in Detroit, however, provides greater clarity about how these challenging socioeconomic circumstances translate into barriers to attendance for Detroit families. We did *not* find that disadvantaged parents were indifferent about their children's attendance. The parents we interviewed conveyed a strong commitment to their children's education and a concerted effort to support their attendance.[12] Rather, the socioeconomic barriers that parents described to us revealed challenging trade-offs between school attendance and other household needs.

Financial Constraints. For some parents with low incomes, financial constraints often led directly to students missing school. One example comes from Denise, a mother of four chronically absent children at a DPSCD elementary-middle school in the northern part of the city. Denise drives her children to school every day, but there are days when she can't afford to fill up her car with gas: "Sometimes if there's problems, like if there's no gas or whatever, then sometimes it's hard, sometimes like if I were in between jobs or anything like that, then yeah, it sometimes can be tough. . . . So sometimes, they'll have to stay home, because there's no gas." When she is short on cash, she tries her best to cover her expenses in other ways: "Like, sometimes the food stamps or something will get pretty low, [so we] will go to a church or something like that to get some food that way, I do have priority for gas and things like that to get the kids to school." Ultimately, however, there are some days when Denise simply cannot afford to bring them to school. As Denise's story suggests, many of these financial limitations ultimately limit families' transportation options, which we will discuss later in greater detail. Families in Detroit's neighborhood public schools face even greater financial constraints on average than families in Detroit charter schools, which helps explain why DPSCD's chronic absenteeism rate is even higher.[13]

Parental Employment and Work Schedules. In other cases, the demands of parents' jobs (which they depend on for household income) created barriers to attendance. Many parents in Detroit have inflexible schedules or work shifts that conflict with school drop-off and pickup times. Indeed, we found that among children whose parents are employed, those whose parents had more flexibility in their work schedules were less likely to be chronically absent.[14] If parents cannot arrange for someone else to pick them up or drop them off, they face a difficult choice: keep their children home from school or miss work and risk unemployment in order to bring them. Gladys's story at the beginning of the chapter provides one example of how work schedules can lead to attendance issues: she depended on her job to secure stable housing for her and her children, but this meant occasionally being unable to drive them to school.

Another example comes from Robin, whose daughter was in kindergarten at a DPSCD elementary school on the west side of Detroit. Robin used to work at a manufacturing plant: "I would go in the morning [around 4:00 a.m.] and get out 2:30." At that time, her schedule made it difficult to get her daughter to and from school: "So in the meantime I would depend on somebody else to help out, which I really don't want to. . . . The person that was helping was my mother. She's kind of old but she's been having back problems . . . then I have to leave work and try to get [my daughter]." Ultimately, Robin decided she could no longer keep her job and support her daughter's attendance, so she quit. When we spoke to her, she was still looking for work: "I pick up a job when I can get one. . . . It's easier to stay at the plant [financially], but the shift is like a twelve-hour shift. It's hard to work around that and her going to school. I gotta wait for something [else]." Gladys's and Robin's situations show how lower-income families may struggle with a trade-off between work and school attendance.

Limits to the Availability of Family, Friends, or Neighbors. A common thread through the examples we've presented so far is the role of social networks. Parents often turn to family members, friends, and neighbors to help them get their children to or from school, especially as a backup option if their usual routine is disrupted by financial constraints or scheduling issues. When parents cannot rely on their family, friends, or neighbors for help in these situations, their children may not be able to attend school.

We consistently found in our interviews that families with chronically absent children had more limited support from family, friends, and neighbors. In a few cases, parents described being truly socially isolated, with no family or friends to whom they could turn. In Gladys's story, for example, there were no family members or friends she could rely on. More often, however, the parents we spoke to had family and friends who were caring and supportive but who were simply not available to help with their children's attendance for one reason or another. For example, Robin's mother would help when she could, but her health issues made it hard for her to drop off or pick up her grandchildren.

Another example comes from Charlene, a mother of two children and guardian of two other children, all of whom attended a DPSCD elementary school on the east side and all of whom were chronically absent in the year we spoke. Charlene was in a difficult financial situation. While her family lived in a relatively affordable low-income housing unit, she was unable to work and received disability payments. Her adult daughter lived with her and usually contributed to the household finances, but she had recently been laid off. With the financial constraints Charlene faced, she could not afford a car. Her children usually took the bus to school, but according to Charlene, "it's been a couple of times that the bus didn't show up at all." On those days, Charlene had to pay her neighbor to take them to school. While her neighbor is "always there for [her]," there were times when she couldn't afford to cover the cost of gas for the trip, and so her children had to miss school.

By contrast, families whose children were not chronically absent often had other family members or friends whom they could turn to as backup options. For example, Lorna's daughter attended a DPSCD elementary school and was not chronically absent. Lorna did have some difficulty getting her daughter to and from school because she lives far away and does not have a car. "If I was staying closer, she would be walking there. . . . I don't have a car now. But I have people that look out for her. Aunties, friends, they look out for her education." In the morning, she takes an Uber to work and makes a stop to drop off her daughter at school. Then, in the afternoon, one of her family members or friends will usually pick her up: "Her auntie has a car, yeah . . . [and] one of my coworkers." There had been times when her daughter missed school due to a lack of transportation: "I just couldn't reach nobody, and I didn't have no money myself at the time to pay for a ride, and we just didn't go. . . . Maybe once a month, if that." But for the most part, she could rely on her family and friends to help her out. Whether or not families could draw on these social resources—family and friends who are regularly available and have a reliable mode of transportation—could often be the difference between missing school and not.

Housing Instability and Homelessness. In addition to persistent socioeconomic barriers such as poverty, work-related constraints, and limited social networks, acute socioeconomic issues also cause students to miss school. Housing instability and homelessness are examples of a shock that can lead to absenteeism.

We found that students who changed residences during the school year were 30–40 percent more likely to be chronically absent than students who did not move, even when controlling for other socioeconomic, school, and neighborhood factors.[15] In addition, we found that students who experienced homelessness or an eviction during the school year were more likely to be severely chronically absent.[16]

Our interviews with parents reinforced these findings: housing instability created major disruptions that led students to miss school. For example, Carmen is the mother of three children attending a DPSCD elementary-middle school on the east side. She and her children used to live a few blocks from the school but were displaced as the result of a house fire: "When we had the house fire, um, we basically were homeless." In this period, while Carmen tried to sort out their living situation, her children missed a good deal of school. When they finally landed in a new apartment farther away from the school, the district provided transportation services to support them: "They was still letting them come to [the same school]. . . . I was in this McKinney-Vento program where, no matter where you are at, the kids can get transportation. They was coming to pick them up from the door and dropping them off at the door."

Carmen and her children had secured new housing, but the transportation services then ended, and this additional disruption forced her into a difficult trade-off between work and her children's attendance. "After we had found us somewhere to stay, they said that we are no longer qualified for that program no more. . . . So it is my responsibility to get them back and forth to school." In order to drive her children to school, Carmen had to leave her full-time job and take more flexible gig work instead. While this new job helped her manage her children's attendance better, it meant that their family struggled more financially: "I want to get back to work. . . . I'm behind on my bills right now because I'm not working. This DoorDash, don't get me wrong, it keeps stuff steady, but I just need something [else] bad. . . . I wanna be home with my kids . . . so I can make dinner and make sure they're straight for the next day." Carmen's experience shows how unstable housing affects student attendance, directly through the disruptions that families experience and indirectly by exacerbating other barriers to attendance.

Student Mobility. *Student mobility* refers to students changing schools during the school year (or between school years before reaching the final grade level offered at their school). Though student mobility is not a direct measure of socioeconomic status, a large body of research shows that school switching during the year is often related to poverty and economic insecurity.[17] We found that for Detroit students in both traditional public and charter schools, those who switch schools during the year were three to four times more likely to be chronically absent than students who do not, even when controlling for residential mobility and other socioeconomic, school, and neighborhood factors.[18] Thus, student mobility is another acute disruption that both reflects and reinforces the socioeconomic barriers to attendance that students face.

Transportation Issues

Ultimately, attendance is about getting to school, and transportation issues are a major cause of chronic absenteeism in Detroit. In our survey data and interviews, we found that most Detroit families drive their children as their primary mode of transportation to and from school, partly due to the limited availability of public transportation and school buses. Yet Detroit also has a high level of transportation insecurity, and we came to understand "getting to school" as a much more complicated issue than whether families owned or regularly used a car. Problems with transportation can be organized into a few categories for most families: regular transportation was generally unreliable; when regular transportation or routines were disrupted, there were no reliable or affordable backups; or concerns about student safety with regular or backup transportation options caused them to miss school. Families in Detroit's neighborhood public schools were less likely to own a car on average than families in Detroit charter schools, which is another factor that helps explain why DPSCD's chronic absenteeism rate is even higher.[19]

Unreliable Regular Transportation. For families whose children were not chronically absent, most had regular ways to get their children to school that almost never failed. Most of these parents, for instance, discussed how they drove their children to school every day. For chronically absent students, however, transportation was frequently cited as a barrier to attendance, usually because there were problems with the regular way to get their children to school. For instance, some parents said that their personal car was unreliable or broke down frequently, that they sometimes did not have money for gas or car repairs, or that the bus was late or unsafe. These occasional transportation issues occurred in the context of other socioeconomic challenges. For example, Denise, whom we discussed earlier, had regular access to a car but sometimes had trouble paying for gas.

Another example comes from Tamara and her son Marcus, who attended a DPSCD high school on the east side. Marcus became chronically absent when the family's car broke down and needed repairs. While they saved money to fix the car, they turned to Tamara's mom (Marcus's grandmother) for help, but her own work schedule and financial limitations got in the way. In Marcus's words, "We ain't had no transportation, because her car was messed up. My grandma had to go to work every morning, so she couldn't take me. She couldn't just hurry up and take me to school. She got to leave out because she works . . . but I ain't go for a whole week, because I ain't had no car, and my grandma said she ain't want to keep on Uber-ing me, keep on sending me Lyfts and stuff. . . . She said it cost $40 just to come pick me up from my school." Marcus missed school frequently until Tamara was able to pay for car repairs.

In DPSCD, K–8 students were eligible to ride the yellow school bus if they attended their neighborhood assigned school and lived more than three-quarters of a mile away from that school. In high school, the district paid for bus passes to allow all students to ride Detroit's public bus system for free. Parents whose children used the bus to regularly get to school generally said it was reliable, but a few raised concerns about the bus getting in the way of regular school attendance. For instance, Rhonda, whose son attended a different high school on the east side, was grateful for the availability of a pass to ride the public buses but also felt constrained by problems with the bus and not having any other options: "The only barrier is those [city] buses not coming on time. . . . I do appreciate the fact that he is allowed to get a bus card for free to get to school every day. That helps me out a lot, because other than that I would literally have to borrow money from my aunt just to make sure he got to school." Unreliable transportation on the bus was the main reason her son missed school. Further, most students in K–8—both in DPSCD and in Detroit charter schools—are not eligible to ride the bus, due to the high rates of school choice and school bus eligibility criteria such as assigned-school attendance and distance from school. In addition, relatively few high school students ride the public buses.[20]

Unreliable Backup Transportation. Unexpected events can disrupt a family's regular routine for getting to school. Even when families had reliable ways to get their children to school, disruptions to their regular routine created new barriers to attendance. Many parents we spoke to regularly drove their children to school, but when their availability changed due to sudden illness or unexpected work commitments, they sometimes struggled to find backup transportation. As previously discussed, financial constraints and a lack of social support left many families with limited transportation options when their routines were disrupted and they had to find a backup to get their children to or from school.

Many families relied on themselves or a single other person to get their children to and from school. When they were sick, or had to work, or had an appointment, they did not have anyone else who could help them get their children to school. One illustrative example comes from Daisy, whose two daughters were not chronically absent. Daisy had a conflict between her work hours and her daughters' high school schedule. So to make sure her daughters got to school every day, she relied on a friend to take part in their daily routine: "My shift starts at 7:00. Up at 4:00, so I can make sure I get breakfast, take my medication, not forget anything, fix my lunch, whatever. Before I leave the house at 6:00, I'm waking my daughters up. They leave at about 7:30. So, since I no longer use the Lyft, I allow a friend of mine to take me to work, come back, grab the kids and take them to school. Then he picks me up at the end of the day and we drive over [to the high school] to get the girls." Daisy emphasized how precarious the arrangement was: "It's been working fine. But I mean, God forbid if something happens to [my friend], then I don't know [what we'll do]." Their arrangements highlight how student attendance can be vulnerable to a lack of backup options.

Concerns About Transportation Safety. Finally, safety concerns contributed to transportation issues. Some parents did not feel comfortable with their children riding public buses (as either a primary or backup mode of transportation) because they felt their children were too young to navigate the city bus system; and others did not feel that their children would be safe walking to or waiting at bus stops. For example, Daisy felt that she and her daughters didn't live "in an area where they would feel safe enough to catch the bus," which is why she did not consider it as a backup option. Similarly, Tamara worried about her son Marcus taking the bus to school because "he doesn't know how to ride the bus. . . . I don't want to put him on the bus because I don't want him to get lost and get on the wrong bus." Marcus had also previously had a violent encounter in their neighborhood, which made him uncomfortable walking or waiting for the bus. Indeed, we found that students living in neighborhoods with higher crime rates and more vacant homes were more likely to be chronically absent, even when accounting for socioeconomic circumstances and school factors.[21]

Even the weather could create safety concerns. Many of the families we spoke to said that bad weather—especially snow and cold temperatures—could get in the way of getting to school, especially if children had to walk to school or wait for a bus. For example, Rhonda's son would sometimes wait for an hour or more before the city bus would arrive. When the weather is bad, that can create a barrier: "It was four times [in the last month]. It's too cold for my son to keep standing out there, or I don't feel like he should be walking." Indeed, in an analysis of weather patterns and attendance, we found that heavy precipitation in the winter made students more likely to be chronically absent.[22]

Student Health

Health is an issue for all families, and getting sick is a reason that just about every student has missed school. All the families that we interviewed recalled instances where their children missed school due to a specific illness (e.g., a cold, the flu, or a virus) or symptoms (e.g., coughing, a fever, or a runny or stuffy nose). For chronically absent students, illnesses were not the only reason that they missed school, but they added a substantial number of days on top of other reasons that students were absent. (We discuss the impact of COVID-19 on attendance in chapter 5.) In addition, when students have chronic health issues (e.g., diabetes, severe asthma, or allergies) that are undertreated or very severe, they are the main driver of chronic absence. Health-related absences are exacerbated by issues with health-care access, such as limited access to transportation, unaffordability of medical care, or the need for frequent or recurring appointments or appointments that can only be scheduled during school hours.

Student Physical Health. Students can miss school due to both acute and chronic illness. The amount of school students missed because of these physical health issues was sometimes exacerbated by challenges accessing health care, especially due to scheduling conflicts and sometimes due to transportation issues. Discussing physical health issues, parents explained that they made decisions about keeping their children home from school based on clear visible signs of illness. They expressed a concern for their children's well-being and in some cases the health of other students at the school.

Acute health issues were common reasons that students missed school. Most families with whom we spoke, whether their children were chronically absent or not, mentioned acute illnesses as a reason that their children missed school. Many specifically recalled instances that their children missed school due to a cold, the flu, a virus, or another acute illness like strep throat, pink eye, or pneumonia. Others spoke more generally about symptoms that led them to keep their children home for the day—coughing, a fever, or a runny or stuffy nose in particular, but also throwing up or diarrhea. For chronically absent students, these acute illnesses were not the *only* reason that they missed school, but they contributed to a student's status as chronically absent, adding a meaningful number of days that they missed school on top of other reasons that students were absent. For example, for Alonza, a severely chronically absent DPSCD high school student, the biggest barrier to attendance was transportation: her mother often could not afford gas to drive the children to school. However, she had also been sick with a cough or a fever a few times during the school year and thus had also missed several days because of that.

Chronic health issues were also a challenge for some students. Asthma was the most common issue we heard about in our interviews. In some cases, students had their asthma under control, and it was not a major reason that they missed school; but for others, it led students to miss a significant amount of school, along with other barriers to attendance. We also heard from students dealing with diabetes, stomach and digestive issues, and severe allergies. In each of these cases, the student's chronic health issue contributed to their chronic absenteeism.

These recurring issues were often major drivers of chronic absenteeism, depending on the severity and level of control over the issue. One example comes from Shanice, a DPSCD high school student who had been recently diagnosed with diabetes. In her mother's words, "Sometimes she's pretty tired and she has to miss school because . . . she didn't have any energy." Another example comes from Julio, a DPSCD high school student with severe allergies. Though Julio does not have asthma, once or twice a month he suffers from body aches, nasal congestion, and difficulty breathing. For both Shanice and Julio, the absences related to their chronic illnesses added up to chronic absenteeism.

Student Mental Health. In addition to students' physical health, their mental health can affect their attendance. Several parents mentioned family tragedies, such as the loss of a family member, as the source of sadness, depression, or anger for students. In some instances, coping with a loss was an acute issue that led students to miss school for some time. Nisha and her two sons, who attended a DPSCD high school, dealt with a family tragedy when her youngest son died. Her two sons missed school during a period of grieving: "In the first stage when my son passed, they didn't go [to school] for maybe about a week." In addition to initial periods of mourning, family tragedies like these could be a persistent reason for students to miss school, especially when students deal with recurring feelings of grief and the memory of a lost one. For example, Tonya is the mother of a DPSCD elementary school student, and her father (her son's grandfather) passed away the prior year. She "did keep him from school one day" as a result of his grandfather's death: "It was around the time his grandfather died, it had only been a year [since he died . . .] and he was really upset in the morning." These examples show how a death in the family can affect students in ways that lead them to stay home or that lead their parents to allow their children time and space to process their grief outside school.

Bullying or student conflict can cause or exacerbate mental health issues in a way that leads to more absences. For some students, bullying or student conflict is upsetting or angering and leads students to want to avoid issues in order to feel better. For example, Rhonda encouraged her son to stay home if he had a conflict with another student: "I don't want him to get into any arguments. . . . If he's feeling frustrated or something might have happened during the day, or one of his friends might have said something that got on his nerves and he didn't say anything about it, I'll give him that personal day, and we'll talk about it." In other cases, conflict with students can inflame mental health issues that students are already dealing with because of other traumatic or tragic experiences. One example comes from Marcus, who shared a traumatic story about witnessing the murder of one of his friends while in middle school. Since then, he frequently woke up feeling angry in the morning. He had some negative experiences with teachers and with other students at his school, and often when he woke up feeling angry, he decided to stay home: "I know if I go, and I'm mad or something, I know I'm going to go there and fight."

Parent Health. Students can also miss school because of their parents' health issues. Many of the families we spoke to could not always rely on someone else to take their children to school, especially if they had a sudden reason for not being able to themselves. So when parents are sick, it can sometimes mean that they are not able to get their children to school. Several of the parents we interviewed recalled one morning that they woke up too sick to bring their children to school. For example, Queen, the mother of a DPSCD middle school student, sometimes woke up with a migraine headache: "One morning I didn't get out of bed because my head was hurting so bad and . . . as far as him getting ready and stuff for school it is mainly my job, and yeah, he just didn't go to school, because I didn't even get out of bed for almost the whole day."

Parent health issues are especially a barrier when a parent has a severe or chronic illness. One example comes from Donna, whose son missed a significant amount of school in a prior school year when she was battling cancer: "Now I got to go to chemo five days a week, six hours a day, that's a job. So it's like, okay, what am I going to do? . . . I couldn't bring him to school certain days." Another example comes from Roger, the father of a DPSCD elementary school student, who sustained an injury from a gunshot to the leg years ago. Roger has limited mobility some mornings as a result: "They didn't want to take out the bullet because they didn't want me to be paralyzed, so it's something I have to live with for the rest of my life. So, like, some days when it's raining real bad, real cold, or snow, so I can't even get out of the bed, and I had to call one of my friends to see if they can drop my kids off at school for me." The problem is severe enough that in the winter it prevents him from being able to drive his children to school almost once a week.

Finally, parents' sleep issues were also a barrier to attendance for some students. As in Gladys's case, these sleep issues can be the result of parents' work schedules. They can also be related to stress or other health issues. For example, Veronica, who is the mother of two students at a DPSCD elementary-middle school, "just [has] trouble sleeping sometimes": "It's been a couple of times that because of my sleep issues they missed school."

Doctor's Appointments. Physical and mental health issues also contribute to absenteeism because students may need to go to a doctor's appointment during school or need time to recover from medical treatment. For acute illnesses, some families we spoke to shared that they had to schedule students to have follow-ups with a doctor at a hospital or urgent care center. In addition, students sometimes missed school for additional days after receiving medical treatment, especially if surgery was involved. For students with chronic health issues, accessing and receiving health care could especially be an issue when students required recurring appointments to monitor their condition or a series of diagnostic appointments to determine an appropriate treatment. Similarly, for mental health, some students have therapy sessions that are relatively frequent and cannot be scheduled outside school hours.

Seeking out and receiving health care also led to absences if parents had a harder time accessing it. These issues were usually related to their work schedule or the doctor's availability. One example comes from Camille, whose son Carter attended a DPSCD middle school. Carter has asthma and is required to see the doctor once every three months: "Sometimes he can only go in the morning, when [the doctor] is there." Transportation also plays a role, because if families do not have easy access to a car, then a trip to the doctor can turn into a full-day absence. For example, Louisa, whose children attended a DPSCD elementary-middle school, did not own a car and relied on the bus to get to and from the doctor. Consequently, "if they have an appointment in the morning time or mid-morning, early afternoon, then they may stay home that day and go to the appointment."

School-Based Factors

In addition to these out-of-school barriers to attendance, some aspects of the school environment itself can contribute to chronic absenteeism. For example, we found that students are more likely to be chronically absent if they go to school with a higher concentration of economically disadvantaged students or if more of their classmates from the previous year have switched schools. These factors may place a strain on schools as they try to mobilize resources to support students and sustain positive peer and student-teacher relationships over time.[23] In addition, students who are suspended tend to miss even more school after their suspensions, which highlights the lingering impact that school discipline can have on students' relationships with and attitudes toward their schools.[24]

Schools with more positive school-family relationships in Detroit also tend to have lower chronic absenteeism rates.[25] On the flip side, poor school-parent relationships can negatively affect student attendance. For example, schools may struggle to find out why students miss school and effectively respond to those barriers to attendance if they do not have strong relationships or open lines of communication.[26]

In addition to parent-teacher relationships, student-teacher relationships can also affect attendance. Positive relationships can help students feel greater support and belonging. For example, Jerome, a high school student, told us, "It's some good teachers in my classes. I like the staff there . . . [and I] like my counselors. They do a whole lot." Similarly, Daisha, another high school student, told us, "My coaches, I got a pretty positive relationship with them. They check up on me, like out of school, which is good." In our interviews, we also heard some examples of negative student-teacher relationships that fueled absenteeism. For example, Donna felt like her son's teacher and other students picked on him: "And he gets mad, 'I don't want to go to the class.' Like, 'She always trying to embarrass me.' You know, teachers do that. 'She always put me on the spot, she know I don't know this and yet she'll still put me on . . . embarrass me in front of the whole class, everybody laughing at me.'" As another example, Marcus had a few instances when he skipped class because he felt the teacher singled him out for not wearing the proper attire and did not hold the other students to the same standard: "She said, 'You ain't wearing the right thing in class,' but I always wear what I wear in class, and no teachers never say nothing but her, and I know. Because she can't say nothing about me, because I've seen a whole bunch of other kids in there wearing their jackets and stuff. And she won't let me wear mine." Perceptions of unfair or uneven treatment can erode students' trust in their teachers and lead to skipping or avoiding class.

School Refusal and School Withdrawal. A common assumption is that if students miss school, it is because they or their parents are either disinterested or unmotivated. Researchers use the term *school refusal* to characterize instances when students actively avoid going to school, and the term *school withdrawal* to describe instances in which parents deliberately do not bring their children to school.[27] Although we found that the vast majority of students and parents we interviewed were committed to regular school attendance, there is no question that students sometimes miss school simply because they do not want to go or because their parents allow them to stay home or choose to keep them home. In other instances, when students or their parents described instances of school refusal or withdrawal, they drew direct connections to school-based factors that shaped their decisions.

For example, we heard from some high school students that a lack of academic support had led them or their peers to miss class on occasion. For example, Madison, a high school student, had a cousin who missed school often because she struggles academically: "I feel as if she misses school because she doesn't know how to do the work. . . . I don't think she's getting the help that she needs, and that's why . . .

she'll just not go." Madison also had skipped her math class a few times because she was struggling to keep up: "My Algebra 2 class. I was struggling so bad with it. . . . I would ask for help, but the help that I was getting wasn't enough help to make me understand any clearer than what I already had. And it completely stressed me out." For both Madison and her cousin, their schools may have been able to boost their attendance by supporting them academically. These examples also speak to the potential negative cycle related to attendance and academics, wherein students miss school (often for the outside-of-school reasons discussed earlier) and fall behind academically, which may then lead to further absences.[28]

Yet supportive teachers and academic experiences can help mitigate that negative cycle. For example, Jerome told us about how his science teacher helped him and his classmates: "Just the way she taught. The way she asked questions, she made sure everybody did understand it before she'd go farther in the lesson." Likewise, Daisha told us about one teacher at her school who was especially supportive: "My teacher, he really a cool teacher. He understands problems that are going on, he tries to help you adjust for those problems."

We also heard about absences on early-dismissal days (e.g., for parent-teacher conferences) or the final days of the school year because students and parents alike often viewed these days as educationally less important, a phenomenon that has also been documented in other school systems.[29] For example, Rose's son often asked to stay home on half days, which she allowed: "Most kids and their parents on half days feel like, why bother going?" Diego, a high school student, skipped most of the last two weeks of school: "I see no purpose in going. . . . I mean, grades had stopped. As soon as grades stopped, I didn't want to go any more. But I mean, attendance was still counting." Diego's attitude probably reflects that of most students and parents across the district, given that attendance tends to fall sharply in the last two weeks.[30] Finally, we heard about some instances where students would skip school to avoid a conflict with another student or a teacher. For example, Diego also skipped class on occasion for this reason: "It was sometimes that I didn't feel like going, because of a certain person. . . . I had a class with the person, and I didn't want to cut up on them." As discussed earlier in the section on student mental health, school refusal can result from conflict between students.

While these examples clearly show that school refusal and withdrawal can be issues—and that they are often linked to school-based issues such as academic support and engagement or safety and relationships—it is important to understand these issues in perspective. In our interviews, barriers to attendance related to transportation and health were much more salient issues than school refusal or withdrawal. For example, Madison did talk about skipping Algebra 2 because she was struggling academically, but most of her absences were due to a chronic health issue related to her stomach. In addition, school refusal and withdrawal do not occur in a vacuum—these decisions are in part a product of students' life circumstances and schooling experiences. For example, while Diego sometimes decided to skip school to avoid an interpersonal conflict, he was enabled to do this because his parents' work schedule meant he was responsible for getting to and from school on his own. So while parent and student interest or motivation play a role, they interact with the broader contextual factors we've discussed.

Acute Versus Persistent Barriers to Attendance

Finally, it is important to note that students who are categorized as "chronically absent" may have dramatically different absence patterns, in addition to different reasons for their missed days. For instance, some students who are chronically absent have what we call an *acute* absence pattern, in which the majority of their absences occurred in groupings one to three times throughout a school year. This pattern might be present for a student who had several severe illnesses (e.g., missed a week of school three times in a year due to the flu or severe allergies). This pattern might also correspond to a student who had a single major crisis in their life—such as an eviction, a death in their immediate family, or a car accident that leaves them without reliable transportation—which can cause them to miss several weeks of school all in a row. Other students have what we call a *persistent* absence pattern, in which their absences are spread somewhat evenly throughout the school year, such as a day or two every other week. This pattern might correspond to a student whose family has unreliable transportation (e.g., lacks regular access to a car or often does not have gas money), or a health issue with frequent flare-ups (e.g., severe fatigue due to diabetes, breathing issues due to undertreated asthma). This distinction between acute and persistent patterns of absenteeism highlights how similar types of issues that lead to chronic absenteeism may affect students differently—and thus may require different solutions to the barriers they face.

ATTENDANCE AS AN "ECOLOGICAL" ISSUE

In sum, chronic absenteeism is an "ecological" issue. While students may have specific immediate reasons for missing school, those reasons tend to be the result of a combination of overlapping conditions and circumstances. These include family income, employment and work schedules, social connections, transportation resources, public and school-based transportation systems, health issues, health-care access, neighborhood safety, and positive school climate and school-family relationships. Not all Detroit families face the same barriers to attendance, and some face more significant barriers while others face relatively few. Yet the broad social and economic inequalities in Detroit—from a history of economic decline and segregation to presently high rates of poverty, unemployment, and crime—help explain why so many students are chronically absent citywide. These structural root causes, as well as the more immediate barriers to attendance, are often outside the direct influence of schools.

On the other hand, for students who are not chronically absent, their families tend to have more favorable conditions and access to a set of resources that help them consistently attend school. This is not to suggest that these families face few or no socioeconomic difficulties. In fact, we often heard from families whose children were not chronically absent that they had to go to great lengths to ensure their children's attendance, stretching their wallets or their social networks or making difficult trade-offs between work and school. Still, what distinguished these families from those whose children were chronically absent was that these resources were available to support their children's attendance.

In the next chapter, we describe how a group of community-based and educational leaders in Detroit turned to the issue of chronic absenteeism. These leaders certainly recognized the multifaceted nature of chronic absenteeism, and in some cases even started out prioritizing efforts that would address out-of-school factors. Yet as they faced the magnitude and complexity of the issue, they narrowed the scope of their efforts. Informed by popular education reform ideas about accountability and school improvement, they prioritized informing and motivating parents and other school-based actions—in other words, "educational" solutions to the problem. That approach, while well-meaning, was simply out of step with an "ecological" understanding of chronic absenteeism and the reality of social and economic inequalities that Detroit families face.

CHAPTER 2

Finding an "Educational" Solution to Chronic Absenteeism in Detroit

Before policy makers and advocates pushed for a national shift in how schools should be held accountable for student attendance in the Every Student Succeeds Act of 2015, community members in Detroit identified absenteeism as a problem they needed to address. These leaders drew on their personal experience working with Detroit families and their professional expertise in social policy, youth development, and systems change to advocate that everyone who cares about kids in Detroit should be paying attention to chronic absenteeism. Their countless hours of deliberation, logic modeling, coalition building, and daily work on the ground in Detroit schools and neighborhoods were largely accomplished alongside their other full-time jobs and professional commitments. They knew from the start that the reasons students missed so much school in Detroit were multifaceted and complex, and would require major shifts in systems within and beyond schools.

After working on the issue for about five years, in 2017, these community leaders set an ambitious goal: reduce Detroit's chronic absence rate to 15 percent by 2027. Though they had started with local neighborhood efforts to improve student attendance, they realized that in order to reach their goal, they would have to activate a larger collective of people and organizations. Given their experience, it made sense to initially strategize around how to support Detroit schools and youth development organizations in reducing chronic absenteeism. We joined their efforts in 2017 to form a research-practice partnership, with the goal that their questions, problems, and new initiatives would inform a research agenda to shed light on the causes of chronic absenteeism in Detroit and the effectiveness of new programs and policies to address it. (The authors were close research partners to the Coalition and the Detroit Public Schools Community District [DPSCD] and participated in decision-making with Coalition leadership.[1] More about the authors' roles and our research process can be found in the appendix.)

In this chapter, we map the trajectory of the Coalition's efforts. In particular, we highlight how, despite starting with a focus on the ecological, root causes of absenteeism, their work came to narrow in on educational solutions and schools as some of the only sites of intervention, driven in part by organizational routines shaped by philanthropic priorities, new school accountability metrics tied to chronic absence, and the availability of school-centered guidance.[2] This focus on educational solutions became the predominant paradigm within which school and community leaders worked to solve chronic absence, limiting the impact of their efforts but also creating opportunities to learn and transform their strategy into one that is now in a stronger position to address the systems that produce such challenging conditions for student attendance in Detroit.

KIDS IN THE STREETS

Although the work of reducing chronic absenteeism in Detroit stretched across many organizations, people, and time, the formalized efforts by community groups, philanthropy, and schools began in two Detroit neighborhoods that we'll call Northwest and Southwest, with two dynamic leaders who have championed this issue for more than a decade. Based on dozens of interviews, hundreds of hours of observation, and document analysis, we trace the history of their early conceptions of the problem of absenteeism, early efforts to solve it, and learning along the way to help us understand and situate the subsequent school-based efforts. Data in this chapter primarily come from interviews in early 2019 with Coalition members, who reflected about the history of the Coalition and their involvement in the issue of chronic absenteeism.

Northwest Detroit

In the early 2010s, Marvin Ashford was a faith leader and a fixture in Northwest Detroit, in a neighborhood that was home to about twelve thousand people. If there was a community picnic, protest, food drive, school event, or meeting in the neighborhood, Marvin probably knew about it, organized it, or was participating in it. In his mid-sixties then, Marvin was a connector within the neighborhood, among the families who lived there and to the municipal, grassroots, and philanthropic community beyond. As a Black pastor at a small local church and the executive director of the nonprofit Northwest Together, Marvin saw both the enormous strengths and beauty in Detroit and the challenges that his and other neighborhoods faced related to poverty, racism, and political neglect.

Detroit's education ecosystem at that time was in turmoil. Student achievement was among the worst in the nation. After the release of the 2009 National Assessment of Educational Progress scores, one national education leader said that "no jurisdiction of any kind in the history of NAEP has ever registered such low numbers." He went on to say, "They are just above what one would expect by chance alone—as if the kids simply guessed at the answers."[3] In 2009, the district was placed under emergency management by the governor; and in 2011, the state created a takeover district for failing schools and subsumed fifteen city schools under the Education Achievement Authority.[4] The traditional public school district was suffering from major financial problems resulting from population decline, enrollment shifts from the district into charter schools and suburban schools of choice, a weak local tax base from which to raise bond monies for capital improvements, and mismanagement by the state.[5]

Longtime community leaders like Marvin were searching for answers to how things got so bad, and what could be done about it. Working with community organizers in the emerging group Grassroots Union, Marvin began asking his congregants and neighbors what they were seeing and what they wanted to change in their neighborhood and beyond. Throughout these conversations, one theme kept coming up. As Marvin later reflected, "We were discussing and talking with people about how we could impact the quality of education, one of the things we [heard] is that there were too many kids running up and down the streets. So, attendance seemed like, of all the things we could do, that was something the community could do without calling on a lot of others to help."

Marvin and his fellow pastors formed an informal collective to improve attendance in Northwest Detroit. They started with the deceptively simple idea that, if kids were missing school, they would use the resources they had—church vans—and go pick them up. They asked schools to identify the students who were missing the most, and the group organized to go to the children's homes each morning, sometimes get them out of bed or make sure they had breakfast, and then drive them to school. For a semester or two, their scheme worked: the children they picked up got to school more often. But it didn't last. Marvin learned through talking with Detroit public school leaders that 75 percent of students in the neighborhood were considered chronically absent at that time—more than one thousand children.

The pastors and their volunteers were dedicated, but they could only do so much. Marvin recalled that one volunteer from a neighboring church was an eighty-year-old white man who stood out in the nearly all-Black community: "He was driving into an area of Detroit in which 500 people had been shot in a six-month period and maybe ten, twenty of them had been killed. He was driving every day with his white hair, eighty-something-year-old-self, into this neighborhood to pick up kids and then bring them back to school, every day. We were doing this every day. . . . We realized that the problem was way larger than our cars could solve, even if they didn't burn out, which they were." Their church vans were breaking down from overuse, and the demands of a high-poverty community were competing for their time.

Southwest Detroit

Twenty miles away, Joni Clark was noticing similar troubles in Southwest Detroit, where she was a leader in a place-based community development organization called Southwest Partnership. In 2012, Joni's organization led a quality-of-life planning process to engage neighborhood residents, stakeholders, and youth in identifying critical needs in the community. Education was one of the seven domains they focused on and, as Joni later shared, "attendance rose to the top as a major issue in the neighborhood." While they looked at student achievement and graduation rate data, they also conducted focus groups with community members and interviewed one hundred influential leaders in the neighborhood, including youth leaders, school principals, and parents. What they heard across all these groups was the same: "Kids aren't going to school." At this point, the organization was not tracking the reasons why kids might be missing school, but there was a growing and collective sense that attendance was an issue, and Joni and her colleagues began to strategize about how to address it.

Southwest Partnership was well-connected and in regular communication with other organizations and schools in Southwest Detroit, many of which were committed to developing a plan to address absenteeism. Building on their model of hyperlocalized community development, they worked with their partners to consider how to leverage existing programs and relationships to better understand the issues keeping kids from school. From the beginning, Southwest Partnership was attempting to coordinate activities that would address attendance issues holistically, from lots of different angles. As Joni shared, they started mentoring "kids who had attendance issues." They also began to think about how to coordinate community school coordinators in several schools in Southwest Detroit and Department of Health and Human Services workers who were working with students and families in neighborhood schools. These partners had "really good relationships with principals" and were seen as key connectors between students and social resources that could support families struggling with poverty. Yet the task of coordinating a holistic model to improve conditions for attendance was a big one, and Southwest Partnership's model was intentionally designed to focus on the small geographic area it served. Joni wondered whether they could implement the needed initiatives given their existing resources and partnerships, asking, "Do we have enough?"

Common Problems

In 2014, through their shared membership in Grassroots Union, Joni and Marvin began working together to think through how to address chronic absenteeism. They traded ideas and experiences with absent students, and they shared what they were learning from their communities. Southwest Partnership held listening sessions to learn about why students were missing school, and they identified two primary causes in their neighborhood. First was health—both everyday childhood illnesses and chronic conditions—likely exacerbated by being "the most polluted ZIP code in Michigan."[6] The second was transportation. Joni shared that many youth in her neighborhood told her, "We have to get ourselves to school." Other barriers to attendance that Southwest Partnership identified included housing instability, suspensions, and uniform requirements.

Likewise, Marvin listened to students and parents in Northwest Detroit and heard about additional challenges. As he shared,

> When kids get to know and they feel they trust you, they start talking. So, we would hear about what was going on at home. Parents who were facing serious challenges who weren't at home 'cause they were at work. Not having water so they couldn't get their clothes clean. . . . One of the families that I was picking up, the mother would never come downstairs. So, she never saw the children off in the

> morning and they would complain about how they would try to wake her up or get her up. What I later came to understand is she's clinically depressed. She really should have been getting mental health services. She should be getting behavioral health services.

What Marvin and Joni recognized, both from their prior work in communities and from their new efforts to better understand attendance problems, was that chronic absenteeism was a complex issue, with multiple, often compounding causes. They began to develop a logic model of what caused chronic absenteeism and what would need to be in place to solve it. It began with the assumption that chronic absenteeism was influenced by "poverty, disciplinary policies, safety, health, transportation, family issues, environmental issues, [and] school structures and resources." It also documented their shared belief that "schools do not have the support or resources to adequately address chronic absences."

They soon realized that they and their small neighborhood organizations could not solve the problem on their own. They began to seek out information, advice, and resources to inform their next steps. With the support of the Skillman Foundation and Grassroots Union, they connected with Showing Up for School, a nonprofit that works with schools and community organizations to shine a light on the problem of chronic absenteeism and promote a multipronged approach to addressing it. Their goal was to provoke a citywide response to what they were quickly coming to think of as an educational crisis.

Two things stand out about this moment. First, absenteeism was an evident problem in cities like Detroit well before the national education reform movement put a spotlight on it and demanded that schools be held accountable for it. Second, community leaders who worked with families every day recognized the problem as complex. In other words, they had an "ecological" framing of the nature of the problem. However, understanding a problem ecologically and coming up with a strategy that addresses the problem ecologically are two different things. Political, economic, and practical forces influenced how the Coalition came to develop and implement their strategy, eventually focusing much of their effort on a school-centered approach.

ELEVATING CHRONIC ABSENTEEISM

As educators across the country grapple with how to manage high rates of chronic absenteeism since the COVID-19 pandemic, Detroit's efforts nearly a decade earlier provide important lessons. They started with small, bespoke solutions to absenteeism in particular neighborhoods but quickly realized they were unsustainable. Then, as we show here, they began pulling in other stakeholders but struggled to convey a clear message about what they were asking these other organizations to do. By 2015, four groups were coming together as a makeshift coalition to work on absenteeism in Detroit: Northwest Together, Southwest Partnership, Grassroots Union, and Community Alliance, another youth-focused nonprofit in Southwest Detroit. They were implementing small pilots in their neighborhoods, like the church vans initiative, and sharing their experiences with the other groups. At this point, they had no funding to support their efforts directly. Instead, they were drawing on unrestricted funds from small philanthropies to work on attendance on top of their other priorities, such as afterschool programming, childcare, food security, and job training. This was unsustainable. As Marvin shared after about six months of picking up students in church vans,

> I don't think you can do this work without staff or the sustained places. It's too intense. It requires a lot of bandwidth. And pastors have a lot on their plates. They have the business of the church; the lights, the gas, the water. They have the theological preaching, teaching and they have the, what I call, Matthew 25: feeding, clothing, and ministering to those in need. That's a lot. And in a community like [Northwest], which is suffering from generational poverty, or often in Southwest you have the issues of an endless rate of murder, coupled with the challenges of poverty, the pastors [were] overwhelmed. And as any pastor will tell you, you can only get people to volunteer for so much at a time.

Similarly, Joni said of this early period, "We have learned enough to know that we needed resources."

The first resources formally allocated to addressing chronic absence in Detroit did not flow to a Detroit-based organization. Instead, Grassroots Union asked the Skillman Foundation to award a grant to Showing Up for School, with the expectation that Showing Up for School would then pay Detroit-based staff to help implement a strategy. This was highly unusual. As Joni recalled, "One of the tensions when they decided to fund Showing Up for School instead of a local entity, was that had never happened anywhere before. [And staff at Showing Up for School] would say, and I think would still say, they don't want Showing Up for School to be the entity that holds the work in a local community." Despite this concern from both Showing Up for School and some Detroit-based community leaders, Grassroots Union had worried that awarding the funds to one Detroit organization, when many were involved, could potentially disrupt the coalitional movement they were trying to build. Ultimately, the decision was made: Showing Up for School would "hold" the work in Detroit, marshal their own staff to provide support to local efforts, and distribute resources to local organizations.

Other than the odd funding arrangement, Marvin, Joni, and other Detroit leaders were glad for the support of Showing Up for School. The organization had helped put chronic absenteeism on the map and led the way in persuading educators and lawmakers to pay attention to it. They had resources—a tool to help the district calculate chronic absenteeism and organize its attendance data, school assessments to identify areas for improvement, and deep knowledge of the emerging research base on the importance of school attendance. They also brought credibility to an issue that Marvin, Joni, and their colleagues were desperately trying to elevate to a larger collective of stakeholders.

And it worked. Soon after Showing Up for School came on board in 2014, leaders from the Detroit public school district (which was still under state takeover at this time) began participating in the group's informal meetings. The goal was to make chronic absence a big-tent issue, with leaders from across education and all other sectors of social and political life coming together to address the problem. Reflecting on the need to elevate the issue to a citywide effort, Marvin shared, "So, as we began to succeed in elevating this issue and engaging community, engaging schools, and elevating the issue to the point that decision makers or policy makers paid attention to what we were saying, we began to wrestle with, 'How do we actually now take this knowing and translating into doing?'" This would become a critical juncture for the Coalition. They had earned the attention of district leadership, an important local philanthropy, and political and business leaders across the region, in part because they were legitimized by their association with Showing Up for School. The problem was, they didn't yet have a message. As Joni would later reflect, "We weren't quite ready to tell them what it is that we needed them to do. For example, Annie, she was at the U.S. District Attorney's office, she would comment that they were doing stuff around safety and she was like, 'I just don't see how I fit into this [chronic absence work].' They weren't committed to the collective work, and I don't know that we did a great job of figuring out what are the commitments we're asking people to make." The informal group had quickly begun to formalize, and it was clear that they had to develop an "ask" for the partners they brought to the table. What did they want them to do, now that they were convinced that chronic absenteeism was a problem worth solving?

ADOPTING AN EDUCATIONAL APPROACH

Identifying cause and effect in the evolution of a movement can be nearly impossible. After all, movements are made up of human beings, each with their own ideas, experiences, interests, passions, and expertise. And these people exist in contexts with certain histories, resources, strengths, and challenges. Still, sometimes certain events or circumstances represent turning points, catalyzing changes in direction that are nearly unmistakable. Such is the case with the movement to reduce chronic absenteeism in Detroit. Based on our analysis of dozens of interviews with Coalition members and their partners, in addition to observation notes from weekly (2017–20) and then biweekly (2021–23) Coalition meetings that we participated in, as well as member checks that we have since conducted with these same individuals, we have identified three primary factors that motivated the Coalition to turn toward an educational approach to reducing chronic absenteeism: (1) organizational routines aligned to prior philanthropic priorities, (2) pressures placed on schools by new chronic absenteeism accountability metrics, and (3) the availability of specific school-centered guidance and tools. Here, we outline how these three dynamics merged to create a set of conditions that led the Coalition members to think of schools as the most critical sites of intervention and to encourage schools in Detroit to adopt an educational approach to solving chronic absence.

Organizational Routines and Philanthropic Priorities

With Marvin, Joni, and their colleagues, the Coalition had decades of experience in community organizing and youth development in neighborhoods across Detroit, and they each represented existing nonprofit organizations that worked in and around schools. They were funded primarily through local philanthropic dollars, with short-term grants of one to two years, in which they were required to implement programs and report back on youth and resident involvement. This would end up being an important dynamic in how Marvin, Joni, and their colleagues decided to invest their time and effort over the next several years. They were not funded directly to work on attendance, they already had more than full-time jobs running programming through nonprofits, and they had early experiences that showed them just how big and complex the issue of chronic absenteeism was.

In 2014, the Skillman Foundation partnered with the United Way for Southeast Michigan, the Detroit Mayor's Office, and the Detroit Regional Chamber to launch the Coalition for the Future of Detroit Schoolchildren (CFDS).[7] The primary goal of this group was to establish priorities for the future of Detroit schools. The Detroit Public Schools were nearly bankrupt, and the Michigan legislature began to debate whether and how to resolve the financial problems that were created under state management—and return local democratic control to the district.[8] Marvin and another early Coalition member were on the steering committee, and they advocated that chronic absenteeism be prioritized in the CFDS recommendations. In 2017, the group's final report included six priorities that "we can act on now." The first was "Get Serious About Attendance."[9] This recommendation was a formal appeal to "do something" about attendance, and it solidified a working relationship between local funders, particularly the Skillman Foundation, and the Coalition. (We have received funding from the Skillman Foundation for our research, including some of the research on attendance and chronic absenteeism included in this book.)

The Coalition members had worked with Skillman before. As the leading local philanthropy focused on K–12 education in Detroit, Skillman played an outsize role in shaping education reform in the city, particularly during state takeover when noneducators led the city's schools. In 2000, the foundation was the thirteenth-largest donor to K–12 education in the country.[10] Some observers believed that it was partially responsible for the unregulated expansion of charter schools in the city, the state takeover of local schools through the Education Achievement Authority, and the expansion of alternative routes to teaching in Detroit, such as Teach for America.[11]

Yet for many nonprofits and community development organizations in Detroit, Skillman was the most reliable funder of their core work—youth out-of-school-time programming. In this portfolio, Skillman typically awarded one-year grants of up to $200,000 to organizations running afterschool enrichment clubs, summer camps, and other youth-engaged programs for Detroit schoolchildren. The organization that Joni ran, Southwest Partnership, was one of them. With these grants, awardees were expected to "deliver" an outcome—enroll a certain number of children, help a certain number of families, or measurably change an outcome prioritized by the foundation. Skillman's funding approach was not unusual, and education-focused organizations and schools nationwide are often subject to the short-term priorities of donors and policy makers.[12] Yet this approach can heavily influence how education and nonprofit institutions set their priorities and plan their programming. Although Skillman leaders and Coalition members recognized the need for systems change, there were few models for how to go about doing that. Instead, following well-worn organizational routines, the Coalition opted to implement two short-term strategies that aligned with their prior work and the funding models they were used to: an afterschool program to reduce chronic absence and a communications campaign to inform Detroiters about the issue.

Southwest Partnership's Chronic Absence Reduction Program was designed as an afterschool program for middle school students who were moderately chronically absent (missing 10–20 percent of school days). The theory was that middle school was a critical juncture for students' social and academic development and that providing an engaging, welcoming space after school for them to do something they enjoyed would entice them to come to school. Research on positive youth development has demonstrated that the relationships formed in afterschool programs can generate positive outcomes for students.[13] Therefore, the Coalition believed they could first incentivize students to come to the program, and then the program could help improve attendance both by being a direct incentive and by improving school-student relationships. The Coalition designed the program so that students would get tutoring for one hour, and in the second hour they would participate in an engaging activity of their choosing, such as art or basketball. Students would not be allowed to participate in the program if they did not attend school that day. The activities offered were chosen by a group of students who helped prepare the request for proposals, reviewed applications, and developed a process for selecting vendors that could provide engaging activities. This program was well aligned with the organizational routines of Coalition members—it was short (one semester), the Coalition could report on the number of students it enrolled and schools it worked in, and it was, at least in theory, connected to the goal of improving student attendance. However, the Coalition encountered significant problems getting the program off the ground in the first year, including delays getting approval to implement the project in district schools, low enrollment of chronically absent students, low attendance among program participants, and no measurable effect on attendance among those enrolled. These kinds of issues were common in the programmatic efforts of the Coalition, and they portended the challenges that would continue for the next several years as Coalition members and philanthropic partners learned the limits of their prior ways of operating when trying to solve absenteeism.

The Coalition's second major initiative in the early years was what they called a "citywide messaging campaign." It was led by Marvin, who had experience with communications from his work in Mayor Coleman Young's administration. The theory was, "If people know better, they'll do better." As Marvin reflected, "The first messaging campaign was to launch a website, do an email, a social media blast and to get pledge cards out." The pledge cards asked students, educators, community members, and business leaders to pledge to help students get to school in whatever way they could. It also included information on what chronic absenteeism was—missing 10 percent of school days or about two days a month—and asked potential partners to "donate" their time and energy to one of several Coalition communications efforts, such as attending weekly meetings, speaking one-on-one with residents, inviting others to the work, posting on social media, or writing news releases. Again, this effort was well aligned to philanthropic priorities and the organizational routines of member organizations. It allowed them to build on their prior experience with grassroots outreach, for instance. The messaging campaign could be "accomplished" within one year, and there were clear deliverables to report back to funders, including the number of page views, the number of pledge cards signed, and the number of people who donated their time to the effort. By the end of the campaign, more than six thousand people, or 1 percent of the population of Detroit, had signed pledge cards committing to improve student attendance.

Yet even in the midst of the campaign, Marvin worried about the efficacy of such an effort, reflecting back on his first experiences picking up children in church vans: "So, the idea is that if people know better, they'll do better. Now, is that gonna solve the problem of the kids who I was speaking of? Whose mother was clinically depressed? . . . No. 'Cause she's got bigger . . . I shouldn't say bigger. She's got different challenges she's got to meet." By the end of the 2017–18 school year, the Coalition was *doing something* about chronic absenteeism, as they were charged to do by the CFDS. But they weren't seeing the results they wanted and needed to meet their "audacious goal" of reducing chronic absenteeism to 15 percent. Both initiatives failed to significantly improve attendance in Detroit, and now the new DPSCD was interested in partnering with community-based organizations to address the problem of absenteeism.

Accountability Pressure on Schools

As discussed in the introduction, the authorization of the federal Every Student Succeeds Act in 2015 solidified chronic absenteeism as an important measure for schools to track, and in 2017, the US Department of Education approved Michigan's revised school accountability plan. In it, 14 percent of a school's accountability index was based on "school quality/student success," with 4 percent for chronic absenteeism.[14] This may not seem like much but, particularly for school systems that persistently failed proficiency and growth targets on standardized tests, chronic absenteeism was an area where schools could potentially make a difference. The stakes for schools performing in the bottom 5 percent of the state were high, with Michigan implementing a new initiative called the Partnership Model for School and District Turnaround that same year, requiring districts with the lowest-performing schools in the state to submit to oversight, improvement monitoring, and coaching by state agents. Districts across Michigan wanted to avoid entering into these agreements, so improving student attendance was one possible way to lift their school accountability scores enough to remain out of the bottom 5 percent.

The Michigan Department of Education had also changed the definition of chronic absenteeism from ten days absent to 10 percent of days absent, aligning it with national norms. This raised the threshold for chronic absenteeism, since 10 percent of school days in most years was around eighteen days for students enrolled the full year. In many districts across the state, this change reduced the number of students who would be counted as chronically absent. In Detroit, it emphasized just how much school many students were missing. In April 2018, near the end of the 2017–18 school year, the US Department of Education released 2015–16 Office of Civil Rights data, which revealed that 47.8 percent of Detroit schoolchildren, across traditional public and charter schools, were chronically absent—the highest percentage of any large urban district in the country and nearly 10 percentage points higher than the next city, Milwaukee.[15]

When the Coalition began engaging with Showing Up for School, they identified a potential champion at the Detroit Public Schools (still under state management at the time), Bobby Jackson. Bobby had come to the central office after a long career in engineering. He was a data and research guy; he was committed to understanding how the district was doing and using data to inform improvement. He was also a Detroiter; he grew up in Black Bottom, a historic Black neighborhood in downtown Detroit that was demolished to make room for the construction of Interstate 75, and he went to Cass Tech, still one of the most prestigious public high schools in the region. When Bobby reflected on the purpose of his work in the Detroit public school district, he shared, "When I think about where I am, my belief in what's achievable or not, I see a city full of students, families like me, that have this unrealized potential. So, the goal is to unleash that potential across the city."

Bobby attended a meeting hosted by Marvin and Joni where he saw a presentation by Showing Up for School, and he was captivated by the data showing the significant connection between chronic absenteeism and student outcomes. His frequent references to particular slide numbers from that presentation became legendary among Coalition members. As a Showing Up for School staff person shared, "We did a session first with some of the schools in the neighborhood. And then we had an evening session with [Bobby] to see if we could cultivate some buy-in from the district, [Bobby] got interested. And then [Bobby] was willing to start to try to take the district data system and crunch the numbers." He started working with Showing Up for School, and through that connection, began attending Coalition meetings. Bobby elevated the issue of chronic absence in the district. He shared the district's understanding of attendance problems before their work with the Coalition, which included concerns related to a state policy that withholds funds from districts for each day in the district's original school calendar with an attendance rate under 75 percent:[16] "Like most groups, most districts, we were focused on average daily attendance, which is different. And we were also focused on the financial implications of dropping below 75% average daily attendance. So, for the most part, while we had attendance agents, we were not aware of what 'chronically absent' was at that time." Bobby began talking about the issue with senior leadership. He convinced Diana Weston, an influential leader in the district, to engage with the group, use data to understand the scale and scope of its chronic absenteeism challenge, and start seeking solutions. It was at this point in 2016 that Diana made us aware of the issue, and we also began working with the Detroit Public Schools (at that time still under state takeover) to understand why so many students were missing so much school.

The interests of the district, the Coalition, and their research partner were aligned. Just as emergency management of the district was ending, the Coalition finally had a willing district partner and a chance to formally collaborate on a larger scale. As a result of state legislation in 2016, Detroit's public schools were reorganized as the Detroit Public Schools Community District.[17] The newly elected and empowered DPSCD school board appointed Nikolai Vitti as superintendent in May 2017. The superintendent installed a director of climate and culture, who would formally supervise the district's attendance initiatives. The district also agreed, with the offer of funding from the Skillman Foundation, to allow the Coalition to work with the twenty-seven schools in the district that were in the bottom 5 percent in the state accountability system. While all district schools would be implementing new practices to reduce chronic absenteeism, these twenty-seven schools would get extra support and coaching from the Coalition. Yet, again, the question became, What would the Coalition ask them to do?

Showing Up for School

Showing Up for School, which had given the Coalition credibility among funders and school leaders and was "holding" the money for the local Detroit strategy, had an answer. The organization had a website with open-source materials, frameworks, and testimonials, and its own staff could provide professional development. Showing Up for School's approach was grounded in the idea that school districts and their communities must work in tandem to produce the conditions for positive student attendance. For districts, the organization promoted shared accountability, capacity building, and the use of actionable data. For communities, the organization argued that adequate, equitable resources should be paired with strategic partnership and positive engagement. Like the Coalition, Showing Up for School conceived of absenteeism as a complex issue with root causes within and beyond schools. Yet while the organization's materials and training emphasized the need for a holistic approach, the most detailed, specific guidance they offered was around their frameworks for schools and districts, particularly a tiered model for organizing attendance data and considering how to align strategies based on the tiers. This tiered approach to reducing chronic absenteeism was catching on across the country, and, as Marvin shared, the State of Michigan and many school districts had already adapted one of the tools that Showing Up for School promoted: "The tier model of tier one, two, and three of Showing Up for School, now being used by Michigan but with some modifications. But the fundamental theoretical approach that Showing Up for School took is even reflected in this new model of the state because even they are tiering one, two, and three."

The tiers framework was an adaptation of other multitiered systems of support used in schools to categorize students with at-risk behaviors and inform interventions.[18] It asked schools to organize attendance strategies by tier, with the idea that most students would respond to prevention strategies like an engaging school climate and recognition of good and improved attendance. Tier 2 strategies were those that could address the barriers to attendance for students who were already chronically absent. Tier 3 strategies were for severely chronically absent students who missed 20 percent or more of school days. Showing Up for School promoted the use and adaptation of this framework, along with encouragement to partner with community-based organizations and a series of other school practices, such as conducting an audit of each school's culture and climate.

Another key dimension of the strategy the Coalition adapted from Showing Up for School was a focus on communication—communication *to* schools and communication *through* schools to parents and students. Marvin remembered that Showing Up for School had shared research on success mentors with the Coalition that suggested that students' attendance will improve if there is someone in the school paying attention to it, no matter who that person is: "It could be the janitor, it could be the secretary or sports man. It could be a teacher but not necessarily one that was in their class." Showing Up for School promoted the idea of key relationships both to improve the overall culture and climate of the school and to create potential pathways through which school staff could learn about the barriers students faced in getting to school. Following this guidance, the Coalition advocated that schools implement attendance teams to identify students who were chronically absent and pair them with an adult in the building who would notice when they were not in school. This practice, along with a focus on data analysis, formed the bedrock of the solution that the Coalition fundraised for, promoted, and implemented themselves, with DPSCD and other school partners in Detroit.

Eventually, the collection of tools, frameworks, and training from Showing Up for School came to be adapted as the Coalition's model for reducing chronic absenteeism in Detroit. As Marvin shared, "Over time, which Showing Up for School encourages, we kind of evolved their method." At first, national Showing Up for School staff would fly in and conduct trainings with Detroit school leaders and attendance agents. But as Joni shared, "we quickly realized . . . there needed to be someone local. We pushed really hard . . . that we want [a local leader] to be the person on the ground working in Detroit." Joni believed this local leader had so much credibility that she could "walk into any school and talk to any principal." Therefore, with the support of the Coalition, Showing Up for School hired her as a consultant and trained her to provide support to schools in Detroit. She then worked with a Showing Up for School staff person to design trainings and present at professional development sessions.

In the 2018–19 school year, the Coalition formally partnered with DPSCD and a small network of Detroit charter schools to provide training to school-based attendance agents, school leaders, and other administrative staff working on climate and culture in schools. Their focus was on providing information on chronic absenteeism, best practices for addressing it, and the tiers framework through technical assistance and coaching. In a few short years, Marvin, Joni, and their colleagues—along with champions in the philanthropic community and Detroit public school district—had elevated chronic absenteeism to an urgent issue that many people across the city believed needed to be solved. Released from state takeover and with a new administration in place, the newly organized DPSCD was actively engaged in reducing chronic absenteeism and sought out partnerships. The Coalition and the district had an educational approach to reducing chronic absenteeism that aligned with existing practices for tracking data, categorizing students into tiers, and implementing strategies based on those tiers. Over the next two chapters, we describe how that approach played out and what lessons can be drawn for other districts newly grappling with this problem.

CHAPTER 3

The Attendance Agents and the Tiers Framework

In the 2018–19 and 2019–20 school years, the Detroit Public Schools Community District (DPSCD) began to implement a new, systematic approach to student attendance. This was informed by the district's strategic blueprint—which the new administration put in place. One of the five district priorities outlined in that blueprint was creating a "transformative culture" in the district: "transform[ing] our culture so that students, families, community members, and staff feel safe, respected, and connected." This pillar included a commitment to "cultivat[ing] a school-going culture that dramatically reduces chronic absenteeism in our district."[1] The new district's early investment in reducing chronic absenteeism began with the premise that there were systemic and structural barriers to attendance that were beyond their reach, but that developing and improving school-based initiatives could make some difference, as articulated in the district's 2018–19 attendance plan: "With a lack of viable systems to address attendance at the foundational level, opportunities for districtwide attendance reform exists [*sic*]."[2]

DPSCD's strategy revolved around two main components. The first was the "attendance agent"—a new, school-based position dedicated solely to addressing attendance issues and coordinating wraparound services. The second was a multitiered system of support (MTSS) framework to organize their work. The attendance agents were overseen by James Robinson, a DPSCD leader who managed initiatives related to school culture and climate. James helped initiate DPSCD's shift from district-level truancy officers to school-based attendance agents:

> Our plan for addressing chronic absenteeism this year [2018–19] was to go about placing an attendance agent in every school. In the past, the district only had a few schools with a school-based agent, and then the other schools, about three-fourths of the district, relied on the central-office attendance agents. Upon my arrival, I did an experiment and just placed all the central agents in a school. . . . It was difficult for one agent who probably had six to seven schools to establish positive working relationships with families and students, without being in the school every day. . . . That's what we did. That was the strategy to make certain that there was a point person in every school that's monitoring attendance, but then having the autonomy to go out and find out what's actually going on.

James also supervised the district's adoption of the "tiers" framework to guide its attendance strategy: "We're also just making certain that our staff understands that [students] should be tiered. We tier kids based on [their attendance]." Today, districts across Michigan and around the country are putting attendance agents and MTSS frameworks in place for their own attendance initiatives.[3] However, DPSCD was a relatively early adopter, in part due to the involvement and support of Showing Up for School and the Coalition. As shown in figure 3.1, in 2018–19, DPSCD's spending on chronic absenteeism initiatives per pupil was nearly nine times the statewide average, and only grew over time. James explained that the district's plan built on the efforts supported by Showing Up for School in the previous school year: "There were some things that needed to be refined in that process, but nothing that we're looking to abandon in the coming school year."

This chapter takes a close look at the attendance agents and the attendance tiers framework—the two main components of DPSCD's plan for the 2018–19 and 2019–20 school years. Together, they represent the "educational" solution to chronic absenteeism that DPSCD and the Coalition embraced. Though the district previously had a position titled "attendance agent," this new attendance agent position would be a reimagining of the role. There was some precedent with the old truancy officer role that it was replacing, but it was also meant to be a departure from that truancy model. The role came to be defined by three competing models that we call the bureaucrat, the school improver, and the caseworker—each of which was rooted in a different underlying theory on how

FIGURE 3.1 DPSCD and state average spending on truancy/absenteeism services per pupil

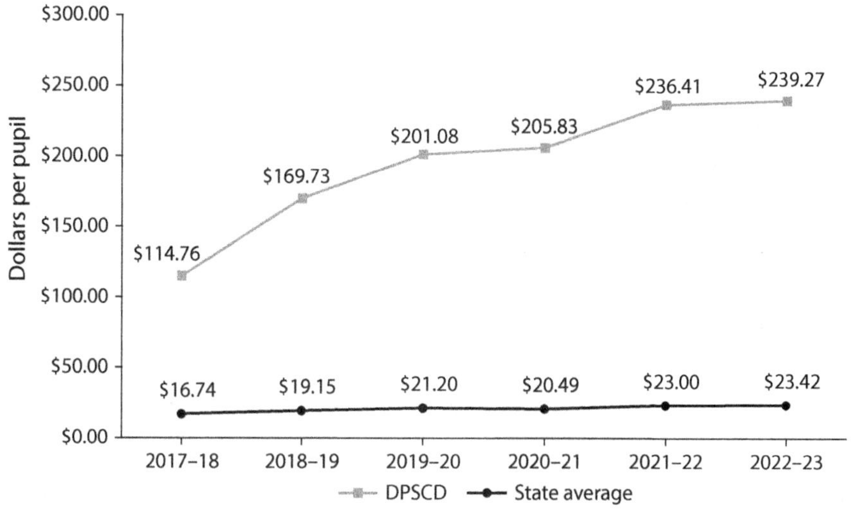

Dollars per pupil	2017–18	2018–19	2019–20	2020–21	2021–22	2022–23
DPSCD	$114.76	$169.73	$201.08	$205.83	$236.41	$239.27
State average	$16.74	$19.15	$21.20	$20.49	$23.00	$23.42

Source: Budget transparency report, MISchoolData.org.
Note: Figures in this graph are adjusted for inflation, with expenditures displayed in 2022 dollars.

to decrease chronic absenteeism, each of which corresponded to a set of familiar routines and tools available to most public schools in the United States, and each of which incorporated necessary and important functions for school-based staff. As district leader Diana Weston shared, "No matter what role you have in the district—teacher, principal, lunchroom aide—you function in these roles. There is always going to be a layer of compliance, such as lunchroom aides needing to serve lunch. And everyone should be contributing to school improvement. And everyone needs to be addressing students' needs." The challenge was determining an appropriate balance of time and resources across these roles, given the scale of the problem of absenteeism in Detroit. While the attendance agent role was new, the tiers framework for attendance had already been popularized by Showing Up for School, and the general concept of MTSS was familiar to educators because it was already used in other areas such as academic intervention and behavior management. The premise of MTSS is that for about 80 percent of students, universal (or "tier 1") practices are adequate to support their outcomes, whereas about 15 percent of students may need targeted (or "tier 2") support, and about 5 percent of students may need intensive (or "tier 3") intervention.[4] Given the magnitude of chronic absenteeism in Detroit, however, this ideal model of MTSS simply did not match the reality that DPSCD faced.

THE ATTENDANCE AGENT ROLE

In the fall of 2018, more than one hundred district personnel started their jobs as school-based attendance agents. The attendance agent role was new for most schools in the district. They were responsible for improving attendance, but how were they supposed to go about this? Initially, the attendance agent position was defined broadly: "to support students who struggle with attending school on a regular basis" and to monitor attendance data so that they could intervene when students accrued a certain number of absences.[5] With this uncertainty around the role, principals started to task attendance agents with odd jobs around the school. As James explained, "What schools were doing was using an agent to stand at the door and write tardy passes, or using an agent to do hallway duty, using an agent to monitor and support cafeteria duty . . . because they couldn't do what they were hired to do." Several months into the school year, James sought to "reset" the position. At the same time, Showing Up for School and the Coalition continued to provide professional development to a set of attendance agents and recommend resources to the district. In sum, the district and Showing Up for School were actively working to clarify and refine the attendance agent role, which included working with the principal and a school-based team to analyze barriers to attendance and implement tiered supports. The district wanted to establish clear job responsibilities and expectations, primarily focusing on the agent rather than the team. Showing Up for School and the Coalition wanted to shift the overall focus and orientation of the district's attendance initiatives. In some ways, their visions for the role complemented each other, and in other ways they diverged.

The work of attendance agents came to be defined by three distinct models. The first was the bureaucratic model, focused on tracking attendance, enforcing laws and policies, and reaching out to families in a routinized way. The second was the school improver model, focused on monitoring data and developing and implementing new school-based strategies to improve attendance. The third was the caseworker model, in which agents worked with individual students and families to identify and address barriers to attendance. Each of these models was emphasized to varying degrees in the DPSCD 2018–19 attendance plan and in training materials from Showing Up for School, which was supported by the

TABLE 3.1 Attendance agent models

Model	*Benefits*	*Drawbacks*
Bureaucrat	Sets clear and manageable job responsibilities and routines	Sets standardized work tasks and compliance orientation; limits innovation
School improver	Provides autonomy and responsiveness to local conditions	Places emphasis on absence rates rather than reasons, has a lack of clear guidance, and focuses on school-based initiatives with limited potential impact
Caseworker	Directly addresses barriers that students and families face	Is costly and time intensive, especially given the magnitude of absenteeism

Coalition. As summarized in table 3.1, each of these models had benefits and drawbacks. Consequently, the attendance agent role took on elements of each.

Attendance Agents as Bureaucrats

The bureaucratic model for attendance agents somewhat represented an evolution of the old truancy officer model described in the introduction—keeping track of students identified as truant, conducting outreach and investigations for those students, and providing formal notices about their truancy status and the related laws and policies. James described several elements of this bureaucratic model when outlining the competencies that he felt attendance agents should have: "When I talked about data, policies and laws, and school-community liaisons, those were the three areas that I asked for our agents. . . . I think the first piece was to definitely deal with [attendance] data. The second piece, once you have the data, was to understand the attendance plan, the code, the compulsory attendance laws . . . things of that nature. Then you need to be a community liaison for your school. How do you bring parents in, attendance team meetings as you see fit." These core competencies—managing and analyzing attendance data, understanding attendance laws and policies, and engaging with the community—resemble the way that truancy officers have done their jobs for over a century.[6] In line with this older kind of education-centric approach to student attendance, the district established a set of specific bureaucratic responsibilities for attendance agents to carry out.

In line with the broader commitment to data-driven practice in education emphasized by the US Department of Education since the passage of No Child

Left Behind, both DPSCD and Showing Up for School described compiling student attendance rates as a necessary starting point for any decision-making and action by school-based practitioners. For example, Janet Knight, a Showing Up for School affiliate who traveled to Detroit to help facilitate training sessions with attendance agents, stated that "this data can turn into something manageable. . . . [It] allows you to compartmentalize the students and meet the needs." Attendance agents were also told, "You can't do anything without data. You don't know what you should be focusing on. If you don't have data, then you don't know what you're working on." The centrality of tracking attendance rates was reinforced by the district's practice of data-focused meetings, during which principals would present data on student achievement, discipline, and attendance to the district superintendent and other district officials to recognize schools for improvement and share ideas for overcoming challenges with their peers and district leaders. Substantial portions of professional development and technical assistance—from both Showing Up for School and the district—were dedicated to showing attendance agents how to properly compile attendance data.

In addition to tracking attendance rates, the district emphasized tracking the reasons students miss school. Generally, attendance agents had strong impressions of why students missed school, often identifying major factors in our research, such as health and transportation (see chapter 1). James believed that attendance agents needed to devote more time to systematically documenting those reasons. For example, at one district-run professional development session, when attendance agents were sharing a variety of reasons why students missed school, James responded, "Let's stop talking about what we think the problem is and start documenting it. The conversation means nothing if there's not documentation. Write it down, document it." Data tracking, therefore, was meant to be both a method of categorizing students into tiers and a systematic way to document barriers to school attendance, which would inform school-based strategies to address them. At the time, however, there was no districtwide method to systematically track the reasons why students missed school, so agents were asked to do this on their own.

Implementing attendance-related laws and policies was another core expectation from the district. Two key policies that the district emphasized were related to initiating truancy proceedings and disenrolling students from the district. For truancy, the district maintained a structured process that required thorough documentation of the actions an attendance agent took to engage the student or family. James encouraged attendance agents to use truancy referrals after attempting other solutions. For example, during a districtwide attendance agent meeting, one attendance agent raised concerns about the large number of chronically absent students who were using school choice to attend their school. James responded with guidance for how to deal with the situation: "The attendance rate is negatively affecting students, so we recommend you enroll your child in the neighborhood school where we can provide transportation. If they don't, and they still don't get them to school, that's where we start court referrals. . . . As soft as you can, by law, as an attendance agent, you're required to do certain next steps: court . . . document all that, exhaust all the temporary resources, but then you have to follow the protocol." James's emphasis on requirements and protocols reflects the—often legally required—bureaucratic nature of the model he and other district personnel were providing for attendance agents.

Guidance on disenrolling (or "dropping") students similarly reinforced this bureaucratic model. The district drops students who it verifies have changed schools, or who are absent for twenty consecutive days, in order to maintain accurate records of its students. Attendance agents were asked to play a role in maintaining rosters by confirming information on student enrollment or investigating students with many consecutive absences. Attendance agents sought clarity on when and how to drop students in part because they were concerned about how these students affected the bottom-line attendance data at their schools—in the words of one attendance agent, how these students would "count against us." At one districtwide attendance agent meeting, for example, James explained to attendance agents that students who are candidates to be dropped "will count against you until we can give evidence that they ended up at another school. If they are not in school, they have to be counted at their last known school." When attendance agents asked about dropping these students to avoid a negative impact on their school's attendance rate, James reiterated that "you can drop them as long as you have the proper documentation," emphasizing that, although attendance agents were to play an important role in complying with the administrative rules regarding student enrollment, dropping students should not be done for the purpose of improving attendance. Like truancy proceedings, the task of dropping students introduced a focus on bureaucratic documentation and recordkeeping.

Finally, the district expected attendance agents to contact families about their children's attendance. As James explained, attendance agents were expected to follow the district's already-existing "3-6-9" policy for contacting families about attendance: "The next thing that we did was continue the system that was already in place, which was the 3-6-9 policy. . . . So if a child missed school up to three days, it was up for a teacher to make a call. At day six, the attendance agent would get involved. . . . At day six, turn it over to the attendance agent with documentation of the attempts that have been made to reach out to the child." At six absences, attendance agents would make phone calls; and at nine absences, they would conduct home visits or other escalated levels of engagement, such as a meeting with a parent to develop an improvement plan for attendance. While attendance agents certainly used these points of contact to identify specific barriers to attendance that students face, their outreach efforts under the 3-6-9 policy resembled a bureaucratic process. For example, Michael Strong, a former DPSCD culture and climate staff member who switched into the attendance agent role, described his daily routine this way: "I usually run my report and compare from yesterday . . . who came to school, who wasn't here throughout the day, how many kids brought in excuses for their absences. . . . If any kids are absent for three days in a row, you know, you need to reach out." Similarly, Valerie Holloway, another attendance agent, explained that her day starts with "look[ing] at data to see who I need to call right away." These were standardized and regimented practices that attendance agents were expected to carry out.

The work of attendance agents was also constrained by their employment status. The attendance agent role was brought under the Detroit Federation of Teachers union contract, which meant there were certain constraints on their time and job functions that made it difficult to reinvent their role. For instance, they were on contract for ten months rather than twelve, limiting the planning and outreach they could have done during the summer to proactively address potential problems with attendance.

In sum, DPSCD, with guidance from Showing Up for School and the Coalition, outlined bureaucratic tasks such as organizing student data into tiers and implementing outreach routines as a core function of their work. As James explained,

> There was a goal or an expectation for the central office to provide capacity to that agent, in the manner of making certain the agent is aware of everything that's in the plan. How to pull reports and documents from our student information system. How to thoroughly and accurately go out, do home visits, to recapture

> students. . . . Let's say it was an attendance agent that was well versed in all of those things that I named. You could move them further along the line, and get them to understand okay, now with Showing Up for School, here are some additional things that you could do to make this work better in your school.

For the first time, DPSCD was employing attendance agents at all schools in the district. In order to provide clear direction for this new position, the district emphasized a set of discrete tasks and procedures to guide their work. In addition, given that several policies around attendance remained in place (e.g., 3-6-9, truancy referrals), the district sought to ensure that attendance agents understood and properly implemented those policies. From James's perspective, attendance agents could engage in additional school improvement strategies for attendance, but only after they mastered the bureaucratic elements of their job.

Attendance Agents as School Improvers

If the bureaucratic model was a kind of evolution of the truancy officer role, then the school improver model for attendance agents represented a starker departure from it. Showing Up for School and the Coalition promoted a shift from the old truancy model to this newer approach through professional development and technical support to the district. Rather than the old model of using the threat of the court system in response to students who were identified as truant, Showing Up for School trainers encouraged school-based attendance agents to address attendance across all three tiers, including using strategies to prevent absenteeism before it began. The shift in practice that Showing Up for School and the Coalition wanted to see in the district mirrors the broader shift in focus from truancy to chronic absenteeism in education reform. In this way, the school improver model epitomized the "educational" solution for chronic absenteeism. Indeed, as with reform efforts in other domains (e.g., instruction), this approach to attendance involved a strong emphasis on creating new organizational infrastructure to implement "best practices" and using data analysis to inform and continuously improve those practices.

As previously discussed, Showing Up for School and the Coalition shared the district's commitment to data as a central component of the attendance agent role. While the district placed a heavy emphasis on using data for monitoring and structured outreach, however, Showing Up for School and the Coalition advocated for a more autonomous form of data-driven practice. This was often done in connection with the tiers framework (discussed later in this chapter). For example, during a Showing Up for School training, Valerie Holloway reflected on how she had used data to inform her practice: "It allowed me to decide what my plan of action should be, which group to focus on more, what strategies to use for kids who are already on point, kids who are at risk of losing their good status, and kids who are already far gone. It helped me to organize and decide where I need to start. Because at the beginning I didn't know where to start." In other words, while general data monitoring (described earlier) was a necessary first step, Valerie was also trying to develop new school-based strategies or interventions based on her analysis. This went beyond the more routinized form of data use associated with the attendance agents' bureaucratic tasks. Janet Knight responded that Valerie had "hit the nail on the head."

The district, often through the training provided by Showing Up for School and the Coalition, also encouraged attendance agents to implement schoolwide (or universal) initiatives to encourage positive attendance. District leaders described these schoolwide initiatives as "the real work" of shifting the school culture so that all children were getting positive messages from adults in the building, getting recognized for their good or improved attendance, and building strong relationships with school staff. These kinds of school-based attendance interventions—strategic communication with students and families, incentives or awards based on attendance, pairing students with mentors—are the types of initiatives that Showing Up for School and the Coalition wanted to see in schools. Their underlying expectation was that attendance agents and school-based attendance teams would lead these improvement efforts, taking the concepts and adapting them for their local context.

Finally, Showing Up for School and the Coalition also encouraged attendance agents to see themselves as facilitators in school-based attendance teams. The school attendance team's purpose was to select attendance initiatives and support their implementation. As Showing Up for School explained in a presentation, the team should include the school's principal, dean of culture, school guidance counselor or social worker, teachers, and the school nurse. The goal was for schools to incorporate attendance practices as a key component of their work, alongside academics and student behavior, for all staff who were interacting with students.

In sum, the attendance team was meant to be a new organizational structure that would bring attendance into the center of schools' improvement efforts.

Accordingly, the primary focus for attendance teams would be in-school factors that affect attendance. DPSCD supported these attendance teams as a lower priority than the routine tasks we outlined earlier. James affirmed that "establishing an attendance team is an expectation of that role. That is also in our attendance plan. . . . The expectation of that attendance team was to look at data, identify where kids are, and tier them for support." He also acknowledged Showing Up for School as a helpful partner for establishing those teams: "We want attendance team meetings. But we didn't identify or solidify an exact structure and function of how it should run. I think what Showing Up for School offers is that piece." At the same time, however, he felt many attendance agents were not yet prepared for that aspect of the role: "We can't be so interested in doing an attendance team because this agent doesn't even have the necessary qualifications, or capacity, to pull data. . . . This is where you had agents not feeling comfortable facilitating an attendance team." As his comments illustrate, attendance agents would need to manage the bureaucratic and school improver elements of their role, both of which served important functions but also required different skills, time, and capacity to execute.

Attendance Agents as Caseworkers

Finally, there was the caseworker model for attendance agents. Both DPSCD and Showing Up for School endorsed the practice of working with students and families to identify and address barriers to attendance. For example, James connected the work of attendance agents to resources that the district provides for special populations: "This is why the Office of Homeless and Foster Care reports to my office. Sometimes we find out those barriers and are able to provide [resources]. . . . By doing that, we try to remove barriers." In this way, the attendance team, with the agent in a key role, was responsible for developing strategies for each tier of students and for addressing attendance barriers that cut across the ecological systems in which students attend school.

Attendance agents themselves also often characterized this element of their work as essential. As agents reached out to families with absent children, they were confronted with the socioeconomic challenges that students and their parents often faced. For example, Earl Jamerson, another attendance agent, listed some of the barriers to attendance he observed: "Parents don't have lights, gas, heat, can't pay rent. They relocate in shelters." Agents routinely sought to identify these issues when making phone calls and conducting home visits. For example, Aretha Johnson said that as she contacted families, she tried to "follow up about what's going on. Why is your kid missing school? So, I come by, and I present myself. . . . 'I'm here to find out why or how we can assist your family, because your son or daughter has this many absences. What is it we can do to support you to bring this up?'" This instinct aligns with a long history of truancy officers positioning themselves as "social field workers" to distance themselves from law-enforcement reputations and establish positive relationships in the communities they served.[7]

Yet both the district and Showing Up for School characterized this part of the job as secondary. DPSCD wanted attendance agents to prioritize tracking student attendance and following district policy on outreach. Identifying and then addressing barriers to attendance might be a by-product of their routinized outreach, but district leaders emphasized following the routine itself. James explained that he mostly viewed parent outreach (e.g., phone calls, home visits) as a way to encourage better attendance rather than addressing barriers: "In most cases . . . when they do make home visits and contact the parents, [the students] start to have better patterns of attendance. What you have to monitor is when they fall off again. . . . I think it's just the constant communication and connection that helps them." While the district wanted attendance agents to target outreach to individual students and families, with other school staff creating schoolwide conditions for student attendance, Showing Up for School encouraged attendance agents to prioritize establishing attendance teams and school-based interventions, with most of their time spent on implementing schoolwide preventive practices and relatively little time spent on individual cases. They promoted this idea in part by advocating that attendance agents should be liaisons between the school and external organizations that could help remove barriers for individual students. In addition, they expected that community-based organizations, including the Coalition, would be involved in directly removing attendance barriers outside school, including through advocacy for structural change to reduce poverty and significant investment in transportation, housing, and health.

One concrete way that the district and attendance agents embraced the caseworker model was in connection with district services for students experiencing homelessness, in compliance with the federal McKinney-Vento Homeless Assistance Act, which provides guidance and resources for supporting youth experiencing homelessness.[8] James incorporated a focus on McKinney-Vento into early attendance agent trainings: the head of the Office of Homeless and Foster Care presented on the legal definitions of homelessness, outlined the resources to which students experiencing homelessness are entitled, and described the process for identifying and referring students experiencing homelessness to their office. In addition, many attendance agents were designated as McKinney-Vento coordinators for their schools, meaning that they were personally responsible for managing the intake and referral process.

Besides homelessness services under the McKinney-Vento Act, however, there were relatively few resources for attendance agents to draw on as they engaged with individual families. The district's Family and Community Engagement Office provided some guidance for engaging with external organizations and accessing social services and resources that might help address barriers to attendance. Attendance agents also worked with their school's "success coach"—a social services navigator placed by the Michigan Department of Health and Human Services (MDHHS) in some schools around the state—to access resources that could help families. Still, attendance agents often felt like they had to compile information about these resources themselves. For example, Valerie Holloway explained,

> One thing that I look for are resources in place. . . . There are some families who don't send [children] to school because they don't have a uniform. . . . I need to have [clean uniforms] already in place. And, I am in the process of getting to our MDHHS worker to get something. Like, what do you have for counseling? So, I could put it on my board, so I don't have to stop, like, "Let me find [the MDHHS worker], let me call somebody else." So, just resources that are available, that we can go to really quick. . . . So those are some things that I need at my fingertips. Clothing, housing information, bus tickets if they need them, transportation, being able to let them know this is who you call, or even just giving them directions. So, that's just the thing, making sure that resources are readily available.

In addition, when attendance agents did have funding directly at their disposal—for example, small grants from the Coalition for attendance initiatives or limited discretionary funds from the district for initiatives related to school culture and climate—they were encouraged to use those resources for schoolwide preventive practices. As Earl Jamerson put it, "Outside of our budget that the district provides, we don't have anything. . . . The way we've been using [those funds] is to provide incentives for students to come to school."

Ultimately, the attendance agent role came to incorporate elements of all three models—the bureaucrat, the school improver, and the caseworker. Agents structured their work around routine tasks such as data monitoring and outreach to families; worked with colleagues to design and implement new school-based initiatives to promote attendance; and, when they were able, identified specific barriers to attendance for students and sought to provide resources that would address them. The tiers framework, which attendance agents used to organize their work, helped incorporate these competing models into different parts of their practice.

THE ATTENDANCE TIERS

In addition to defining the attendance agent role, DPSCD sought a method to organize their work. Showing Up for School provided an MTSS framework for attendance—attendance tiers—which is meant to promote a data-driven and evidence-based approach to chronic absenteeism. The framework classifies students into tiers for intervention based on their attendance rate, accompanied by a menu of practices that could be used for each tier (figure 3.2).[9]

Students in tier 1 are not chronically absent (i.e., fewer than 10 percent of days absent). The framework called for preventive schoolwide practices to promote attendance for tier 1 students, such as communicating with families and students about the importance of attendance and their own attendance rates, providing positive reinforcement through incentives or awards, and maintaining a positive school climate. Students in tier 2 are moderately chronically absent (i.e., 10–19 percent of days absent), and students in tier 3 are severely chronically absent (i.e., 20 percent or more of days absent). For tier 2 students, the framework called for early intervention. Potential interventions recommended by Showing Up for School included adult or peer mentorship, tutoring, and check-in/check-out between staff and students. The idea was that these tier 2 relationship-building practices would yield information about common barriers to attendance that could then be incorporated into tier 1, schoolwide supports.

For tier 3 students, the framework called for specialized support, such as case management involving resources from external agencies, and (as a last resort) legal action through truancy prosecution. Training materials encouraged school staff to conduct root cause analyses and document particular reasons for absences to inform their selection of strategies within and across the tiers.

FIGURE 3.2 The tiers framework

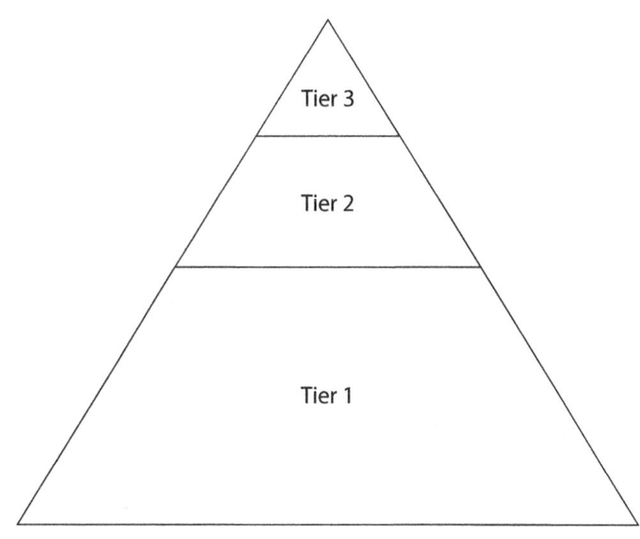

Tier	Percentage of days absent	Expected share of students	Intervention type
1	0%–4% (Satisfactory) 5%–9% (At risk)	80%	Universal and preventative practices
2	10%–19% (Moderately chronically absent)	15%	Targeted support
3	20% or more (Severely chronically absent)	5%	Intensive support

The conventional logic underlying this sort of MTSS is that tier 1 strategies (i.e., universal) are low cost (e.g., \$10–\$15 per student) and should be effective for around 80 percent of students, whereas tier 3 strategies (i.e., intensive interventions) are high cost (e.g., \$25,000 or more per student according to one early research paper) but will only be necessary for 5 percent of students.[10] With such high rates of chronic absenteeism, however, the distribution of students by tier—and thus the interventions needed to improve student attendance—did not match up with this ideal. This misalignment highlights the fundamental incompatibility of an "educational" solution—as embodied by the tiers framework—with the problem of chronic absenteeism in a place like Detroit. Allocating \$25,000 for every student in tier 3 would cost more than \$400 million, or more than half of the district's revenue in 2019.[11] While Showing Up for School and the Coalition encouraged the implementation of community-based efforts such as community schools, which may have helped reduce these high costs, such efforts were not prioritized during this time.

Adopting the Tiers Framework in DPSCD

For DPSCD, the tiers framework was meant to guide attendance agents' practice. In some ways, it helped reconcile the competing models of the attendance agent role. Overall, the tiers aligned with the school improver model, as they encouraged attendance agents to use data analysis and their professional judgment to design and implement attendance initiatives. More generally, the prioritization of universal tier 1 strategies aligned with the emphasis on school improvement efforts. At the same time, however, attendance agents could incorporate their required bureaucratic tasks into the tiers framework as well. For example, organizing students into tiers provided a structure for data monitoring. In addition, attendance agents could use their required phone calls as a tier 1 universal strategy and home visits as a tier 2 early intervention strategy. Finally, since the tiers framework anticipated that attendance agents would need to spend relatively limited time on tier 3 specialized supports, it reinforced the deprioritization of casework-type activities.

Showing Up for School and the Coalition promoted the tiers framework through professional development for attendance agents and technical support for district leaders. As Janet explained at an early training session for attendance agents and other attendance team members, "This year, [there] will be work sessions to look at data and to make plans for students in each tier. Each session will have a timeline, who is responsible and then report out. We are going to learn and grow from each other's mistakes." Using the tiers framework was the foundational practice that Showing Up for School sought to instill in attendance agents. Like most other districts, DPSCD was in the early phases of developing a robust data infrastructure that would allow school staff to identify students who were at risk for chronic absenteeism, so there were expected growing pains in implementing this framework. Showing Up for School and the Coalition encouraged the district to implement school-based attendance teams to support agents in analyzing and acting on tiered data, including through root cause analysis. DPSCD formally adopted the tiers framework for its attendance strategy.

DPSCD did make one adjustment for its version of the tiers framework. The district's framework distinguished between "recovery possible" students, who were chronically absent relative to the number of school days so far but had not yet crossed the threshold of eighteen days, and "severe" students, who had already missed eighteen days. This was meant to distinguish students who were currently chronically absent but could be "recovered" for this school year from students who could not be recovered. Thus, DPSCD's approach emphasized that attendance agents and other school-based staff should prioritize students based on whether they could reasonably be prevented from reaching the chronic absenteeism threshold. This approach supported the district's efforts to reduce chronic absenteeism in line with state and federal expectations, given the enormous scale of the problem and the limited capacity of schools to solve it. However, it highlights the gap between what is reasonable to expect schools to do and what is required to improve attendance in places with such deep social inequality.

In sum, Showing Up for School and the Coalition promoted the tiers framework, and DPSCD adopted it to organize the attendance agents' work. As Janet told attendance agents during one training session, "It's just a system to compartmentalize . . . to be able to put students in a different container. It helps to manage the work. There are different strategies that can be equally effective." Yet the tiers framework was misaligned to the magnitude of chronic absenteeism in Detroit, and, as implemented in DPSCD, the framework emphasized specific strategies based on a student's attendance level rather than the reason for their absences.

A Mismatch Between the MTSS Ideal and DPSCD's Reality

The "ideal" MTSS is based on a distribution in which 80 percent of students are in tier 1, 15 percent of students are in tier 2, and 5 percent of students are in tier 3, but the reality for chronic absenteeism in DPSCD is far from that ideal. Figure 3.3 shows the distribution of students by attendance tiers in 2018–19 compared with the ideal assumed by the tiers framework. Far from most students, only 38 percent of students were in tier 1 (i.e., "not chronically absent") at the end of the 2018–19 school year. In addition, 29 percent of students were in tier 2, and 33 percent of students were in tier 3. Simply put, significantly more students would need intervention and specialized support than the tiers framework anticipated, which was especially problematic considering the financial limitations in DPSCD. No district in the country—DPSCD included—has adequate

FIGURE 3.3 Mismatch between the MTSS ideal and reality for DPSCD, 2018–19

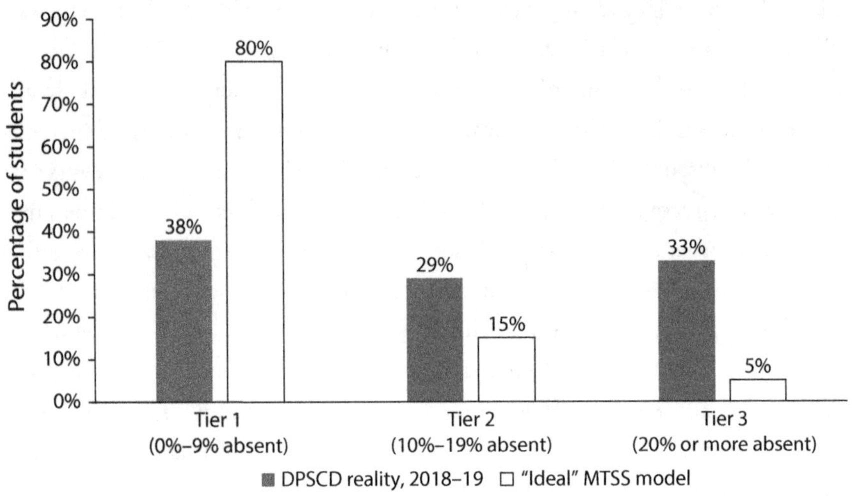

Source: Data provided by DPSCD.

resources to provide sufficient targeted and intensive support at this level of chronic absenteeism.

Despite the reality that most DPSCD students were in tier 2 or 3, Showing Up for School and the Coalition promoted the ideal version of the tiers framework to attendance agents. In training sessions, they encouraged attendance agents to prioritize universal school-based initiatives to help prevent absences. For example, Janet Knight told attendance agents, "Ideally, if you have $5, tier 1 gets $3, tier 2 gets $1.50, and tier 3 gets $0.50. Ninety percent of your time and talents should go to prevention." The idea was that by devoting most of their time to tier 1, agents could prevent students from slipping into tiers 2 and 3, saving time and resources in the long run.

In high-absenteeism contexts, schoolwide strategies can include a focus on common barriers to attendance, such as schoolwide access to meals, health services, or transportation.[12] Yet Showing Up for School and the Coalition focused on schoolwide strategies that were more clearly in the control of attendance agents and school-based teams. For example, during one training session, the facilitators presented a slide with the following "tier 1 prevention example strategies":

- teacher involvement
- mentoring

- incentives
- school structures: assemblies, clubs, advisories, homerooms, monitor meetings, youth involvement/voice
- messaging campaigns: use morning/afternoon announcements, newsletter, bulletin boards, T-shirts, attendance awareness campaigns targeting parents, communities, social media
- engagement activities: schoolwide competitions by grade level, subject, teacher

Although Showing Up for School did not present this list as comprehensive of all of the strategies that schools might employ, it illustrates how communication- and incentive-based practices were promoted over specific strategies that would remove barriers to attendance. Those efforts were reserved for tier 2 and especially tier 3, on which attendance agents were encouraged to spend less time and effort and fewer resources.

Conflating the Level of Absenteeism with Specific Interventions

Finally, while the tiers framework focuses practitioners on the amount of school that students miss, it does not directly address the reasons that they miss school. In training, Showing Up for School communicated to attendance agents that the tiers should be seen as a starting point to further investigate the causes of student absences. For example, a self-evaluation rubric provided to attendance agents defined "proficient" data use the following way: "Data is analyzed to develop . . . strategies based on reasons for absences."

As attendance agents sought more concrete recommendations to inform their practice, however, the trainers provided them with specific strategies to use for each tier. As discussed in detail earlier, recommendations for tier 1 often focused on communication with students and their families or schoolwide culture and climate initiatives such as incentives or competitions. Showing Up for School advocated for relationship building as a two-pronged approach to reducing chronic absence. First, strong relationships could directly improve attendance by motivating some students to come to school. Second, strong relationships could indirectly improve attendance by creating a trusting dialogue between families and school staff, where families share about the barriers keeping their children from school so that the staff members could address them. One challenge in communicating the second prong, however, was that there was no systematic way for agents to keep track of the barriers students and families mentioned, so agents could not identify patterns across classrooms, grades, or schools. Therefore, while trainers encouraged agents to identify root causes of absenteeism, the technical assistance they provided focused more on the first prong than the second prong.

Recommendations for tier 2 included engaging in more intensive personal outreach, in the form of phone calls and home visits, and pairing students with adult mentors inside the building as a form of intervention. For example, a slide on "tier 2 early interventions" during one Showing Up for School training session presented specific examples for attendance agents, including "home visits" and "mentoring." A later slide encouraged attendance agents to select "two Tier 2 strategies that you can implement in your school within the next two to three weeks." The district also encouraged attendance agents to use specific strategies for tier 2, such as conducting home visits, pairing every chronically absent student with an adult in the building for check-ins, and developing individual attendance plans. For example, during one training session, James Robinson told attendance agents, "If a kid gets to tier 2 at this point . . . there should be an attendance contract. That's something the school should know school-wide: when the child misses six days, parents and students get attendance contracts. [That is] the whole purpose of MTSS."

For tier 3 interventions, the district and Showing Up for School recommended that attendance agents turn to their homelessness liaison as a resource if families were homeless or housing unstable. (As noted earlier, in many cases, attendance agents themselves were the designated homelessness liaison.) They also reminded attendance agents that most schools had a representative from MDHHS located in their building, who could assist families in need with accessing social services and on a limited basis could help with transit resources such as bus tickets or gift cards for gas. As James reminded attendance agents in one training session, "Your MDHHS staff person should also be on your attendance teams." Finally, they reminded attendance agents that they could use legal interventions via court referrals, but identified these as a "last resort."

While Showing Up for School trainers emphasized that attendance agents and their teams should use their professional judgment about the best strategies for their schools, the takeaway for attendance agents was often to implement or adjust their implementation of specific strategies. For example, Earl Jamerson reflected on the trainings this way: "I learned we was doing this wrong, we need to do this. Or, we was giving the incentives wrong, we need to do it this way. We were doing tier two wrong, we need to do it this way. It's always real informative."

In effect, by strongly emphasizing an association between each tier and specific strategies without infrastructure to support the systematic documentation and analysis of the reasons students missed school, guidance provided to the attendance agents sometimes sent the message that the level of student absences could translate directly into the specific interventions they should implement. As we discuss in the next chapter, this led attendance agents to focus much more on implementing a standard set of strategies for students rather than on identifying and addressing the specific reasons for their absences.

ATTENDANCE AGENTS AND THE TIERS FRAMEWORK AS "EDUCATIONAL" SOLUTIONS

Adapting guidance from Showing Up for School and the Coalition, DPSCD implemented a new attendance strategy, centered on school-based attendance agents and a tiered framework for analyzing and responding to chronic absenteeism. The design of this strategy, reviewed in this chapter, provides a clearer sense of what it means to seek an "educational" solution to the problem of chronic absenteeism. The attendance agent role, like the truancy officer role that preceded it, was informed by multiple competing occupational models.[13] Attendance agents ultimately embraced (or were required to embrace) elements of each: the routinized monitoring and outreach practices of a bureaucrat, the focus on effective schoolwide systems and practices of a school improver, and the attention to root causes and external resources of a caseworker. The district also turned to the tiers framework to organize attendance agents' work, and Showing Up for School and the Coalition provided training and support around the framework. They promoted an "ideal" version of the framework, encouraging attendance agents and their teams to focus most of their time and effort on tier 1 schoolwide and preventive practices, even though most students fell into tier 2 and tier 3 in terms of their levels of attendance and school staff were understandably unable to address the most pervasive systemwide barriers to attendance (e.g., transportation, housing instability). At the same time, the Coalition directed most of their resources toward this "educational" or school-centered approach, meaning that there was not a parallel strategy to address the systemwide barriers in the way that Showing Up for School promoted.

The organizational infrastructure that DPSCD built around the attendance agent role and the tiers framework solidified the district's and the Coalition's embrace of "educational" tools and strategies for addressing chronic absenteeism—those focused on communication, information, motivation, and in some cases punishment. As a result, their strategy directed limited attention to developing the resources and capacity needed to address root causes of absenteeism. As we discuss in the next chapter, attendance agents were often overwhelmed by the magnitude of the issue and the limited progress they saw from schoolwide practices in which they invested significant time and effort, and in some cases shifted toward more negative and punitive engagement with families.

CHAPTER 4

Implementing the Attendance Strategy in Detroit's Public School District

Now that the new attendance strategy was in place in the district and supported by the Coalition, it had to be implemented. In education, as in most sectors, implementation is often where the best-laid plans go awry, and it can also be where new innovations are developed that respond to the needs of local contexts.[1] Several kinds of problems can arise during the implementation of new initiatives in schools. Due to lack of training or buy-in, educators may circumvent new mandates and revert to the status quo. Implementation can be highly uneven, shaped by varying conditions in schools such as resources, administrative leadership, and student needs. Even when educators implement new initiatives as designed, sometimes the consequences of implementation are unexpected or undesirable. In these cases, often the problem lies in the mismatch between the policy design and the problem the policy is trying to solve.

In this chapter, we explain how the attendance strategy was implemented in the Detroit Public Schools Community District (DPSCD) in its first two years, 2018–19 and 2019–20, drawing from interviews conducted during those school years with school and district staff working on attendance issues. First, we show how attendance agents came to embody the three models of their role described in chapter 3 (bureaucrat, school improver, and caseworker) and how these roles conflicted with each other for priority and time. We demonstrate how these models reflect common organizational structures and routines in schools and discuss the implications for improving absenteeism given these common ways of operating. Then we analyze how the multitiered system of support framework significantly shaped the practices of attendance agents and led to unintended consequences for educators and students. Finally, we describe how the lack of progress experienced by most attendance agents led some to characterize chronically absent students and their parents as being uncommitted, uncaring, or out of touch, even while others acknowledged the racial and socioeconomic inequalities that created such difficult conditions for student attendance in Detroit. While there are some lessons here about how schools and districts might implement their attendance initiatives more effectively, the main takeaway remains this: any effort to substantially reduce chronic absenteeism in Detroit, or any other high-absenteeism district, will not succeed if it depends on the resources, tools, and capacity of schools alone.

EMBODYING THE ATTENDANCE AGENT ROLES

As introduced in chapter 3, DPSCD attendance agents were asked to embody three role types in varying degrees as they implemented the district attendance strategy: bureaucrat, school improver, and caseworker. The guidance they received from district leadership and the Coalition (largely through professional development provided by Showing Up for School) created a blueprint for their work, and they each implemented that blueprint in various ways while embedded in unique school contexts throughout the city. Through nearly thirty hours of observation of attendance agent district meetings and school-level attendance team meetings, seventy interviews with district staff and Coalition members, a survey of attendance agents and deans, and analysis of eighty artifacts such as attendance plans and professional development guidance, we documented the extent to which attendance agents implemented these roles, how the guidance they received shaped their priorities and practices, and how their work ultimately affected students and families who were struggling to get to school. In our case schools, we observed attendance agents put a lot of effort into the strategies that the district and Showing Up for School promoted: they held regular attendance team meetings with other school-based staff, analyzed data and categorized students into tiers, made phone calls and conducted home visits regularly, and enlisted other staff in the school as mentors or to help with phone calls. Yet they spent far less time on strategies that would alleviate attendance barriers through additional resources or social services.

Results from our districtwide survey reflected these observations from our case-study schools (figure 4.1). Nearly all attendance agents reported frequently

FIGURE 4.1 Percentage of attendance agents who used strategy frequently, fall 2019

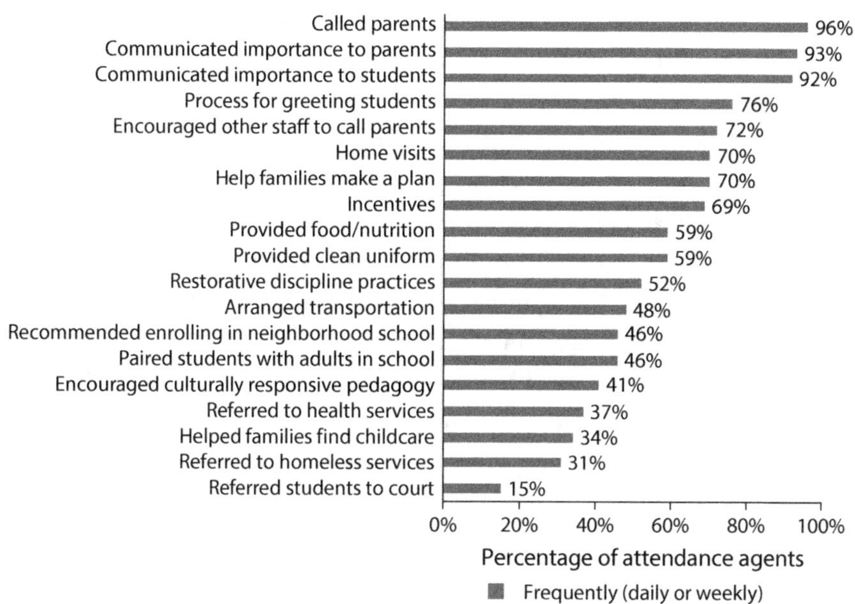

making phone calls, and about 70 percent reported frequently working on incentives for attendance and conducting home visits; yet fewer than 50 percent reported frequently helping families with transportation, health services, childcare, or homelessness services. Guided by the tiers framework and eager for concrete means to address ambiguous ends, attendance agents identified students to support based on their attendance tiers but intervened based on tier-associated strategies rather than in response to the reasons students were missing school.

Bureaucratic Work

The Detroit public school system (first as the Detroit Public Schools and later as DPSCD) had long employed attendance agents who worked with extremely truant students and their families. These agents, who were deputized and carried badges indicating their association with law enforcement and the judicial system, largely spent their time visiting truant students' homes and warning parents that, if their children did not start attending school more regularly, they would be given a citation and asked to attend a hearing in the Third Judicial Circuit of Michigan. This punitive approach was meant to incentivize students and families to begin coming to school more regularly and, sometimes, to ensure that the family had the resources they needed to support regular attendance. Although the shift to school-based attendance agents and the multitiered system of support approach moved away from court referrals, attendance agents, some of whom had been in this role before the shift, still spent much of their time on bureaucratic tasks that resembled the routinized, recordkeeping aspect of the deputized agents' roles. In fact, we found that most attendance agents spent most of their time during the 2018–19 and 2019–20 school years (before the start of the COVID-19 pandemic) on bureaucratic tasks that supported recordkeeping and compliance.

To determine the students and families to contact during a given week, attendance agents compiled student attendance data, ran reports, and categorized students into tiers to determine interventions. The three activities that took up most of the agents' time during this period were analyzing data, making phone calls to families, and conducting home visits. Although home visits were sometimes used to build rapport with families and provide resources to remove barriers (which we discuss later in this chapter), agents typically conceived of home visits as compliance tasks, in which they had a list of families and a predetermined number of visits to do in a day or week, and agents documented that they had visited all of the homes on their list, whether or not that visit led to any sort of intervention plan.

Attendance agents and other school-based staff were consistently using data on attendance rates in their work on chronic absenteeism, and in fact they often relied on the data they analyzed as they made sense of their roles. For example, Aretha Johnson told us, "In the beginning of the year, I wasn't using [my data]. . . . Now that my time is really centered and focused, I really look at the student percent of absence, the days missed." Earl Jamerson explained how this focus on data helped him shift from the old truancy approach to a more systematic one: "My initiative was to take three [students], and kind of get them to a point where they were at least coming to school. Then my [percentage of students in tier 3] started to grow, because I was missing all the [students in tier 2]. I was like, 'Ahhh man. Now I've got another three. Now I gotta wait two weeks for this kid to be back at a Tier Two.' You get what I'm saying? I had to realize how to switch my focus." Data on attendance rates were also regularly part of the attendance agents' collaboration with school leaders and other school-based staff. Across our case schools, we observed school-based staff using data on students' attendance rates as a central part of their practice.

While the data were a useful foundation for attendance agents' practice, compiling and monitoring attendance rates became one of their predominant work activities. Substantial portions of Showing Up for School and DPSCD professional development sessions in 2018–19 and 2019–20 were devoted to compiling attendance data and "tiering" students, and attendance agents and school leaders referred to tiering students as a core practice related to attendance. Principal Camille Ford shared how her attendance team used data: "We disaggregate the data, divide tier one, tier two, tier three, and then we just monitor and again reach out to the families. And we talk to the students, we stop by the classroom to check to see if they're there, and have a good day, great to see you today. So again, just monitoring. Just definitely monitoring." Importantly, the data processes at the center of this work created challenges for school-based staff, as they were asked not only to monitor attendance data but also to do the technical work of running reports, merging information from multiple data systems, and analyzing data within software that was unfamiliar to most of them.

Much of the difficulty that attendance agents dealt with in these data processes stemmed from a poor data infrastructure that DPSCD had inherited from the era of state takeover. Under the state's management, the district used an outdated student information system with limited functionality, which degraded in quality over time. From the start, updating its data system was a priority for the new DPSCD, but it took several years to carefully select a student information system vendor, map out the transition and overhaul of data systems, replace the old system with this new system, and integrate that system with the rest of the district's technical and organizational infrastructure.

In the meantime, attendance agents had to follow a complicated set of steps to sort students into tiers: downloading PDFs, copy-pasting into spreadsheets, deleting certain rows and columns, adjusting some raw data, and excluding certain students based on enrollment counts. Attendance agents were often doing this process weekly, and it would sometimes take them much longer than the district expected. As district-level attendance coach Ben Hunter said,

> You want the principal to be informed and know everything they know about the data; meet with your principal, sit down with them and explain it so that they understand; that is of the utmost importance that you do that. Do your school's data over and over and over again; memorize all the steps, know them, and you'll be able to do them in about fifteen to twenty minutes; do it at least every ten days

> if not more [frequently] to keep up with the data in your school. [You] need to know who in your school is in what tier, need to know all of that—need to be experts on the data for the district; 'til we get a program on PowerSchool [a student information system] we need to be able to do this.

School-based attendance agent Valerie Holloway described the time it took to pull her data: "Lately [I'm] spending so much time with data that it takes away from me actually doing the work, doing the phone calls, getting out to the homes, pulling the children into the office." In this way, attendance agents and other school staff were spending so much time organizing their data into the tiers framework that they were often not spending as much time on the other dimensions of their role—namely, developing authentic relationships with families and strategies to remove attendance barriers. To a degree, these issues were resolved through upgrades to the data dashboards that were available to the district's culture and climate support staff during the latter part of the 2019–20 school year. With the click of a few buttons, these central office staff could now easily pull the attendance data for any school and send them to attendance agents for their use.

While attendance agents devoted a significant amount of time to documenting attendance rates, they spent less time documenting the reasons that individual students were chronically absent. On official paperwork that the district asked attendance agents to submit, there were spots for both the school's attendance rates and the top three common barriers to attendance that students faced, and some agents developed an "attendance barrier tracker" for their schools. Yet it was not clear what was being done with this information or whether the barriers that a significant number of students faced were given additional attention by district or school leaders. For the most part, school-based staff spoke anecdotally and in generalities about why students missed school rather than citing specific data or evidence, and professional development sessions in 2018–19 and 2019–20 did not include opportunities for agents to strategize about how to deal with the most common barriers they cited, such as transportation.

Attendance agents also spent considerable time making phone calls to families and conducting home visits. Throughout 2018–19 and 2019–20, agents and teachers were encouraged to use phone calls as their "first line of defense," after which students would be referred for more intensive outreach and intervention. Often, agents would use the data processes just described to produce a call sheet that they (and sometimes teachers in their buildings) would need to work through over a day or week. This outreach ranged from perfunctory calls and visits, where agents would sometimes just need to get through their list to report that they had completed it, to more intensive or strategic outreach, where agents and other school staff would call or visit homes with a plan for improving students' attendance.

An illustrative example comes from Andrea Washington, a DPSCD high school principal, who was deeply involved in her attendance team. On one hand, she spoke about the ineffectiveness of the bureaucratic approach to outreach: "You call the parent and make a threat, and then the student comes the next day. And then they're gone again." On the other hand, the same principal described how intensive outreach can lead to improvement for a small set of students:

> So, I have one specific student, [she] is being raised by her brother. Her brother is three years older than her. And they live in this big house down the street. [She] wasn't going to class. So, I just called her brother every single day. And so, I think I got on his nerves. But I was doing it in a nice way like, "Hey, I just want her to go to class. She's here every day. She looks like she's smart. I have no clue, 'cause she's always in the hallway." Two weeks, [she] has been in class. She makes it a point to come and tell me that she's going to class. That's huge, you know what I'm saying? I have one winner right now. I'm taking that and saying, "Okay, if I can get her to go to class, I can get anybody to go to class, 'cause she don't never go to class." So, there are some successes. Now she's doing track after school because we've been able to develop a relationship that's positive even though you don't wanna go to class, now you know I care about you, and I want you to be better. So, it's a work in progress. Our school is small enough that we can have an impact, you know what I'm saying? The teachers are kind of tired, and I understand. I'm tired, too. But our team is big enough that if we just take on four or five kids, we're still having an impact.

This was a common refrain from attendance agents and other attendance team members in schools—they spent a lot of their time on tasks that, while laying the foundation for data-informed engagement with students and families, ultimately did not do much to address the barriers to attendance that many students faced, although they occasionally saw success with a handful of students whom they were able to connect with and for whom the barriers to coming to school were within their grasp to solve. As attendance agent Carlos Rivera said, "I would say that the students that are really missing for reasons out of their control are much harder to get in contact with."

School Improver Work

The tiers framework and the guidance offered by the district and the Coalition also shaped attendance agents' work in ways aligned with the school improvement and accountability logic of modern educational reform. As described in the introduction, chronic absence was first integrated into federal and state education policy through school accountability ratings that made districts and schools accountable for the percentage of students who missed 10 percent or more of their enrolled days. In turn, the tiers framework translated chronic absence rates into tiers that were easy to discuss and measure. Attendance agents used the tiers framework and embodied the role of school improver in two primary ways. First, they focused much more on the number of days students missed school than on the reasons they missed or the patterns in their absences. Second, they emphasized tier 1 approaches to reducing chronic absence over approaches designed to identify and address students' root barriers to attendance.

Chronic absenteeism was a major problem for the district, both because it undermined the ambitious instructional improvements they hoped for and because the state held them accountable for high rates of chronically absent students. In addition, the state reduced their funding each time their daily attendance fell below 75 percent. Mike Lennon, principal of a K–8 school on Detroit's west side, described how chronic absenteeism became a districtwide issue that everyone was paying attention to and working to address:

> From the beginning of the year, Dr. [Nikolai] Vitti did a great job as far as setting the tone for the year and one of those tones was addressing chronic absenteeism. And so, on my end, I really strategize to do that and so, we came up with specific goals for ourselves and I think I even had one of them hanging [in the office]. So, you see it? It says 25% reduction of chronic absenteeism so, at the beginning of our professional development at the school, we highlighted that. . . . We've been really diligently working hard on that and so everyone in our building is aware, and they're also aware that it is a big district initiative as well.

Each principal had to present their chronic absenteeism data in districtwide data-sharing sessions, attended by the superintendent, principals, and key central office leaders. In addition to principals, district leaders in charge of attendance were asked to provide data on attendance and to report on "how good the attendance agent is" at each building.

This emphasis on chronic absence rates in each building significantly influenced how attendance agents spent their time and how they conceived of success. While the tiers provided an easy container to organize attendance data, they led some attendance agents to feel frustrated with the lack of progress they could demonstrate. The district focused on chronic absenteeism, which meant that some of the progress attendance agents experienced with certain students was not visible in the reports they provided to central office leaders, particularly if those students were still counted as chronically absent. An example from a veteran attendance agent, George Hamilton, illustrates this conundrum well:

> So, if I get to you and you've missed fourteen days, you are a Tier Three student that I'll work with for the entire year. . . . According to how we're tiering and identifying our students, you could have 90% or 100% attendance after I get to you because I addressed that barrier and you got a ride every day. But you are going to complete that whole year as a Tier Three kid. You'll never be identified as nothing else but a Tier Three kid. So, there's room for improvement with how we classify and categorize a student who had poor attendance. And I just don't think that's healthy. I don't think that's a really holistic approach. I'm trying to change your mindset. . . . So, if you're a chronically absent student, once you are in rhythm and you're coming to school on a regular basis and you're engaged, I don't want to remind you that, "Oh, hey, by the way, you're doing really good for a chronically absent student." I don't ever want to say that to you. I want to say that you're doing excellent because now you're embracing what we're doing here.

According to the accountability framework used by the state and translated through the district to schools, the student just described would likely still be categorized as chronically absent by the end of the year, counting against the agent, his principal, and the district. For some attendance agents, this possibility meant that it was not an efficient use of their time to work with students who would ultimately still count against them. If the goal was to reduce the rate of chronic absenteeism, then focusing on students who were more likely to come in under that threshold was reasonable, especially given their time, capacity, and resource constraints.

Attendance agent Hank Terry shared that, before they had to analyze data in this way, they were able to focus more on understanding and removing attendance barriers for families: "Last year—it was a lot less being asked for. . . . The thing that really improves the numbers is going to the homes, the leg work basically.

If you focus on 'the numbers' more than improving the numbers . . . that's where the conflict is." The emphasis on "the numbers" embodied in the school improver role led many agents to feel that any success that did not show up in improvements within the tiers was not seen by supervisors, external partners, or state policy makers.

Since attendance agents and other school staff were focused on "the numbers," they designed strategies that they believed would lead to immediate improvement in their chronic absence rate and that felt immediately within their capacity. They emphasized what Showing Up for School described as tier 1 strategies, particularly incentives and communication with parents, as they implemented the multitiered system of support. For example, Showing Up for School encouraged attendance agents to develop incentives for student attendance. In fall 2019, nearly 70 percent of attendance agents said they used incentives daily or weekly to encourage better attendance, despite limited research evidence of their effectiveness and some evidence that attendance awards can be counterproductive.[2] Attendance agent Earl Jamerson shared how a focus on tier 1 strategies like incentives could emphasize school improver tasks such as data monitoring that took up so much time. He shared that he monitored attendance levels for every homeroom to determine if they had 90 percent average daily attendance, which would result in the class getting a "free dress Friday." He said he monitored the data "every week" and further explained, "I have daily percentages outside my door for every class pre-K to 8, and outside every classroom too so they know where they're at and they know how to get there; also have lower elementary, upper elementary compete with each other." The winner got a pass to avoid punishment for a low-level infraction, or the opportunity to trade a punishment for a higher infraction for a lower one, such as trading an "A-level infraction for a B or C one."

When school leaders or attendance agents received additional funds to support their attendance efforts, they almost exclusively used those funds for incentives or awards for perfect or improved attendance. For instance, in 2018–19, Showing Up for School helped to facilitate a mini-grant program for Detroit schools to fund an attendance initiative. Camille Ford's school won a grant, and when asked what her school did with the funds, she shared, "We use those funds for incentives. Acknowledging the children, rewarding the children for their perfect attendance. And we do also acknowledge children with improved attendance as well. So, it's not just always the ones for perfect attendance. We do acknowledge the students with improved attendance." The Coalition helped Showing Up for School review the mini-grant applications, and they observed that nearly all the applicants requested money to support incentives for children to come to school, which reflected schools' comfort and familiarity with this type of strategy. Incentives were also included in guidance from Showing Up for School and the Coalition, although it emphasized how incentives should be incorporated within a broader effort to prevent absenteeism and remove barriers.

As a short-term strategy, agents often described using incentives like trophies for the classroom with the best attendance, schoolwide announcements for students with perfect attendance, special parties with food, and even prizes like Detroit Pistons tickets. Many of these practices were developed over the years to increase attendance on Fall Count Day, the day when all school districts in Michigan must count all of their enrolled students for the purposes of allocating state funding. As is typical with other districts throughout the state, the district has long had its best attendance on Fall Count Day, and agents tended to believe that the same strategies should work on any other day. However, there was a lack of resources to sustain that level of incentivizing every school day, and it would likely be ineffective in the long term for many students with transportation, housing, or health barriers to school.

Case Management Work

While attendance agents spent most of their time analyzing data, making phone calls, and doing routine home visits, they spent far less time on activities that would connect families with resources or remove attendance barriers. For example, less than half reported helping to arrange transportation services for students daily or weekly, and less than a third reported helping to connect families with health services daily or weekly. The biggest hurdle for this type of casework was undoubtedly the resource constraints of the district, which is not equipped to resolve the myriad social and economic inequalities that Detroit families face. It is thus not the case that attendance agents could have fully eliminated the barriers to attendance that most students faced, even if they focused primarily on these activities. Still, there were some district- and community-based resources that attendance agents could provide for families. The caseworker role was one that many attendance agents took pride in, and it was often where they saw the most success when they were able to devote the appropriate time and resources to it.

One way that attendance agents supported families was by helping them when they were experiencing homelessness or housing instability. Attendance agent Aretha Johnson described a typical day working with families to address housing barriers:

> This morning, like I transition from coming to work to assist a parent who got here early. I signed her up for McKinney services and so eventually, when her application is cleared, transportation will pick up her kids cause she qualifies. She's doubled up with another family. But she came in to let me know that she got her vehicle fixed, so she's requesting gas cards now instead of transportation. So then, she wanted some additional support. . . . After her, I got another McKinney-Vento cause we have a high population of homeless students. We got two shelters within a half mile radius.

Aretha's principal also told us that she uses a van to "bring kids to school left and right." He went on to share that the superintendent "was looking at some possible solutions to providing services around this as far as he really wanted to strategize and possibly have selected schools, have like a smaller bus that could go out in the community." Later on, the district did purchase a fleet of small vans to support school attendance for some students with transportation barriers.

Attendance agents and their colleagues often went above and beyond to provide resources to families in need. For example, agent Carlos Rivera shared a story about a family whom the staff pulled together to help:

> Last year, we had a family that was displaced as the result of arson. They lost their home, and there were three, at that time, four children here, four students. We were able to gather resources . . . and they received, I guess I'll say a stipend. So, they had housing for about a week in a local hotel or something like that. . . . Obviously, you can't fund them for too long, but then as a staff, we all pulled together and just grabbed nonperishables and bags and bags of clothing and pull together as a team.

Similarly, Earl Jamerson described how he and his colleagues helped families with clothing and food:

> We have been in situations where staff here, they paid out of pocket for kids to have a uniform shirt. I bought uniform shirts for three, four students already. We've come out of our pocket to fill up Thanksgiving baskets for families, everything to that nature. So, the team here, even if we don't have the resource at hand, we'll figure out a way to get a child a resource for them to be successful.

> We also have a [Michigan Department of Health and Human Services] worker that handles all the benefits, that if a child needs any benefits, she can start up a case for them and they can get her what they need to be successful, not only in school, but at home as well, 'cause we know that's where it starts.

This kind of intensive intervention with students could be highly effective but could not be feasibly provided by one attendance agent to even a fraction of the total number of chronically absent students in their schools. And it was simply unsustainable (and not at all a district expectation) for attendance agents and other educators to use their own money to help students, even if they sometimes did so out of the kindness of their hearts. Still, attendance agents often discussed examples like this to illustrate moments when they felt success.

Beyond the competing role priorities described earlier, the size of potential caseloads and the lack of district resources to support those loads prevented many agents from prioritizing case management as a key part of their role. For instance, Aretha worked at a school with over 500 students, and more than 70 percent were chronically absent, which means a caseload of more than 350 chronically absent students—more than ten times the recommended caseload for child welfare workers.[3] In addition, financial limitations meant that in 2020, the district could only afford one person in the McKinney-Vento office, who was responsible for coordinating the support of between 5,000 and 10,000 students experiencing homelessness.[4] Central office attendance agent Jonathan Smith said:

> There is one man . . . and he is over the McKinney-Vento office . . . and when we identify the family's needs and we determine that this family does not have a consistent and regular place of residence . . . they are paired with other family members, they're living with friends, they're living from shelter to shelter, they don't have clothing, adequate clothing, shoes and that kind of thing, or they have experienced a fire that destroyed their clothing and that kind of thing . . . so McKinney-Vento provides those things. However, when you are talking about a school district the size of DPSCD, then you are talking about one individual who is over this program. . . . So, that is a major problem.

Balancing the many needs of chronically absent students and their families weighed on attendance agents, and they felt the competing pressures of time and accountability as they determined when to address the root causes of absenteeism. As attendance agent Earl Jamerson shared in reflecting on the different aspects of his job, "That's two different jobs in a way, and maybe they need another attendance stat person or something like that because to be doing the stats and going out to do things that improve the stats—that's two different jobs."

Our interviews with parents and students mostly focused on the barriers to attendance that they face, but we did ask what the school does when their children miss school and whether the school does anything to help with their children's attendance. Many parents shared that they received automated calls when their children missed school. Some complained that the robocalls went to parents on days that students were present in addition to days that the students were absent. Fewer parents said that they received phone calls from staff members. Of those who did, some said they heard from a teacher at the school after a few absences, and some said that they heard from attendance agents after their children missed many school days. Only a few families mentioned specific initiatives that the school had put in place; for example, one parent shared that she communicated with teachers about attendance through the ClassDojo app, and one recalled that the school was using incentives like pizza or snacks to motivate students. Another parent recalled recently reviewing her son's attendance record with the attendance agent at that school. Only a few families shared that they received a home visit or that the school was helping them with resources, such as a fifty-dollar gas card each month or help applying to Section 8 housing.

While these responses do not constitute the results of a representative survey, they do suggest that information about in-school efforts had not penetrated to the parent level; that teacher and attendance agent phone calls were happening but not at the rate that was expected by the district; and that attendance agents had not successfully carried out a large volume of other time-intensive attendance agents' activities, such as conducting home visits and connecting families with resources. (It's important to note that some parents' phone numbers changed frequently, which complicated outreach efforts.) When we followed up by asking what would help parents out, the most common response was some form of transportation support, and in particular, access to a school bus. A combination of limited transportation resources and widespread school choice within the district made it difficult for the district to address those needs.

WORKLOAD

Attendance agents in this period were working incredibly hard—putting in long hours, relentlessly engaging with students and families, and managing complex systems that were often not set up efficiently. Most agents were doing their best to implement all three roles to varying degrees, leading to a high workload that many described as unsustainable. As Earl Jamerson shared, "There is always work to do. . . . I have things to do 24/7." There were three main causes of their overwork. First, they were trying to fulfill multiple attendance roles, as described earlier, many of which conflicted with each other for priority and resources. While most schools did have attendance teams that discussed attendance data, the design and implementation of attendance initiatives fell largely on the shoulders of attendance agents. Second, many of their caseloads were more than ten times the maximum number recommended by child welfare agencies,[5] ensuring that even those agents who did their best to fulfill their mandate to communicate with and support all chronically absent families were simply unable to do so. Third, they were often pulled into non-attendance-related work in schools.

For nearly all attendance agents, the number of chronically absent students in their buildings was too large to realistically monitor and problem-solve attendance challenges. The DPSCD handbook gave guidance that read, "At day six of absence, the student will be referred to the attendance agents for intervention which may include home visits, meeting with parents or daily and check-in monitoring with students. In most instances this level of intervention will provide the necessary wrap-around services to assist students with attending [school]." By the sixtieth day of school in 2018 (November 30), for instance, 43 percent of the nearly 48,000 students enrolled in the district at that time had already missed six days of school. That means that, across the one hundred or so attendance agents working in the district, each had an average of more than 200 students for whom they were asked to conduct a home visit and provide the necessary wraparound services to assist students in coming to school. By the 120th day of school, that number had risen to 72 percent, or about 345 students per agent on average.

Although attendance agents were encouraged and trained to work with teams to fulfill their roles, many agents felt on their own in the face of extremely high numbers of chronically absent students. As Aretha Johnson put it, "Nobody helps me with attendance. . . . It just always feels like there's a lot to do. Like between the lists and the incentives and the educating." Another factor was the time intensiveness of certain activities. Phone calls and home visits, for example, required a lot of time and preparation, especially given that agents were often not able to reach families. Aretha remarked, "A lot of times folks aren't there. Like I went to eight, nine homes Friday and I think two people were home. . . . I think I talked to one or two parents, and I only got two parents to call me back." The time intensity of attendance agents' work was rooted in the fact that many of their efforts were relational—building trust and getting to the heart of issues with students and families. Beyond home visits and phone calls, the district encouraged agents to create mentoring programs where every chronically absent student would have an adult in the building looking out for them and monitoring their attendance. As James Robinson said, "The best way to do it, is tie students to the teacher of record. Those teachers should be responsible. But some teachers may have more students than average. You need to tie students to other teachers or counselors, social workers, deans, principals, assistant principals, etc. if some teachers have way too many students to call." Attendance agents described difficult time constraints related to reaching students and families and spending time working with them, especially given the large number of chronically absent students in a given school.

In addition, attendance agents were supervised by school principals who were responsible for the functioning and success of all aspects of the school. That meant that they sometimes repurposed attendance agents for tasks outside of their focus on attendance, as inadequate funding would often create staffing issues in other parts of the school. As attendance agent leader Jonathan Smith shared,

> Many . . . and when I say many, I mean many . . . many of the principals, when these people hired in as attendance agents, did not understand the job of attendance agent or the roles or the duties. They would assign them jobs, tasks, duties, that have nothing to do with attendance. . . . And it ranges from hall monitoring to lunchroom duty, to playground duty, to covering a classroom when teachers are absent, to clerical work, to some other things that I probably don't even know about, but it prevents the assigned attendance agent from doing the best job they can as it is defined by their job description.

When these issues were elevated to district leadership, they were addressed and corrected, but agents were ultimately supervised by their principals and wanted to contribute as team players to the overall functioning of their schools.

Attendance agents felt pressure from the sporadic nature of their work and the challenge of managing daily issues that can interfere with more medium- and long-term planning. As Valerie Holloway explained, "I do have a paper routine, but rarely does it go according to the paper." The challenge of managing daily issues was especially salient as attendance agents negotiated the role within the school more broadly. The culture and climate office explicitly asked schools not to pull attendance agents into responsibilities outside their purview. However, as Hank Terry explained, the centrality of attendance to the school and to student issues created a "gray area": "I mean, cause that's what I say my primary job is, just monitoring the kids and going out [on home visits], you know, and getting percentages [of attendance] and whatnot. But it's just, anything, you know, sometimes like random things come up." Many agents described these competing priorities and the lack of autonomy they felt to make decisions about how to spend their time to improve student attendance.

Latasha Williams, a high school attendance agent who had worked in the district for eighteen years, discussed the feeling of burnout she experienced given the enormity of the task of reducing absenteeism in a district with limited resources to solve the underlying barriers:

> We're expected to give everything we have, not only physically, mentally, emotionally, but financially as well. And that's not fair. Because what are we showing them? We're showing them that we're worn out, we're tired, we work every day, and the cycle is still going. When there are things in place, there are ideas that will be phenomenal for this district, and they know all of these things. I don't wanna continue to be recognized as a school who's not doing what they're supposed to be doing. We're doing it above and beyond with nothing, so imagine if we had something, you know what I mean?

In the next section, we describe how the competing priorities, heavy workload, and feelings of burnout led to unintended consequences for attendance agents and the students they were charged with serving.

"TRIAGING" ATTENDANCE AGENT PRACTICE WITH THE TIERS FRAMEWORK

Along with the difficult workload and competing approaches, the tiers framework played a significant role in shaping attendance agents' practices. The framework was intended to help attendance agents move away from the old truancy approach, which involved giving all of their attention to a handful of high-absence students, and toward schoolwide practices and interventions. It was also intended to help the attendance agents make sense of the nature and magnitude of the issue of chronic absence in their schools so that they would take a more systematic and data-driven approach. It was intended to move practitioners from short-term or reactive thinking to more strategic action and long-term thinking; and it would be a tool through which attendance agents could prioritize how they spent their time and resources, including which students and interventions to focus on.

In its implementation, however, attendance agents used the tiers framework to "triage" their workload—to prioritize some interventions and some students over others.[6] The fact is that the attendance agents faced a problem far beyond their capacity to solve: the sheer magnitude of chronic absenteeism in Detroit and the depth of social and economic inequality at its root called for greater investments in schools and in the agencies and community organizations that provide resources and services directly to families. In that context, attendance agents received advice to prioritize tier 1 strategies that were universal and could shape school culture (e.g., messaging, schoolwide incentives). Later on, they were told to focus on tier 2 students who could "realistically" be prevented from ending the year as chronically absent. In these instances, specific interventions were recommended for "bubble kids"—those on the cusp of the chronic absenteeism threshold.[7] These interventions were more rooted in standard tier 2 strategies (e.g., conducting home visits, assigning mentors, making phone calls) than they were focused on specific barriers. Attendance agents, struggling with their workload and guided by the tiers framework, ultimately devoted less time to addressing specific barriers to attendance and to working with tier 3 students.

Attendance agents and school-based staff worked hard to implement tier 1 initiatives. As discussed earlier, many attendance agents created new awards and rewards to recognize and incentivize better attendance; and others incorporated attendance goals into already-existing incentive structures, such as those associated with a school's Positive Behavior Intervention and Support systems. Attendance agents explained their focus on tier 1 strategies in terms of this shift from the truancy model to a more preventive and strategic approach. Carlos Rivera, an attendance agent at a DPSCD high school, explained it this way: "So, my focus primarily being on 'Tier 3,' right, as an attendance agent, again pursuing those legal issues . . . [Showing Up for School] suggested flipping it and focusing more on the 'Tier 1' and the 'Tier 2.' . . . Keeping them out of that upper tier, right, the prevention area kind of thing."

The focus on students categorized in tier 1 and tier 2 reflected a form of "educational triage" wherein district personnel encouraged staff members to target students on the cusp of chronic absenteeism.[8] Especially in the second half of the school year, district staff and Showing Up for School coaches stressed to attendance agents that they should focus on students who could most realistically be prevented from missing 10 percent of the total days. The district communicated this clearly, asking attendance agents to distinguish between students who had missed more than 10 percent of total days from "recovery possible" students who had missed 10 percent of days so far but not more than 10 percent of total days in the school year. James Robinson explained, "When you look at the tiers of individual students, that chronic 'recovery possible' group, we have a bigger target on them." He went on to say, "We can be halfway in a school year, and if we identify kids that have already missed twelve days of the school year, they would be a part of that chronic absence recovery where we could see, if we were at the end of the school year, they would fall in that tier. Those kids that are chronically absent, have missed the eighteen days, regardless, wherever we are." Likewise, Showing Up for School promoted a focus on tier 2 in their professional development sessions. For example, one presentation suggested "focusing on moderately chronically absent students ('Tier 2') as a third and fourth quarter attendance strategy." District staff repeated the sentiment. For example, Ben Hunter stated at a professional development session for attendance agents that they "have to focus on the Tier 2 kids. If you deal with them right now, you can prevent them from falling into Tier 3." School leaders and attendance agents embraced this approach. As Principal Camille Ford said, "Our focus here is the Tier 2 students because we certainly don't want them to become Tier 3. So . . . the students [in tier 2] were assigned attendance mentors."

Schools targeted students categorized in tier 2 with more resource-intensive strategies, including connecting with families through phone calls and home visits, enrolling students in mentorship programs, and having families and students sign attendance contracts. The precise strategies varied among schools and even among attendance agents within schools. For example, George Hamilton described how he and his colleague Malik Wilson, another attendance agent at his school, took slightly different tier 2 approaches: "He does check-ins [with students]. I do attendance tracking, so I'll give him a sheet for the week. They're going to take it out every day to their class. Take it home with them on Friday, have mom sign it, bring it back to me Monday. And I try to, before we get to the next level of tiers, I'm conscious to call [and say], 'Come in and see me before it gets bad.' So that's what I'm doing on my end . . . but how he's doing his check-ins, I'm doing tracking." This description not only provides a rich example of how attendance agents translated tier 2 strategies into action but also shows how these efforts were more targeted and time intensive than schoolwide initiatives. At the same time, it illuminates how these more intensive strategies were mostly focused on more intensely interacting with and motivating students rather than addressing students' external barriers to attendance.

While schools targeted moderately chronically absent students (categorized in tier 2) with interventions that required more personnel and time, they tended to neglect more severe cases of chronic absence. As Principal Richard Hernandez told us, "I think Tier 1 and Tier 2 are happening. I don't think enough Tier 3—deep dive, finding resources, and removing obstacles for chronically absent kids—is happening." Part of the problem stemmed from uncertainty on the part of district and Showing Up for School staff regarding how to effectively address the out-of-school barriers they associated with severely absent students. Although trainers and district leaders acknowledged that many of the root causes stemmed from issues outside the school and that required community approaches or systems change, there were few concrete resources or guidelines available to show school staff how to initiate partnerships toward that end. This lack of resources to address attendance barriers could also get in the way of sustaining trusting relationships with families. As Valerie Holloway shared, "If resources are not in place when you start this business, it's almost setting yourself up for defeat, . . . because it's like, 'How is it that you're going to find out what's going on with me and you can't offer me anything?'" In their communication with families, agents often described learning about the challenging barriers that kept students from school, but they had limited time, tools, and resources with which to address those barriers.

Ultimately, the emphasis on tier 1 or universal strategies, the lack of guidance for how to support severely chronically absent students, and the accountability demands on the district (which were passed on to schools) led the district and attendance agents to treat many students as too hard to reach. The tiers framework reinforced a cycle in which school-based staff did not substantively address out-of-school barriers and largely focused on moderately rather than severely chronically absent students. District and Showing Up for School staff implied that moderate chronic absence (tier 2) could be addressed with a set of school-based attendance interventions—mentoring, check-ins, home visits, attendance contracts, phone calls—and encouraged schools to use their limited time and personnel resources on these efforts in addition to schoolwide culture and climate initiatives (tier 1 strategies). Consequently, school-based staff spent less time investigating and addressing out-of-school barriers that were preventing the most severely chronically absent students from coming to school. In fact, students missing school across the tiers may have faced similar out-of-school barriers, but identifying these potential common barriers was deemphasized.

As we discussed, attendance agents were working very hard, but they were not seeing the progress they hoped for, which was often discouraging. Attendance agent Latasha Williams shared,

> It's just like being given a task and not given everything that you need in order to achieve that task. You're given the task and you're expected to figure it out yourself. And that's what they want us to do with the kids, too. You want us to take a student who comes in here, and this is just an example, and has failed every single class or hasn't been in school for 180 days, but they're still supposed to take the SAT and achieve a score that is nationally recognized. And if they don't, you might lose your job, 'cause you're not teaching. Or "We want you to make all these kids come to school every day, and I don't care how you get them there. You can't pick them up in your car, 'cause now that's a liability. And we're gonna give you the bus cards whenever we get ready to give them to you. But they better be in school 'cause I'm looking at your attendance rate."

As Latasha's examples reflect, many attendance agents felt tremendous pressure to improve their students' attendance but often felt they did not have the resources they needed. Legal and risk management constraints also hindered the ability of the district to be as flexible or responsive to student needs as they might have liked (e.g., providing rides to school). Unfortunately, to reconcile this gap between their efforts and results, some agents directed blame at parents and students themselves.

DEFICIT PERCEPTIONS OF ABSENT STUDENTS AND THEIR PARENTS

Many, if not most, district leaders and school staff recognized the systemic barriers to regular school attendance that Detroit students faced. As central office attendance agent Ben Hunter said, "We got a mass problem with poverty in this city that a lot of folks don't talk about when they talk about attendance. And you really can't separate one from the other." Similarly, central office attendance agent Charlie Woodward reflected,

> The root of [chronic absence], in my opinion, is systemic racism. I think everything boils back to public education was built on the sole principle of exclusion. So, none of the constitution, the preamble . . . "we the people" wasn't "us the people." So, every single system, especially from the public sector, was built on the sole principle of exclusion. To me, that's the achievement gap. That is every academic or social indicator that can be revealed in the K–12 system, has a foundation in historical racism. So how policies are designed, especially around discipline, is why African-American males are the most marginalized in the K–12 system, highest diagnosed as special ed, lowest high school completion rate, lowest college enrollment rate, and lowest college completion rate. So, I think a lot of the stuff is rooted in policies, procedures, and practices that need to be reformed, dismantled, destroyed, rebuilt, or completely thrown away to an extent.

Despite the widespread understanding of the systemic racial and socioeconomic inequalities that influence Detroit's high chronic absence rate, an unintended consequence of the challenges in implementation of the attendance strategy was a desire among some attendance agents to place the blame for their lack of progress on students and, in particular, their parents.

Initial interviews in 2018–19 of district staff, community partners, and staff in case-study schools (thirty-two people in total) highlighted school-level, community-based, and policy-based barriers to attendance. At the school level, interviewees pointed to classroom factors like ineffective instruction and permissive classroom policies along with frequent staff turnover; and school culture and climate issues like student behavior, poor school morale, and inadequate relationships in the school. At the community level, interviewees highlighted socioeconomic issues related to transportation, health care, and homelessness. At the policy level, interviewees pointed to the impact of school choice and open enrollment (leading to student turnover and the choice of schools far from home), as well as inadequate resources to address absenteeism, such as lack of guidance from the district and insufficient staff to address the number of students who were chronically absent.

However, many also framed parents from a deficit perspective, as being unresponsive, unmotivated, or not understanding the issue of absenteeism. These

FIGURE 4.2 Percentage of attendance agents who placed barrier in top three, fall 2019

Barrier	Percentage of attendance agents
Transportation	60%
Parent motivation or involvement	31%
Housing or homelessness	25%
Health	23%
Poverty and related issues	12%
Family-related challenges	9%
Uniforms or apparel	7%
Employment or parent schedules	6%
Traveling or immigration	5%
Negative student experiences about school	5%

Note: N = 71.

sentiments were reflected in a 2019–20 districtwide survey that asked attendance agents to rank the prevalence of these barriers, both listing the top three barriers to attendance that students at their school face (figure 4.2) and indicating the percentage of students at their school who face each barrier to attendance (figure 4.3). Transportation stood out as the most prevalent issue: 85 percent of attendance agents identified transportation as one of their school's top three barriers to attendance, and on average attendance agents estimated that over 60 percent of students had transportation issues. Yet school-based staff also saw parental attitudes and dispositions as a major barrier, indicating on average that parents' misunderstanding of absenteeism was an issue for over 60 percent of students and that unmotivated and unresponsive parents were a barrier for more than 50 percent of their students. About one-third of agents listed a barrier related to parent motivation or involvement as one of the top three barriers to attendance in their schools.

These numbers point to an attitude among many attendance agents that Detroit parents do not care if their children are in school, which contradicts the extensive evidence on the great lengths to which many Detroit parents go to ensure educational opportunity for their children,[9] and the reasons we described in chapter 1 for why many Detroit families miss so much school. It also conflicts with the district's official "core values," which have been consistent since 2018–19, including "students first," "equity," and "service."

FIGURE 4.3 Attendance agent ranking of factors negatively affecting student attendance, fall 2019

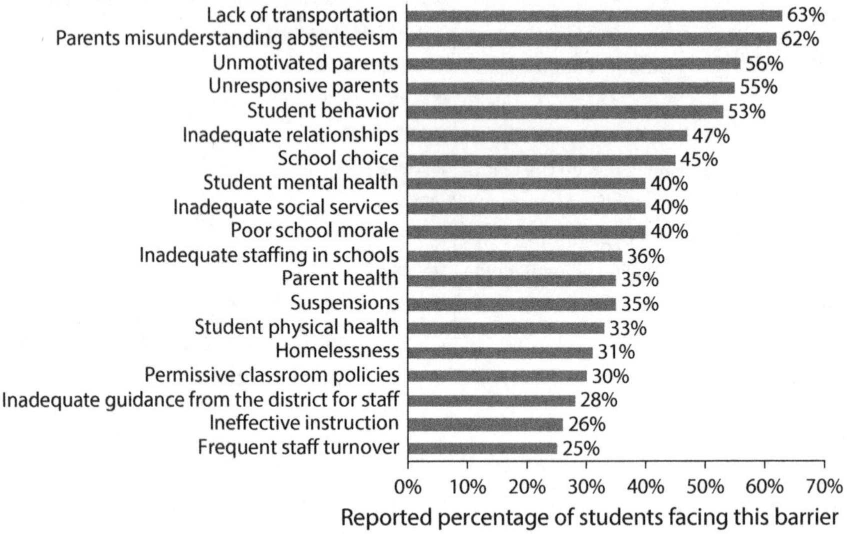

Lack of transportation 63%
Parents misunderstanding absenteeism 62%
Unmotivated parents 56%
Unresponsive parents 55%
Student behavior 53%
Inadequate relationships 47%
School choice 45%
Student mental health 40%
Inadequate social services 40%
Poor school morale 40%
Inadequate staffing in schools 36%
Parent health 35%
Suspensions 35%
Student physical health 33%
Homelessness 31%
Permissive classroom policies 30%
Inadequate guidance from the district for staff 28%
Ineffective instruction 26%
Frequent staff turnover 25%

0% 10% 20% 30% 40% 50% 60% 70%
Reported percentage of students facing this barrier

Still, contrary to the district's official values and expectations for staff, some attendance agents adopted a deficit-based perspective on chronic absenteeism. This attitude is exemplified in the way Jonathan Smith, an attendance agent leader, compared tier 1 and tier 3 students:

> Tier one are the students who are going to do the same things consistently, in other words, they come from families that the parent is engaged with the education of their children, the children know what the expectations are, the children want to go to learn, the children don't go to school and question what the norms of that school are, because their parents have already informed them. The students in tier three are those students who have been culturally deprived of being in a home that has an intact nuclear family, being in a home that has modeled acceptable behavior, being in a home that stresses the benefits of education, being in a home where socialization is close to normal, and students recognize that, other than the academic benefits, there are other benefits in terms of being able to socialize with their peers and that kind of thing. But culturally, the [tier 3] students I find, are those students who, where there's a history of noncompliance, has nothing to do with them directly, but indirectly, from their parents, because the parents have not modeled the acceptable behavior, the parents have not modeled the kind of behavior that would cause a student to understand what is appropriate and what is not appropriate. And in some of those families in tier

> three, the homes are . . . there's a problem with substance abuse, be it alcohol, be it drugs, be it abuse, that kind of thing. So, in terms of the court process, a lot of students in tier three fall into that category and will have to go through that legal process to grab their attention.

This example illustrates the way that some staff held competing ideas about Detroit families and their problems with school attendance. Examples from other staff included how parents "are only going to come [to a meeting with school personnel] when it's a problem. Most of them haven't finished school themselves"; or that "I am constantly try to talk to the parents but like I said, the parents are out of control too." We documented many instances of attendance agents who, wanting to explain how their hard work and dedication were not paying off, shifted to blame and judgment when discussing the families they worked with. These sentiments are not unique to Detroit, and they undergird efforts by lawmakers and state attorneys across the country who have sought to prosecute and punish parents who they believe are neglectful because their children are absent too frequently.[10]

The survey results described earlier and our interviews with agents suggest that they often pointed to parent motivation and involvement as an explanation of last resort. They felt like they were doing everything they could, and their chronic absence rates were often not improving, so they focused on what parents were doing wrong, even when they did not believe that the majority of their chronically absent students had neglectful parents. A conversation with James Robinson illustrates this tension between the amount of time spent discussing and problem-solving around students and families who were viewed as uncaring and uncommitted and the percentage of families whom even the district would categorize in that way. James talked about the need to "get tougher on parents just that are blatantly truant." When we asked James to elaborate on the difference between the students he called "blatantly truant" and others, he shared,

> You reach out to the families either through a home visit or a call and they're like, "Don't call my house anymore. Don't come over here again. They'll come to school when I want them to come to school." That is what I'm talking about. That's blatant. . . . Now, the parents that have legitimate struggles, childcare, and they have the older sibling keeping a younger sibling or the child is missing the majority of the day until the relief can come. Some with illnesses that are legitimate reasons for chronic absenteeism that don't have the opportunity for

> affordable health care. Those are legitimate reasons that you don't want to go a punitive route, but the district has been working toward helping remove those barriers. And that's the difference between the two.

After James described this distinction, we asked how many students he would categorize as "blatant," and he responded, "I actually analyzed and looked at that data asking the attendance agents to report back, I would say less than 5%." The perceived extent of this kind of blatant truancy (as James put it) would certainly vary somewhat among the district staff, but those we spoke to universally acknowledged that the share of families who could be called neglectful or in need of court intervention was very small. The district's own 2018–19 attendance plan documented how "responsiveness by parents has been noted by attendance agents as having reported less than 5% of parents as resistant or unresponsive. More than half of the parents contacted have requested follow-up conferences to assist with monitoring daily attendance."[11] However, the time attendance agents and others in the district spent discussing these "blatantly truant" families was out of balance with the small share of families who they believed needed punitive intervention. In fact, district staff often spent large portions of their time lamenting the parents who "don't care" or are not responsive to outreach, even while acknowledging that most chronically absent students did not have parents whom they would describe this way.

One consequence of these deficit perspectives was a reliance on the threat of truancy prosecution. Over time, as school and district staff found their efforts ineffective, they turned to the threat of legal action. The number of actual instances of court-based prosecution remained low, which is a testament to the district leadership's commitment to protecting and supporting rather than punishing and criminalizing families. And as shown in figure 4.1, less than 20 percent of attendance agents said that they referred students or parents to court on a daily or weekly basis.

Still, attendance agents often planned to threaten families with court-based prosecution—either verbally or by issuing formal letters in the mail—as an additional attendance strategy. Earl Jamerson, describing one interaction with a parent, explained the logic behind this approach: "I'm just trying to scare [her]. . . . I have to try something more aggressive." These kinds of interactions could rupture the relationship between families and their schools. For example, one parent told us about a time when her children missed several weeks of school after a family tragedy and the attendance agent threatened to send her to court: "I was in such a tough situation, it didn't matter to them, but it matters to me and my kids."

More generally, attendance agents and other school personnel expressed a desire for more punishments or consequences related to chronic absenteeism. A common refrain was that parents and students needed to be held "accountable." For example, George Hamilton, reflecting on his efforts, stated, "It's getting to that point where someone has to be held accountable. . . . We're being held accountable. The student is not held accountable. . . . Punitive measures aren't the answer. No, they're not. But they are necessary." Claudette Rogers, a DPSCD principal on the east side, suggested that parent and student accountability was more important than additional resources for parents and students: "I honestly don't think more money is the answer. I think parents need to be held more accountable, because right now the way we see things is we do everything . . . we do everything for the children except wake them up in the morning and put them to bed at night." These quotes reflect the mix of deficit perceptions and difficult work demands that often bubbled up. Attendance agents and others involved in their work felt increasingly like the strategies available to them were not effective, and that parents and students needed to be held accountable for chronic absenteeism.

The experiences of attendance agents in 2018–19 and 2019–20 reinforce the limitations of "educational" solutions for chronic absenteeism, because they offer a detailed account of how one such effort played out in implementation. DPSCD's systematic attendance initiative was years ahead of most other high-absenteeism districts in Michigan. Being one of the first major districts to try to solve such a big problem was bound to be difficult and ultimately yield important lessons. There are certainly ways that the district's efforts could have been implemented more effectively. But as we discussed in chapter 3, the attendance agent role and the tiers framework—promoted by the Coalition and Showing Up for School and adopted by the district—were already misaligned with the nature and magnitude of chronic absenteeism in Detroit. The sheer number of students missing 10 percent or more days of school, and deep inequality underlying those numbers, meant that the tools and resources available to attendance agents were simply inadequate to substantially improve attendance.

Before the start of the COVID-19 pandemic in March 2020, DPSCD was on track to be at a similar level of chronic absenteeism to 2018–19. Then the world shut down and attendance agents, like all students and educators in the district, shifted online. In the next chapter, we explain how the district responded to student attendance problems during the 2020–21 and 2021–22 school years, building on these strategies and perceptions. We also document how the Coalition and the district began to adopt a more ecological understanding of the needed solutions to chronic absenteeism and how that move translated into new policies, practices, and challenges.

CHAPTER 5

Chronic Absenteeism Through the COVID-19 Pandemic

In Detroit, as in communities throughout the country and around the world, the COVID-19 pandemic brought about sudden and significant disruptions for students and their families. On March 12, 2020, the governor of Michigan announced a statewide closure of all K–12 schools. Though the school closures were initially scheduled for only a few weeks, they were extended until the end of the 2019–20 school year and continued for many students through the 2020–21 school year.[1] Detroit became one of the early epicenters of the pandemic, with very high rates of COVID-19 infection, hospitalization, and death in the spring of 2020.[2] In a survey we conducted in summer 2021, more than half of Detroit Public Schools Community District (DPSCD) families reported increased financial, mental health, and logistical challenges during the first year of the pandemic.[3]

In those early days of the pandemic, with schools closed for the remainder of the school year, DPSCD and the Coalition focused on meeting families' basic needs and adjusting to the new reality. For example, DPSCD set up school-based hubs for Detroit families (whether they had children enrolled in the district or not) to pick up free meals.[4] James Robinson explained that attendance agents and non-instructional staff shifted their focus to calling families and "making sure students have their basic needs met." The district also implemented a "continuity of learning" plan that involved a combination of take-home materials and online instruction.[5] Likewise, the Coalition pivoted to focusing on student and family health and safety. Marvin Ashford, Joni Clark, and other members of the Coalition joined weekly COVID-19 calls with organizations working closely with youth to strategize how best to support them. Carla Garza, another key leader in the Coalition, worked closely with Showing Up for School to develop guidance for schools on the new problems they were facing, such as how to find students who had stopped engaging with school online.

This chapter is about the way that DPSCD and the Coalition responded to rising chronic absenteeism rates during the COVID-19 pandemic, as well as how they started to adjust their approach to attendance in its wake. To do so, we draw on quantitative analyses of survey and administrative data, as well as interviews with DPSCD parents, school and district personnel, and Coalition leaders during the pandemic (2020–21 and 2021–22) and afterward (2022–23 and 2023–24).

Due to the pandemic, DPSCD's chronic absenteeism rate increased to just under 69 percent in 2020–21 and increased again to 77 percent in 2021–22 (figure 5.1). DPSCD was not alone here—the national chronic absenteeism rate nearly doubled.[6] Similarly, Michigan's statewide chronic absenteeism rate

FIGURE 5.1 DPSCD and statewide chronic absenteeism rates through the COVID-19 pandemic

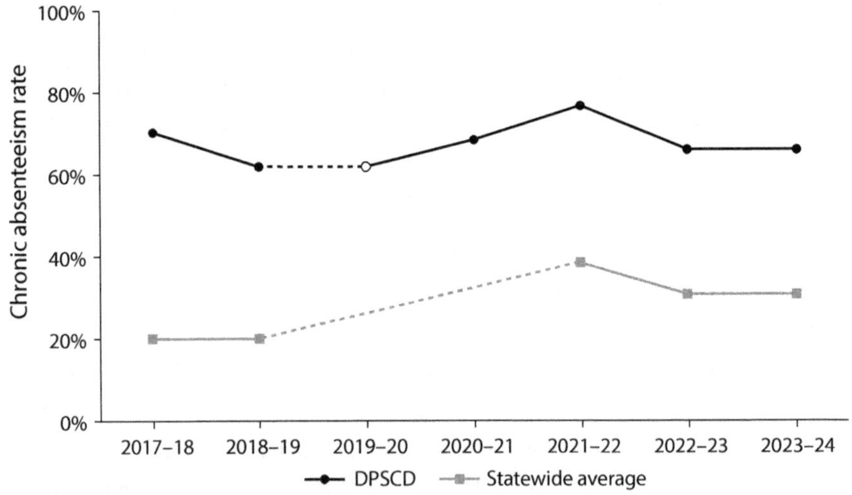

Sources: DPSCD and MISchoolData.org.

Notes: Chronic absenteeism rates for 2019–20 and 2020–21 as provided by the State of Michigan do not reflect actual attendance rates, as pupil accounting was modified under pandemic-era policy. The open circle for DPSCD in 2019–20 represents a "projected" chronic absenteeism rate and is based on district-provided data, which showed that chronic absenteeism in 2019–20 was on track to be at a similar level as in 2018–19. The chronic absenteeism rate for DPSCD in 2020–21 comes from district-provided data.

increased from 20 percent in 2018–19 to 39 percent in 2021–22.[7] During this time, DPSCD leaned into many of its existing attendance initiatives, but attendance agents struggled with increased workloads and difficulty addressing students' barriers to attendance, some of which existed before the pandemic and others of which were unique to the pandemic context. During this time, the Coalition began to rethink their "educational" approach to chronic absenteeism, but several constraints limited their ability to enact an alternative approach. In 2022–23, DPSCD's chronic absenteeism rates decreased to 66 percent, and stayed the same in 2023–24. The fact that the district's absenteeism rate returned to near pre-pandemic levels faster than much of the rest of the country is a testament to the impact that its existing practices had; and the fact that its chronic absence rate remains so high speaks to the persistent social and economic inequalities that drive absenteeism in Detroit. The district began to rethink the role of the attendance agent and began exploring different school and district strategies, including new partnerships. The district and the Coalition both began to pivot toward a longer-term and more holistic approach to addressing the root causes of chronic absenteeism, even while continuing to manage the high levels of absenteeism of students currently in the system. While the effects of these pivots are still to be seen, they represent significant learning about the opportunities and limits in an educational approach to reducing chronic absence and point toward a new way of operating that may have more promise to meet the needs of students and families in Detroit and beyond.

ADDRESSING CHRONIC ABSENCE THROUGH A PANDEMIC: 2020–21 AND 2021–22

The pandemic created unique circumstances for attendance in the 2020–21 and 2021–22 school years. In 2020–21, based on feedback from families and negotiations with the Detroit Federation of Teachers, the district opened the school year with three options for students: remote learning, in-person learning with teachers, and "learning centers" where students could log on to their virtual classes under the supervision of a district employee.[8] (Most charter schools in the city also reopened in remote learning.)[9] The shift to remote learning posed new challenges for families statewide and across the country, including in DPSCD.[10] In our summer 2021 survey of DPSCD parents, just under half of parents reported that computer or internet issues were a reason their child was often or always absent. Even after controlling for other key predictors of absenteeism (including prior-year attendance), students whose parents reported always having computer issues were 35 percent more likely to be chronically absent compared with those who never had computer issues.

Rita, a mother of two DPSCD elementary-middle school students, described running into technical issues when trying to access remote learning: "A lot of days they have trouble with the computer. . . . Because my daughter can't even get into her Microsoft Teams for some reason. And she hasn't been sitting [in class] for a week." Many parents experienced these kinds of technical issues with their devices, low-cost Wi-Fi access (which was provided by the State of Michigan), or both. These problems were exacerbated by financial strain.[11] As Rita explained, she had to rely on the low-cost Wi-Fi, which often did not work as well as she needed: "I have the $10-a-month Wi-Fi. So, I don't know if I have to pay more money. I can't afford it right now . . . but half the time the Wi-Fi doesn't work."

Increased parent and student mental health challenges also contributed to attendance issues. On our survey, 57 percent of parents agreed or strongly agreed that mental health had been a challenge during the pandemic. Lucia, a mother of four DPSCD elementary-middle school students, described how these issues looked for her children: "They're telling me that they can't focus, they're having too hard of a time focusing, being able to concentrate. So, yeah definitely, the mental aspect is very difficult. . . . You know, because one thing that I take very seriously with my kids is school."

In addition to these new challenges, ongoing socioeconomic inequalities continued to drive chronic absenteeism. As in the years before the pandemic, families with lower incomes, those with lower levels of employment, and those who experienced housing instability were more likely to be chronically absent.[12] In addition, as we discussed in chapter 1, attendance issues often arose when parents had limited social support for getting their children to and from school. Even though students mostly participated in school from home, the challenges of limited social support were exacerbated during the pandemic. Parents in many districts across the country were now responsible for overseeing their children's online education, which could be difficult. Rita described the challenges she faced this way: "Them going to school in-person helped me out so much. And with them being out of school, it's such a burden on me, with me being a single mom. I don't have no support or help. This is all on me, so it's so hard right now." Schedule conflicts often arose due to work or errands, which made it hard for parents to ensure their children's participation in remote learning. For example, LaToya, whose three children all attended DPSCD schools, reflected on how she had trouble ensuring they were logged on for school while she was at work: "It was actually kind of hard for me to keep up with them in the morning because I worked like 6:30 a.m. to 4:00 p.m. And when I would call, they would all be asleep." As another example, Rita explained that having her children at home for remote learning created new logistical challenges: "I can't leave the kids home alone when they can't go to school." She sometimes had to bring her children with her to run errands, which would lead them to miss school. LaToya's and Rita's experiences highlight how additional social support, or the lack thereof, remained an influential factor, even with a different context for attending school.

In 2021–22, students returned to in-person learning, though the pandemic continued to negatively affect student attendance. Rates of COVID-19 transmission remained high in Detroit, including a sharp increase in infections that led DPSCD to temporarily return to remote learning for most of January 2022. Student attendance dropped during this period.[13] In addition, in adherence with guidance issued by the Detroit Health Department for all Detroit schools, the district implemented quarantine protocols related to COVID-19 infections in schools: students who were exposed to COVID-19 (i.e., a classmate or their teacher tested positive) were asked to quarantine for seven to ten days and participate in remote learning for that period. On top of persistent socioeconomic inequalities and lingering negative impacts of the pandemic on student and parent well-being, the high rates of quarantining fueled an increase in absenteeism.[14]

DPSCD's Response to Attendance Issues at the Height of the Pandemic

In response to attendance issues during the COVID-19 pandemic, the district relied on some of the approaches it had been implementing for the prior school years, leaning heavily on attendance agents, while expanding its strategy to include more initiatives to remove attendance barriers and partner with external organizations. Consistent with prior years, attendance staff most frequently used communication-based strategies. The predominant form of outreach families received about attendance was through phone calls. On our survey, 72 percent of families reported being contacted by phone. Less frequent forms of communication reported by families included text messages (27 percent) and emails (19 percent).

While phone calls were the most frequent form of outreach experienced by parents and reported by attendance staff, home visits were perhaps the greatest demand on attendance agents during the 2020–21 school year. Home visits were initially seen as controversial, given concerns about COVID-19 transmission, but the district eventually prioritized them as an important strategy, and many agents were willing to take on some degree of health risk to connect with families at home during this difficult time. In addition, DPSCD experienced a decline in student enrollment in the 2020–21 school year, as did many other districts across the state and nation.[15] Thus, attendance staff who were able to work in person were asked to conduct home visits not only for attendance problems but also to identify students to encourage to come back to school or drop from the rolls. Attendance agent Hank Terry explained, "Last week, the principal sent me a list of students. It was about thirty kids or something like that. She's wanting an update on all of them. . . . The list was pretty much from students that we were trying to see who we should drop. From that list, some students they said when the learning center starts back up, they'll be back in school." Consequently, as Valerie Holloway noted, "the volume [of home visits] had really increased." Similarly, Michael Strong described the changes in his work during the pandemic as "home visits through the roof." As much as home visits preoccupied attendance agents, however, only 8 percent of parents who answered our survey reported receiving a home visit for attendance. This is partly because parents were not always home when attendance agents arrived for a visit, and partly because attendance staff were limited in the number of visits they could reasonably conduct. Aretha Johnson explained, "On a typical day, I've got eight to ten families I'm going to visit," and her time each week was split between home visits, other family communication, and school-based responsibilities.

Overall, attendance staff expressed challenges with knowing how to prioritize their time given limited resources and new demands. Valerie put it this way: "There are more severely chronic children. The number has like tripled. . . . So you have to decide, and then you look at your [moderately] chronic children and that number, of course, had gone down a little, because they had all moved to that [severe] category. So now, it's deciding how to go about your work. Those [moderate] students or those at risk students. . . . Where are you going to put your focus?" Attendance agents faced an even more demanding job than before the pandemic, leading many to feel overwhelmed. The result was a situation in which school staff were working tirelessly while still not fully meeting families' needs to alleviate attendance barriers.

In addition to ongoing communication efforts and home visits, DPSCD implemented new technology initiatives to support student attendance in online learning. The district partnered with a number of businesses and philanthropic organizations to provide a laptop with LTE data (enabling internet access without a wired connection) to students in DPSCD and some Detroit charter schools through a program called Connected Futures.[16] Though the computers were essential for providing students with access to online learning, some parents we interviewed shared that they had problems using the devices for all-day online schooling. As Rita said, "The computers keep messing up. I have to keep taking the computers to get fixed." Alexis, a mother of two DPSCD elementary-middle school children, similarly said, "The computers are constantly lagging, shutting down. They couldn't get in their classes."

Starting in December 2020, the district created technology hubs in thirteen school buildings throughout the city. The purpose of the hubs was to provide technical support for families: parents could go to the hubs during school hours to get their children's computers repaired and ask questions about the online platforms.[17] Most of these hubs were open two days a week, from 10:00 a.m. to 6:00 p.m., and one location per city region stayed open until 7:00 p.m. each Wednesday.[18] Our survey showed that 49 percent of district families used a technology hub at least once. Among those families who did not use a hub, 20 percent reported that they could not get to a hub when they needed support and 9 percent reported that the hubs were not open during hours convenient to them. For example, Gabriela, whose two children attended a DPSCD elementary-middle school, explained, "They did tell me that they had sites, but I haven't been able to make it because the hours they have, I'm still at work." Thus, while the district offered support for families, difficulties with transportation and school-work schedule conflicts made it difficult for some families to access that support. Even in a virtual context, these social and economic challenges were contributing to absenteeism.

In addition to their responsibilities from previous years, attendance agents also had to assist with technology distribution and technical problems. As attendance agent Valerie Holloway said, "So at the beginning, . . . the priority was to make sure all of those Connected Future devices have been deployed to the students because, of course, if they didn't have those devices they could not connect academically to learning. . . . So, I assisted with the deployment of those devices, calling those parents, going to the home." This additional tech support role was one more way that attendance agents' jobs became more demanding.

When students missed school due to technology issues, the attendance agent or someone else from their school usually contacted them over the phone. Parents had mixed experiences with this type of support. For some parents, this kind of communication was viewed as helpful, or it improved over the year. Elise, a mother of six children at a DPSCD elementary-middle school, said, "They started sending emails and telling us exactly how to log on." Alexis also shared later in the year, "It's getting better, finally. I'm in more communication now with her teacher." School staff reiterated that online instruction created a learning curve for all parties and that support improved over time. For example, Michael Strong noted that "virtual is something new to everybody. It was new to the teachers, it was new to the principals and everybody. It's a new world. Make sure that the kids can log on. That was the biggest part because if they can't log on, then they're not attending class." Overall, despite increased efforts to engage students in online learning and adjust to this new normal in 2020–21, many students still faced technology issues and were not able to access the provided support (e.g., technology hubs). Attendance agents struggled to manage their suite of responsibilities in the face of rising absenteeism rates.

In 2021–22, DPSCD and its families sought to "return to normal" after a year of pandemic-related disruptions. The district conducted a great deal of community engagement to inform its reopening plan and resumed in-person learning with relevant health protocols in place (e.g., mask requirements, physical distancing, additional sanitation measures for facilities, weekly COVID-19 testing for employees, symptom screening and temperature checks for students and staff, and contract-tracing and quarantining protocols).[19] The district continued to provide a virtual school option, in which about 4 percent of its students enrolled.[20]

Given the increase in chronic absenteeism, the district placed an even greater emphasis on addressing student attendance. Amina Youssef was a new district leader overseeing attendance and other culture and climate initiatives. Amina came into the role from the district's office that oversaw student equity, advocacy, and civil rights, and she shared how addressing absenteeism became more integrated with other district priorities during this time, including creating "more equitably funded realities for our students and families"; ensuring that students felt "loved, challenged, and prepared" in their schools (which the district measured using a student survey); and improving academic performance. She explained that improving culture and climate and decreasing chronic absenteeism were two of the district's focus areas because "you can't drive math and reading scores if you have a culture that's negative and if kids aren't attending school." Other district leaders echoed this shift. For instance, Sam Henry, another leader in the culture and climate office, shared how the district's blueprint outlined the transformation they wanted to see: "We want to really make it engaging and give kids a voice in the schools now. That's something that I see how we're transforming the culture for students coming to school."

In her new role, Amina sought to establish better internal processes for documenting root causes and addressing them earlier, which would reduce the amount of time attendance agents spent trying to figure out why students were missing school:

> One of the specific areas I really want to focus on is how we internally track, report and talk about attendance in our district. . . . We're just tackling "kids are absent, kids are absent, kids are absent." And we're driving it simply by numbers and tallying of numbers of absence. . . . How we're treating families, and how we distinguish that, needs to be nuanced. It's very different to approach a family that maybe has had a death in the family and a religious observance and maybe one sickness and now they've tallied up enough absences to fall into that chronic state. Very different than someone who's just skipping every day or not coming to school, or that is having resource-related problems. And yet, because we are not differentiating that on the front end, our attendance agents have to do a lot of work trying to dig and really unravel the layers or peel back the layers of the onion to figure out what the root cause of the attendance issue is. And I think we would be able to target our resources in a more equitable way and really live into our responsible stewardship, guiding principle of the district, if we report it and talk about our absences internally a little differently.

Amina believed that reorienting the district's efforts toward root causes would allow them to "target [their] resources in a more equitable way." In addition, Amina explained that the district's senior leadership was trying to increase pressure on the issue of chronic absenteeism "at the building level with principals": "I feel like there's incredible pressure that is being felt by the principals to move that [chronic absence] number."

While principals might have felt even greater pressure, they described similar strategies as in previous years. This was as true for principals who were trying to strengthen their attendance efforts as it was for those with fully developed school systems and routines. Jamila Thompson, a high school principal, explained that their school was trying to reinstate prior attendance practices after a change in staffing: "In 2018–19, I had one attendance agent, and he made phone calls, home visits, did incentives . . . but then things fell off because of COVID. . . . We got a new attendance agent who we have now . . . so we're trying to support him." The main components of her plan—phone calls, home visits, and incentives, all driven by the attendance agent—reflected the district's existing approach. Nia Jordan, an elementary-middle school principal, described a similar approach that had been in place since before the pandemic:

> We've always had a lot of attendance initiatives. The district has the 3-6-9 process in terms of when students are absent three consecutive days, contacting the home to ascertain where the child is. . . . [During the pandemic] we still did a lot of things in terms of recognizing students with perfect attendance weekly. We still conducted home visits. . . . I've had parent meetings, every opportunity that I get, I am talking about attendance. . . . Another one of my mantras is, "attendance is everybody's business" . . . although we have [an attendance agent], it's all hands on deck. . . . I have a team that contacts the parents to find out where they are, when they're returning, and what barriers, what is preventing the child from attendance. So that's what we have in place this year. Just being very consistent. I am getting ready to meet with my students, my tier two students. . . . And I've also assigned mentors to the kids earlier.

Thus, while Amina and her department had developed some new goals for attendance practices in the district, principals often returned to strategies and initiatives that were in place before the pandemic.

Aretha Johnson, who was now in her fourth year as an attendance agent, provided a useful example for how attendance agents continued to use similar strategies but began to adjust their priorities and the time spent on certain tasks. First, Aretha shared that she decided to focus less on running reports and analyzing attendance data, so she could dedicate more of her time to contacting families: "I used to think about reports, and reports, and reports and reports. . . . These reports, that's not where the work is. I understand that that helps other people look at data. That's not helping me reach parents. . . . I was looking at data. I was looking at a lot of data. . . . That's not helping me get to know the student, the parent, the situation, or figure out what that parent needs." Aretha also decided to deprioritize school-based practices such as attendance incentives and pairing students with adult mentors, in part because of her lack of capacity to implement these initiatives on her own. Although the district and Showing Up for School had promoted a team approach, schools varied significantly in their implementation of teams before the pandemic. During the pandemic, many agents reverted to working in isolation, without the support of a team. As Aretha shared,

> How realistic is it to think that one person, one agent, can do all of this? Here's an example. They want us to do a buddy pair, right? . . . So if they got a chronic absent student, that student should be buddied up. That's like 400 kids. Who's supposed to be doing that? Who's supposed to be doing all that pairing up? There's supposed to be a grade-level liaison for each grade. It's nice, you make the list, and nothing happens. Who's supposed to do that? It's too much. It's just, there has to be a better way.

As her comments show, Aretha did not feel that she could realistically carry out many of the school-based tier 1 and tier 2 practices, given the magnitude of the problem, constraints on her own time, and the resources and personnel available to her.

Thus, while Aretha prioritized connecting with parents and students, she also decided to reduce her caseload, which she felt made her efforts more manageable: "I'm trying to be really good about following up with just a few parents, because a lot of our kids are chronically absent. So, then my goal is, when I get a good case, I want to follow that one through." She explained that the school's chronic absenteeism rate was simply too great for her to work with every family with a chronically absent student:

> There's not a home visit I won't do, and if I feel uncomfortable, I'll take somebody with me. There's not a call I won't make. But if you're asking me to do X amount, I have lost things because of the stress in preparing to do all these home visits the way they want. Like the notes even behind the visits . . . because I'm going to have contact with the parent again, so then that gives me reference. So, then I'm taking twenty minutes or half an hour to write notes, which is very common for me. . . . I've done twenty home visits in a day. But by the end of the day, like I had to spend my extra time, own time, writing the notes, so I'm not trying to do that.

In addition, Aretha continued to assist with school and district needs beyond her role's immediate scope. For the most part, her principal let her focus on her role as an attendance agent: "I love my principal. I love the autonomy he gives me. . . . Before, there was an expectation by my [former] principal that I do lunch duty and cover classes. . . . [My current principal] gives me a lot of freedom." Yet with the pandemic continuing to affect students and their families—and with pandemic-related quarantines driving up chronic absenteeism—Aretha and other attendance agents were asked to help secure consent from families for COVID-19 testing and vaccines: "I was still doing the COVID consent, up until the week before last. Right, the COVID consent was supposed to be done in January. But it wasn't done for me, until the beginning of March."

Alongside her shift in practice, Aretha also began to rethink the district's overall approach. She felt that her school and the district needed to find a way to better address the various out-of-school factors driving chronic absenteeism: "I think there needs to be more education on trauma, on compassion. . . . Like how can we help parents and students address their stuff? . . . I don't know how that looks. But I know that has to be a piece of it. . . . Like we do have this and we do have a lot of health issues. We do have a lot of transportation issues. We do have a lot of this and we do have a lot of that. So then the question is, how can we bring this together?" Though she wasn't sure how, or whether she had the capacity to do so, Aretha wanted to do a better job at addressing the root causes of her students' attendance issues.

Many other agents also began to recognize the need to better align their practices with the root causes that students were facing and problem-solve alongside parents, even if that meant they may reach fewer families. For instance, attendance agent Felice Pope shared that "we need to be honest with the parents, and the parents . . . honest with us. If the parents are being honest with us that they're having transportation problems . . . let's see if we can resolve those problems." Another attendance agent, Steve Lynn, shared a similar assessment: "It's in my job description to assist with those barriers and knock them down. That's what I'm here for, so I . . . tell [parents], 'If you're honest with me, I'm going to help you.'" While central office leaders and attendance agents evolved their thinking about how best to address the root causes of chronic absenteeism, the state reduced the number of Michigan Department of Health and Human Services (MDHHS) workers in schools, meaning that agents had more work than ever, with fewer human resources to support them. Attendance agent Lisa Mays explained the effect on her work: "We used to have an MDHHS worker. So that would be my backup. . . . But because they're rapidly dismantling my team I'm back down to really a one-woman show once again. Myself." Just like Aretha and her fellow agents, members of the Coalition were also starting to rethink their approach to chronic absenteeism and adjust their efforts accordingly, though they too faced many constraints.

The Coalition Starts to Rethink Chronic Absenteeism but Faces Constraints

The start of the COVID-19 pandemic coincided with the end of our first major research study in partnership with the Coalition, a developmental evaluation of DPSCD's attendance strategy, which relied heavily on support and resources from the Coalition. We had presented interim findings from that study throughout the two-year evaluation period, using continuous improvement cycles to identify areas for adaptation in implementation. Yet the final evaluation report and subsequent engagement with the Coalition around it led many Coalition members to begin to rethink their approach to reducing chronic absenteeism in Detroit. The technical assistance provided by the Coalition, including professional development, tools, and coaching, was valued by school staff, such as a principal who said that they "always leave rejuvenated" after training sessions and another who appreciated the opportunity "to connect with other principals" and share strategies. However, reductions in chronic absenteeism were not statistically different in schools that received Coalition support compared with those that did not. Although chronic absenteeism districtwide had fallen a few percentage points, it was still sky-high, and the pandemic created additional challenges to attendance and student engagement.

While many Coalition members pivoted their organizational capacity to addressing the unique challenges of the pandemic, particularly around basic needs support and COVID-19 containment measures, they also reoriented their conception of what the Coalition was for and what it should be doing to achieve its goals. They began to consider what it would mean to focus on understanding and addressing systemic barriers to attendance. Marvin described the shift this way during a citywide meeting: "The group has evolved in terms of how we define the work. . . . How do we 'see' the challenges to getting to school more clearly?" At the same meeting, Coalition members were asked to reflect on what it would take to "adopt a school-going culture in Detroit." The responses focused on several out-of-school issues and domains of action: transportation, mental health and trauma, policy and legislation, community-based support (defined as multiple actors to help kids get to school across different sectors), student perceptions of educational quality, and systemic and institutional racism. These issues all require resources and interventions beyond the scope of the district.

This reorientation in the Coalition's conception of their work led to a series of strategic planning sessions throughout 2020 and 2021, as they stepped back from some technical assistance and direct service activities while schools were mostly online. Through this strategic planning process, the Coalition formally adopted an "ecological" framework as the centerpiece of its theory of the problem of absenteeism. In strategic planning documents, they coauthored the following tenets of their framework:

- Absenteeism is an *ecological* problem, with multiple interacting and dynamic factors that contribute to whether preK–12 students are present and engaged in school.
- Chronic absenteeism is both a proxy indicator for youth, family, and community wellness *and* a contributing factor to future youth success in school.
- This means that how frequently Detroit children attend school tells us important information about how well their families and communities are doing. It also points toward what schools and communities may need to do to support them.

This refined framework acknowledged the interconnected factors across educational ecosystems that contributed to absenteeism and envisioned how to leverage their resources and organizational strengths to address those factors.

The Coalition also formalized theories of change for each of the four "pillars" of their work to improve school attendance across the educational ecosystem: communications, technical assistance, wraparound supports, and research. In notes during one of their strategic planning sessions, they wrote that the communications pillar could be "the mechanism/device by which [the Coalition] exchanges information with persons exercising power and implementing policy from the individual to macro level," conveying how communications strategies were focused on informing not only parents but also those with the power to create policy change in support of students. Likewise, for wraparound supports, they wrote about "removing barriers at the micro level" and working with schools and community-based organizations to establish "a coordinated system to address barriers at the meso level." Ultimately, their new theory of change included the following pillars that they believed would result in systems change, improved attendance, and better engagement:

- *Research:* Take a continuous improvement approach to understanding barriers to attendance and testing potential solutions across educational and community ecosystems.
- *Technical Assistance:* Develop the capacity of all stakeholders to improve practice around attendance and engagement toward academic success.
- *Communications:* Engage in a multidirectional exchange of information with people exercising power and implementing policy from the individual to the macro level.
- *Wraparound Supports:* Remove barriers at the micro level and create opportunities for students and their families to reengage in school.

These changes to the Coalition's strategic plan demonstrated a marked shift from a narrow conceptualization of the problem of absenteeism to one that explicitly adopts an ecological frame and designs strategies to cut across educational ecosystems.

While the Coalition clearly shifted its conception of the problem of absenteeism and how best to solve it, its core activities—implementing in-school and out-of-school programs, providing technical assistance to schools, and working directly with families—continued to focus on individualized interventions rather than systemic change. Detroit's highly decentralized educational system, with nearly two hundred public schools operated by more than fifty independent districts, created significant hurdles for centralized educational advocacy and governance. This fragmentation bred a competitive environment where institutions prioritized their own interests over collaboration for systemwide improvement. The disunity made it difficult to implement the ecological framework consistently across the educational system, despite its adoption as a guiding principle.

In addition, the Coalition's organizational structure created challenges to developing and advancing a coherent ecological approach to reducing chronic absenteeism. All members of the Coalition's leadership team had full-time jobs or schooling commitments outside of their work on the Coalition, and most were minimally compensated for their participation. The Coalition did not have a formal leader. Although Marvin and Joni were viewed as the cofounders and de facto leaders of the group, the Coalition made decisions by consensus and the leaders of each pillar had a great deal of autonomy about how they would enact their newly developed theories of change. Without a central organizing entity and personnel, this led to misaligned efforts and, in some instances, inaction for some periods of time. The consensus model also led to handwringing and delays in decisions needed to move the work of the Coalition forward. Pressure from local funders continued to create a dynamic in which some members of the Coalition were worried about focusing on systemic change, because of the difficulty of showing positive outcomes within one-year grant periods and the perceived "fundability" of more programmatic efforts to reduce chronic absenteeism.

Despite embracing an ecological framework to address chronic absenteeism, the Coalition and district encountered significant hurdles in implementing an ecological approach. Both organizations—largely in tandem with each other—had invested significant time and resources in a school-based model of improving attendance in Detroit. This investment made sense given what they knew at the time and the resources they had to deploy against the enormous problem of student absenteeism. Over two years, they had created significant organizational infrastructure around their existing attendance initiatives, which shaped whether and how they adapted, particularly in the difficult years during the pandemic. In the next section, we focus on the evolution of strategies to reduce chronic absenteeism following the peak of the pandemic, how the Coalition and district continued to refine their conception of the problem and strategies to solve it, their successes, and their persistent challenges.

EXPANDING CONCEPTIONS AND INITIATIVES TO ADDRESS ABSENTEEISM: 2022–23 AND 2023–24

The school years of 2022–23 and 2023–24 brought new challenges and opportunities to DPSCD and Coalition leaders as they encountered a postpandemic context in which students in Detroit—as nationwide—were more disengaged and less present in school than in any previous time in recent memory.[21] Students and families were facing new and worsened barriers to attendance, such as serious mental health issues, slowed academic progress, shortages among city and school bus drivers, and new parent work routines that sometimes helped and sometimes hindered student attendance.[22] Following the "all hands on deck" mandate at the height of the pandemic, this period saw community and district leaders seek to put into action their evolved conception of the problem of and solutions to absenteeism as ecological, and not simply a matter of schools needing to do better to entice students to attend more regularly. It also meant a recognition by the Coalition that reaching their goal of reducing chronic absence to 15 percent by 2027 (which even at the beginning was considered a "reach") would require a long-term approach to systems change, alongside technical and relational improvements in schools. In this section, we detail the still-evolving strategies of our partners, documenting some significant improvements in district operations that point to the possibility of improved attendance in future years, as well as disappointing results in the Coalition's new strategy, which led leaders to rethink their role in solving chronic absenteeism.

The Coalition Doubles Down in Schools

In the second half of the 2021–22 school year, the Coalition began to develop a new strategy for their work. Up until this point, the four pillars of the Coalition had worked somewhat autonomously from each other, with Marvin leading communications with schools and the broader community, Joni leading wraparound supports through her organization, Carla leading technical assistance by coaching principals and bringing in resources from Showing Up for School, and our team leading research efforts about their work. Although there was consistent strategizing across the pillars, the leaders of each made decisions that were not coordinated with the others. In developing their new strategic plan and formalized conception of the problem of absenteeism, Coalition leaders decided that one way they could put into practice their ecological understanding of chronic absence would be to fully coordinate their efforts across pillars and within specific schools that were interested in partnering. They coined the initiative the 4 Pillars Project and developed a vision for how each pillar would work within a school and provide support to the educators who worked there, connect with families to identify needed wraparound services, and promote research-based practices to improve attendance. As Marvin shared,

> We decided we needed an example. We settled on wraparound services as being a . . . component that marshaled the existing resources of the community to address the challenges that families were facing getting their children to school.

> Their communications was another aspect of this that, things were happening in school about which people did not know and that hyper local communicating designed by community, students, and parents would facilitate, would elevate that level of knowledge and also motivate students to be present. There was technical assistance for school leaders who were wrestling with, "how do you deal with this chronic absence thing that you all are talking about?" Then research which helped to educate and illuminate for us dimensions of the problem that we have.

Likewise, Joni shared that the focus was to "go deep in four schools, try out some strategies and models, and then scale them." Carla acknowledged Detroit's unique context for attendance and shared that the 4 Pillars Project arose out of "a collective interest to see if we can come up with a replicable and sustainable model to address attendance in schools in Detroit, because Detroit is so diverse and so different than other large urban settings because of its high needs, and high poverty, and the systemic issues that have been identified." To implement the vision of the 4 Pillars Project, the Coalition partnered with four schools they had existing relationships with: two DPSCD schools where Marvin and Joni had the deepest connections (one in Southwest Detroit and one in Northwest Detroit) and two charter schools, both in Northwest Detroit. (The Coalition initially partnered with an additional charter school but could not get full buy-in from school leadership to implement the project.)

Several Coalition members had previous experience working in and with community schools, and 4 Pillars was conceived to further adapt a model of community schools for the Detroit context, with an emphasis on attendance. In fact, some of the literature on community schools describes the components of the model as four "pillars": integrated student supports, expanded learning time and opportunities, family and community engagement, and collaborative leadership and practices.[23] As Carla shared, "We knew that we had implemented the community schools model a few years ago, actually, that was sustained for about five years and it ended or wrapped up in 2016, so a little bit before the pandemic. However, we knew that was somewhat of a successful way to support schools in Detroit. With that in mind, we knew that community schools needs a little bit of extra support, and the model itself was great, but it needed adjustments or personalization for Detroit." The Coalition's primary resource in the four schools was human capital brought in to support the facilitation of meetings among family and community members, meetings among staff to plan attendance strategies, and meetings with and between school principals in the four schools, where they were coached by Carla. The Coalition facilitated the hiring of AmeriCorps members to serve in the schools as additional staff to support attendance initiatives and trained them in the Check & Connect method, which has been shown to have positive effects on some student outcomes.[24] These staff played a significant role in developing relationships with students and following up with them when they were absent. The Coalition also developed a database to help schools track their partnerships with external agencies and identify where additional resources were needed to address barriers to attendance. For the most part, the schools believed they had adequate partnerships in place but needed help in activating them appropriately to fill gaps that school staff could not address.

Although several Coalition leaders believed that advocacy for greater funding and poverty-reduction efforts should be the focus of the Coalition, others still championed a school-centered approach and wanted the Coalition to implement a direct service model for schools. The Coalition had not spearheaded any direct advocacy for greater resources from state policy makers, the City of Detroit, or others. The most significant investment in resources that the Coalition helped to arrange was a donation from a professional sports team in Detroit. The team's players made one-time cash donations to help schools create a resource hub with health, hygiene, and other products that students might need. (While the donation was helpful at the time, it did not sustain ongoing funding for the initiatives, as is common with corporate donations.)[25] The players also participated in a coat drive for students in the school. Coalition members described this initiative as important in building trust with schools and getting them to buy into the 4 Pillars Project, but they also felt that, given what they had learned about the drivers of chronic absenteeism, it was unlikely to improve attendance much. Joni described this initiative as part of a "low-hanging fruit" strategy in which school and partner interests were aligned in wanting to provide attendance incentives. While it was unlikely that these initiatives would systematically improve attendance at scale, Coalition members believed they could boost attendance on certain days, such as toward the end of the school year when absenteeism tended to increase. While the Coalition recognized the limits to these low-hanging-fruit initiatives, they viewed them as a step in the right direction, even if they did not ultimately change the overall rate of chronic absenteeism in the city very much.

Through pre- and post- surveys and interviews with school staff and Coalition members during the 2022–23 school year, we found that the Coalition's influence on attendance practices in the 4 Pillars schools was minimal. We identified two main challenges to their success. First, there continued to be misalignment between root causes and the amount of time the Coalition's 4 Pillars staff spent on strategies unlikely to have a big impact—coaching on data analysis, parent and student communication, and incentives. Second, the schools had competing priorities that often made it difficult for the Coalition to shift practice. As Carla said when describing one of the hardest things about her work with principals, "I think it's a really fine dance of always paying attention to what are priorities that we want to support the school with, but then being careful to understand what they need and what they want." Another Coalition member summed up the twin challenges in this way: "The challenge I think was multifaceted, but part of it had to do with expectations and everyone being on the same page, both within [the Coalition], but also with our partners at the schools. I don't think there were clear expectations that everybody signed onto because potentially we didn't have enough vision to know what we were going to need to ask from the schools, and so I think that was a big issue."

Ultimately, staff in the schools perceived a strong culture of attendance in their buildings even before the 4 Pillars Project, and perceptions and practices did not meaningfully improve after one year of implementation. For instance, in fall 2022, 98 percent of the forty-four school personnel who were surveyed in the two 4 Pillars schools in DPSCD agreed that staff in their school work together to try to improve attendance. The results for this item remained similarly high when staff were resurveyed near the end of the school year. These results implied that the Coalition's core strategy might not have been needed, and that they should have invested their time and resources in efforts more likely to improve conditions for student attendance for Detroit schoolchildren.

Coalition leaders felt frustrated about their lack of progress and began to question their investment in the 4 Pillars Project as their primary strategy. Although they set out to learn how to prioritize efforts toward systems change, they found that they struggled to get strategies they championed adopted by schools, and they worried about the sustainability of an initiative that relied so heavily on an external partner for school-based interventions for attendance. Joni shared her hope for what they would learn from the 4 Pillars Project early on in implementation: "Our chronic absenteeism rates indicate that we have a systems issue. So, hopefully, we'll have a better idea of what those systems issues are. We'll be able to say, 'Okay, how do we prioritize that?' And then, 'what are the levers that you pull?'" After one year of implementation, Coalition leaders felt that they had learned a lot, but it was unclear what to do with that learning, as Joni reflected: "I think even though it wasn't implemented as expected, I think we learned a lot. We didn't implement what we thought we would implement, but . . . I feel like we followed what we said we were going to do. We were going to look at things. If it worked, you know, great. If it didn't, we would move on and do something different and make adjustments. So, I think from that perspective, it was good." Both the internal process challenges described earlier and the difficulty of shifting school practice as an outside entity led Coalition members to pause the 4 Pillars Project in the 2023–24 school year. In its place, they convened to take stock of all that they had learned and accomplished, and all that still needed to be done. They facilitated learning sessions to review our previous research on chronic absenteeism in Detroit. They began to consider what it might mean to transition the goals of the Coalition into another entity or a collective of organizations that could take up the fight. They determined that both awareness of the issue and advocacy for systems change were necessary to reduce chronic absenteeism in Detroit, and they did not believe that the current organizations within the Coalition were well positioned to lead that charge. At the time of this writing, they were still deciding how best to transition the Coalition and perhaps plant cuttings of their work in other organizations where they might grow.

DPSCD Expands Responsibility and Strategies for Attendance

Meanwhile, DPSCD began to articulate a more ecological framing of the problem of absenteeism and develop new strategies to address it, even while the core building blocks of their attendance agent strategy remained the same. DPSCD maintained the attendance agent role and increased demands on agents by requiring them to intervene when a student had three unexcused absences. According to the 3-6-9 protocol in the 2023–24 Code of Conduct, this intervention could include home visits, daily check-in monitoring, or a meeting with parents.[26] At each increasing level of days missed, attendance agents were required to continue intervening. At day 9, agents were asked to develop an attendance intervention plan. The district added a new external intervention for when students reached more than 9 days absent—referral to the Truancy Intervention Project (TIP) run by the Wayne County Prosecutor's Office. Like previous iterations, the code maintained that after 6 absences, attendance agents were expected to "provide the necessary wrap-around services to assist students with attending school."[27] In other words, although the district continued to develop new ways to address chronic absenteeism, official policy still emphasized the central role of the attendance agent.

In 2022–23, attendance agents in the two district schools where we conducted case studies were implementing many of the same kinds of practices that we had documented in 2018–19 and 2019–20, yet they shared more proactive ideas about how to remove barriers for students. Many of these ideas were connected to new initiatives beyond the agents that the district had begun or expanded. For instance, the district invested in creating more school bus stops and made it clearer that, even if students did not technically live in the zone to be eligible to ride the bus, they were welcome to ride a bus if they could find a bus stop that worked for them. DPSCD also created an online tool on the district website that allowed parents to search for bus stops close to their homes. With the expanded bus stops, some students could ride a bus to a nonzoned school by accessing a stop close to home. As attendance agent Lindsay Somers said,

> So we do home visits. Like I said, I do the phone calls. . . . We run data, to see who's chronically absent, who's severe. And then sometimes looking at our low risk. Let's not let it get so bad when you get into the chronic category. Families, I will talk to them, and they'll say, "Well, the car broke down, or this . . ." I'll say, "Well . . ." I'll look at the address and see if they're in the boundary area. Say, "Well, let's get a bus. Do you mind?" I do ask because a lot of parents don't want their kid to take a bus, and that's understandable. But you also have to say, "Yeah, that would be a good idea."

So while Lindsay described practices that were very similar to those used before the pandemic, she was able to draw on more and different resources to potentially remove barriers for students. Similarly, attendance agent Dalia Lopez shared how busy she was, but she also had many resources that she could draw on for the families she worked with: "It's a hectic job. It's not for the shy. You have to be very proactive with the parents. You have to think out of the box, you have to be compassionate because we really need to find out what barriers parents and children are facing getting to school. So instead of pointing fingers, we try to help because

I have access to a lot of organizations that can provide assistance for parents." The district had expanded the resources and partnerships that attendance agents could draw on to support families. For instance, the Family Resource Distribution Center offered all district families free access to hygiene products, food, water, and school supplies. Families could visit the center on their own, or attendance agents could retrieve items for them.[28]

Another major investment DPSCD made at this time was in health. The district announced a three-year plan to establish twelve "health hubs" in neighborhood high schools, with five opening during the 2023–24 school year and another three scheduled to open during the 2024–25 school year. This initiative was explicitly tied to improving attendance. As Superintendent Nikolai Vitti said in the press release announcing the initiative, the health hubs were designed to "address behavioral, mental and physical needs to support our students and families. We know that academic growth and consistent attendance require our students and families to be healthy and stable."[29] In addition to the health hubs, the district hired a school nurse for every building, initially using one-time COVID-19 funding and then allocating district budget dollars to maintain them, in part because of the potential benefit to attendance. As Diana Weston shared, "We had about 120,000 visits to school nurses and 88% of students went back to class. If the nurse hadn't been there, they probably would have gone home." These investments are reflected in attendance agent Valerie Holloway's description of her work—alongside many of the initiatives that she implemented before the pandemic, she also relied on new resources and partnerships:

> First of all, just making sure our parents have knowledge of what the office of the attendance is for here at the school. We sent out flyers at the beginning of the year. It explains my position and those things that I support. It states the law and it lets them know, that attendance is the law. . . . The next piece is the strategies that we put in place, if there is an issue with attendance. We recognize our students for their behavior through shout outs. Every other Friday we're celebrating, just their achievement in attendance. Another strategy is the mentoring program. We try and tie a student with an adult, to do check-in, check-out to build relationship with the students, wanting the student to feel comfortable. If there's an issue and they need support, we want to reach out to that family and provide those supports. So, having resources available if they're saying they have issues with not just uniform. We've not made that such a big focus now. We just want them to come to school, clean clothes, appropriately dressed. So, we try and eliminate

> those type of barriers. . . . If families are experiencing sicknesses, illnesses, children with asthma, allergies, we ask them to partner with our nurse, to get information from the doctors, where they can have inhalers or whatever here, to keep them from missing so much from those type of things. So the resources being provided, we have a social worker, counselor. If issues are going on, we want them to connect with someone in the building to support those families, so that they're not out of school on a regular basis.

While agents were still stressed and overworked, they also had more resources and more time to work directly with families.

One of the major changes that DPSCD made in this period was to update the reporting tools that are integrated with their student information system, so that agents and other school staff could more easily pull student attendance reports. A report that organized students in a school by their percentage of days missed or the number of days missed in the last two weeks used to take agents hours to produce. Now, thanks to a data dashboard developed by the district's data services team, those reports and many others are available with the click of a few buttons. This simplified agents' work and significantly reduced the time burden of data analysis to support their outreach and engagement with families.

Recognizing that housing instability was a major driver of chronic absenteeism, the district also worked hard to increase their identification of housing-unstable students who would qualify under the federal McKinney-Vento Homeless Assistance Act. The district had historically only identified a fraction of the students who would qualify under the act, which would provide resources and support, such as transportation between wherever the child was staying and school. Yet, in the last few years, the district's homeless liaison developed additional strategies to increase the rate of identification, going from identifying just 1 percent of students as homeless to more than 5 percent in 2022–23 (a higher identification rate than that in the city's charter schools). While this is still far less than the estimated 17 percent of students who should qualify for McKinney-Vento resources, it is a step in the right direction to support the district's most vulnerable students, nearly all of whom tend to be chronically absent.[30]

In 2024, the district formally adopted a more ecological approach to addressing chronic absenteeism in its new strategic plan, Blueprint 2027.[31] In it, the

FIGURE 5.2 Literacy proficiency rates of DPSCD class of 2031 compared with statewide averages

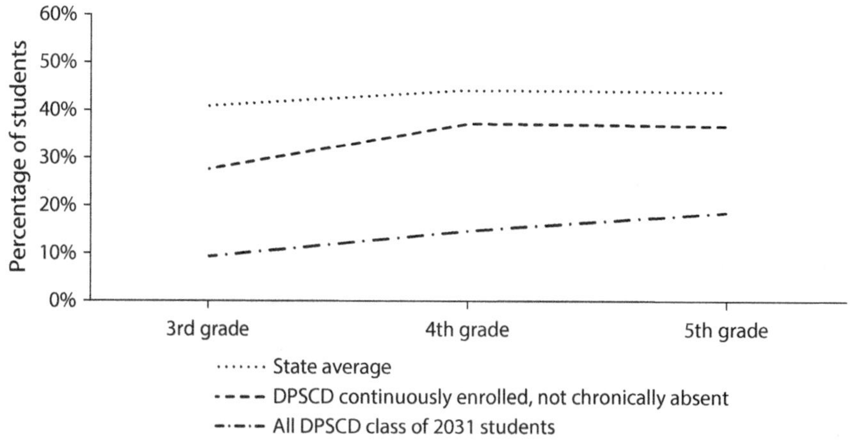

Source: DPSCD superintendent board meeting report, March 19, 2024.

district laid out a plan for improving attendance, including reducing chronic absence to 43 percent and increasing average daily attendance to 90 percent by 2027. These goals reflected a much longer view of what it would take to improve conditions for student attendance in Detroit, change attendance patterns, and ultimately improve student outcomes. Indeed, an internal analysis by the district showed that students who had been continuously enrolled in the district and who were not chronically absent demonstrated academic performance in literacy nearly as high as the state average (figure 5.2).

The tactics the district expected would help them meet their new attendance goals illustrated a new commitment to viewing absenteeism as more than just an educational problem that requires more than educational solutions. They included the following:

- *Access to Physical and Mental Health Care:* Strengthen partnerships with local health-care providers to offer on-site physical and mental health services, including the health hubs.
- *Resources for Families:* Expand the services and use of Family Resource Distribution Centers to meet basic needs and address barriers to attendance.
- *Connected Community:* Continue to expand participation in community engagement structures such as listening sessions, councils (faith based,

alumni, multilingual, school advisory), parent-teacher associations, and board community events.

- *Expectations and Outreach:* Increase attendance expectations and outreach to remove barriers to attendance.

The district was at an inflection point. By the beginning of the 2023–24 school year, the district was down to eighty-six attendance agents, from over one hundred in 2019. They began to reorganize attendance agents and pull some of them back into central office positions, in part due to reductions in funding, while staffing other schools with more agents when they had higher numbers of chronically absent students.[32] They focused the school-based agents on neighborhood schools with larger numbers of chronically absent students. Specialty schools like those that required an application or exam and career and technical education schools, as well as very small schools, did not receive school-based agents. Instead, central office agents were assigned to support several schools in the same way as school-based agents: analyze attendance data to identify students in need of support, conduct phone calls and home visits, and support schools with their strategies.

The initiatives district leaders have invested in to improve attendance cut across the major barriers we've documented in our research—transportation, housing, and health—and leaders are hopeful that they will see a decline in chronic absenteeism in the coming years. Yet they also recognize the limits of what they can do in the district, and they have indicated interest in developing partnerships with external organizations that could help with some of the targeted student support required to identify and remove attendance barriers. One challenge to these kinds of partnerships was the capacity of their external partners. An illustrative example was TIP, with the Thirty-Sixth District Court, where attendance agents could refer families for further support after documented interventions had failed to result in better attendance. Central office leader Angel Burlingame was excited about the potential of the partnership and the fact that the court said "they can take whatever number we send them," but she also worried about how they would adequately support all the students who might be referred: "They had five to six working with TIP, now they are down to two. They don't have clerical support anymore either. Only two people in the office now and they're trying to work out organizational challenges." Likewise, data privacy rules limited the district's ability to partner with external organizations. Such rules often prevented the district from receiving and sharing crucial information about students and their parents, making it more difficult to coordinate external resources and services. As Superintendent Vitti shared in a fall 2023 news interview: "We could envision our district portal system providing access to partners so they can respond to negative attendance trends. However, this would take signoff from families and significant upgrades to the system we are building now. This would be impossible without a robust technology system. You cannot rely on spreadsheets to make this work."[33] As reflected in the superintendent's statement, the district is committed to continuously improving its systems, practices, and partnerships in its effort to reduce chronic absenteeism. Ultimately, achieving their goals will require significant additional resources from the state or other entities. What students and parents in Detroit really need is advocacy for new investments in the state, city, and districts that will dramatically change the conditions for student attendance. Without this, educators and community organizations are bound to struggle with a problem for which they are only one part of the solution. In our final chapter, we provide recommendations to policy makers, districts and schools, and community leaders for realizing this approach to chronic absenteeism.

CHAPTER 6

Rethinking Chronic Absenteeism

We believe that what we've learned about chronic absenteeism in Detroit—after eight years studying the issue and efforts by the district and community-based organizations to address it—can inform educators, policy makers, and community leaders across the country, particularly those in other high-absenteeism districts. Chronic absenteeism is an "ecological" issue, meaning that a complex combination of factors can lead to attendance problems. Those factors will vary among students and families and may even differ for the same students over time. But broadly speaking, the barriers to regular attendance that many students face are due to a combination of family, school, and contextual factors, often resulting from or exacerbated by social and economic inequalities. Deep social inequality creates extremely challenging conditions for student attendance in places like Detroit.

Consequently, while chronic absenteeism is a problem for students and schools, it requires more than an "educational" solution. As we discuss in chapter 3, districts and schools only have certain tools and resources available to them, which are not necessarily aligned with or adequate for the task of alleviating the barriers to attendance that many families face. This is especially the case in high-absenteeism districts, given the magnitude of chronic absenteeism; but it is also true in other school districts more broadly, where supplemental resources and services are often necessary to meet families' needs. As we highlight in chapters 4 and 5, some school-based solutions may have a positive impact (e.g., engaging in effective communication with families about attendance, providing school-based health services or school-based transportation), while others may be ineffective, or even counterproductive if they erode school-family relationships or punish students.

To solve the problem of chronic absenteeism, we need to address it as a societal problem rather than an educational one. Policy makers and community leaders must commit to improving the conditions for student attendance outside school, just as educators are committed to improving conditions inside schools. This means policy makers must allocate additional resources and facilitate collaboration across multiple sectors (e.g., health care, housing, transportation, social services) to meet student and family needs. In the meantime, schools and districts should address factors within their locus of control like communication, focus on supportive relationships, and help families navigate and access existing resources that can address attendance barriers. In this concluding chapter, we offer our recommendations for how policy makers, district and school leaders, and community-based organizations can move toward a more ecological approach to solving chronic absenteeism.

RECOMMENDATIONS FOR POLICY MAKERS

The core argument of this book is that while chronic absenteeism is a problem for education, it requires more than just an educational solution. In other words, while schools are part of the solution, organizations and agencies from other sectors must also play a role. We outline several key recommendations for policy makers that will support noneducational solutions to solving chronic absenteeism, grounded in the concept of "reciprocal accountability," including the following:

- Substantially increase efforts to reduce poverty and invest in well-coordinated resources for youth and families in areas such as transportation, housing, health care, and employment.
- Reduce administrative burdens in accessing existing resources and invest in coordination systems in and beyond schools to ensure that families who need resources can access them.
- Eliminate punishments for schools and students based on attendance and shift toward shared responsibility, wherein districts and policy makers are similarly accountable to families and to each other for creating the conditions for regular school attendance.
- Reduce the emphasis on chronic absenteeism in school accountability and instead support districts in monitoring attendance improvement trajectories, patterns of absent days, and reasons for missing school.

Invest Additional Resources in Programs and Agencies That Support Students and Their Families

There is no getting around the fact that deep social and economic inequalities are the fundamental cause of high chronic absenteeism rates in Detroit and similar districts. Cross-sector coordination is a necessary condition for connecting families with resources and services that can remove barriers to student attendance, but better coordination alone will be insufficient in many contexts. Thus, to truly address chronic absenteeism, policy makers must make substantial investments to reduce material inequalities—for example, by increasing families' economic security, housing affordability and stability, access to health care and healthy environments, and access to transportation.

There are a range of policies that federal and state policy makers can consider. Cash transfer policies such as the Child Tax Credit or a guaranteed basic income have the potential to directly and immediately reduce family poverty.[1] Policies that invest in job creation, increase minimum wages, increase worker power, and guarantee paid family and sick leave can also reduce poverty and increase economic stability.[2] Neighborhood and community development efforts are also vital to economic development in persistently disadvantaged areas.[3] Schools should be an integral part of such efforts: physical improvements and new investments should include a goal of providing all families with consistent and reliable access to a school in their community.[4] A comprehensive approach to housing—including increased housing supply and less restrictive zoning alongside increased affordable housing development and housing subsidies—can reduce the cost of housing and improve housing stability.[5] Universal health-care coverage, along with price- and cost-reduction measures, can ensure that all families can access and afford health care.[6] Policies to reduce air pollution and increase clean energy use can create healthier environments for children and their families.[7] Investments in public transportation systems and school-based transportation can help provide families a way to and from school.[8] As policy makers make these investments, researchers can study their impact on student attendance over time.

Providing additional resources directly to families and communities would go a long way in reducing inequality and improving conditions for regular school attendance, if they were coordinated effectively. Thus, in addition to increasing funding across these sectors, states may need to increase the number of "navigators" who could help families access these resources.[9] For example, the Michigan Department of Health and Human Services (MDHHS) has a program that places "success coaches" in schools to help families access available social services. This is one example of an agency coordinating with schools to engage more directly with families. Indeed, one criterion MDHHS uses to place success coaches is whether a school has above-average rates of chronic absenteeism.[10] Yet MDHHS only has success coaches placed in about 240 schools across the state of Michigan, whereas there are nearly 3,000 schools in the state—and more than half of them have chronic absenteeism rates above the statewide average.[11] This is just one example that highlights the lack of adequate personnel to help ensure families can access useful social services and resources. Thus, investments in greater resources should be accompanied by an investment in additional personnel who can help families navigate and access those resources.

Greater investment in schools themselves is also necessary, as many schools receive funding far below what is adequate to provide high-quality learning opportunities and positive school environments, which are important aspects of what schools can do to improve student attendance.[12] Staffing, school-based transportation, and high-quality facilities are examples of areas where additional funding would benefit schools.[13] State policy makers should recognize that high levels of chronic absenteeism are indicative of inequitable conditions for educational opportunity and increase funding to ensure that schools can adequately support student attendance. In addition to increasing funding, states should consider removing current restrictions on how districts can spend federal grant dollars, allowing for more flexibility in response to local needs. As shown in chapter 3, the Detroit Public Schools Community District (DPSCD) spent nine to ten times more per pupil than the state average on truancy and absenteeism services, all of which came out of its general fund. High-absenteeism districts need additional dollars to invest in chronic absenteeism strategies, so that their students do not lose out on educational opportunities that are afforded to those in districts with lower chronic absenteeism rates. Districts also need fully adequate funding to meet students' academic needs, so that addressing students' social, emotional, and material needs does not require them to divert funds from their instructional efforts.[14]

All these investments should be guided by the notion of "reciprocal accountability" between states and their schools. Educational historian and policy scholar

Jack Schneider writes that if schools are held responsible for students' learning outcomes, then "it is the responsibility of state and local agencies to ensure that resources delivered to schools are sufficient."[15] Extending this logic to school attendance requires extending the reach of this reciprocal accountability from school resources to communities. Districts and schools should be held accountable for doing the best job they can to address the causes of chronic absenteeism for which they can be reasonably held responsible. Yet state policy makers and agencies should similarly be held responsible for adequately and effectively providing families with resources and services that create conditions for regular attendance by addressing barriers beyond schools' control. The magnitude of existing inequalities requires far greater levels of investment and redistribution. And in fact, as we learned in Detroit, these existing inequalities often erode schools' ability to improve school-based efforts and effectively coordinate external resources, due to limited capacity. Only in the context of true reciprocal accountability—wherein the state is responsible for addressing and resolving inequalities beyond the scope of schooling just as much as schools are responsible for addressing and resolving educational issues—can all districts and schools be expected to effectively support student attendance.

Facilitate Cross-Sector Collaboration to Support Student Attendance

Schools go to great lengths to coordinate and distribute external resources to students, to meet their social, emotional, and material needs.[16] The implicit expectation that schools play this central coordinating role is understandable: they are well-established community hubs, and educators interact frequently with students and parents. It certainly makes sense for schools to serve as a key site for interaction and intervention with students and their families, and there is strong evidence that the community schools approach, in which schools intentionally integrate and coordinate with external service providers, can greatly benefit students when adequately resourced and effectively implemented.[17]

Yet there are drawbacks to placing the responsibility for cross-sector collaboration and resource coordination on schools. First, with a few exceptions (e.g., school lunches, school-based transportation, school nurses), districts and schools do not have direct authority over the resources and social services they seek to provide students (e.g., management of personnel, allocation of resources). Consequently, schools' coordinating efforts may end with referrals, whereas additional follow-through is necessary to ensure that students and families register and take up those resources.[18] In addition, while schools may have some experience coordinating external resources and services, equipping educators with the necessary knowledge, expertise, and organizational routines and systems requires ongoing training, greater capacity building, and additional personnel.[19] Finally, while districts and schools might be able to develop those necessary competencies and systems, it is possible that committing time, effort, and resources to coordinating these resources and services will strain their capacity and coherence around instructional improvement efforts.[20]

There are several ways that federal, state, county, and municipal governments, as well as community-based organizations—which provide an array of resources that can support student attendance—can relieve some of the burden on districts and schools for developing new infrastructure and marshaling new resources for barriers to attendance that they are already better positioned to address. First, they can improve the delivery and take-up of services they already offer. Many families who are eligible for existing social services such as supplemental nutrition assistance, temporary cash assistance, and housing assistance do not receive them.[21] Part of the reason is that these programs are underfunded by the federal government and states.[22] But in addition to adequately funding these programs, policy makers need to minimize administrative burdens—for example, by simplifying enrollment processes or automatically enrolling eligible families.[23] Instead of relying on schools and districts to recommend these services to families, policy makers can coordinate with districts to actively promote these programs and recruit families to enroll.

There are existing models for facilitating such partnerships. For example, the "community schools" model has shown evidence of positive effects on attendance.[24] Yet effectively connecting families with new resources and services requires dedicated personnel, strong school-family relationships, well-developed organizational infrastructure, and adequate access to the resources or social services themselves.[25] Expecting schools to be the sole or central coordinating entity for addressing families' nonacademic needs is asking too much. Thus, policy makers must strike the right balance between providing services and resources directly to families and funneling resources through or in coordination with schools. Any additional administrative responsibilities for districts would need to be adequately funded and staffed.

In addition, policy makers can facilitate better coordination between school systems and other sectors. For example, in cities with public transportation systems, students can often ride public transportation for free or a discounted rate.[26] Yet even if students can ride the bus for free, the bus lines and schedules may not align with student commuter patterns or school start times.[27] In that case, city leaders could help coordinate the school and transportation systems to improve the utility of public transportation for school attendance. Likewise, policy makers should pass laws in other sectors that are likely to positively affect student attendance. For example, city governments can pass eviction bans for families with children during the school year to minimize housing instability for students.[28] They can also create ordinances that prohibit certain businesses (e.g., gas stations or corner stores) from selling to minors during the school day. In addition, state policy makers can pass laws or work with large employers to set standards that afford parents flexibility in their schedules around school drop-off and pickup.[29] Policy makers may also need to adjust laws or regulations governing data sharing, since federal and state privacy requirements can make it difficult for districts and organizations in other sectors to share data that are necessary to effectively coordinate services and resources. In sum, coordination and collaboration across sectors can direct existing resources and services to families to help their children to regularly attend school; and this kind of coordination will be necessary to ensure newly invested resources are effective. A Broader, Bolder Approach to Education—a national campaign that promotes comprehensive and cross-sector approaches to education—provides illustrative case studies of this type of coordination in districts across the country, from Florida to Washington and Minnesota to Mississippi.[30]

Curtail Punishments for Students and Schools Based on Attendance

Policy makers should remove punishments for students and schools based on attendance. Students, their parents, and their schools all bear responsibility for attendance; but truancy laws and attendance-based accountability policies create unproductive starting points for thinking about and approaching the issue of chronic absenteeism. School attendance policies and practices should be built on a supportive foundation, rather than a punitive one.

In terms of students and their families, states should repeal, or at least substantially modify, their punitive truancy policies. Truancy-based punishments—from suspensions to monetary fines to jail time—are built on a faulty assumption that if students and parents are threatened with punishment, then they will change their behavior and attendance will improve. For example, Michigan law not only allows for court-based prosecution of chronically absent children or their parents but also allows the state to revoke or withhold access to public assistance programs such as Temporary Assistance for Needy Families.[31] As we have discussed, however, the causes of chronic absenteeism are complex. Parents and students already recognize the importance of attendance and the value of education, and they mostly need help overcoming the barriers to regular attendance that they face. Even in cases where chronically absent students are willfully skipping school, that behavior is driven by social and emotional factors that are best met with socioemotional support rather than punishment.[32] And as we learned in Detroit, threatening truancy prosecution can often make the issue worse, by displacing a more central focus on identifying and addressing students' barriers to attendance while rupturing school-family relationships. There are certainly cases where the weight of the legal system may be necessary, such as instances of abuse or neglect. Yet as is the case in other legal action related to child welfare (e.g., child protective services), the root issues in most cases that merit intervention are due to socioeconomic hardship and inequality.[33]

Instead of responding to truancy with the courts, states should require a response to chronic absenteeism that involves social services and supports. This would be one way to foster the kind of cross-sector support that is necessary. Instead of referring students for investigation and prosecution, schools would refer students to an organization or agency meant to holistically evaluate a student's barriers to attendance and provide supports—from financial or employment assistance to housing to transportation to health care to ongoing counseling and social work. This approach can be informed by the "community response" model for child welfare that has been implemented in states such as Wisconsin, Colorado, and Nebraska.[34] While it will take time and investment to build such a system, states can take a first step now by rolling back the punitive truancy laws they still have in place. For example, Kentucky and South Dakota saw substantial decreases in the number of children committed to juvenile detention after reforming their truancy laws.[35] (By contrast, stricter and more punitive truancy laws are associated with higher rates of chronic absenteeism.)[36]

In terms of schools, states should revise attendance-based accountability policies by adopting the principle of reciprocal accountability. For example, many states penalize schools financially when their daily attendance falls below a certain threshold.[37] These laws unfairly withhold funding from the schools that need it the most. More generally, most states include chronic absenteeism as a component of their state accountability policy.[38] This means that those districts and schools whose families face the most significant social and economic inequalities are more likely to face increased pressure and scrutiny from lawmakers and state education agencies, without corresponding investments to help address any underlying issues beyond a school's control.[39] Instead of punishment, policy makers should respond to high chronic absenteeism rates and low average daily attendance by assessing local conditions and allocating adequate resources and services to meet families' needs, alongside a combination of support and reasonable accountability for schools as they focus on improving their instruction, culture and climate, and school-family relationships.

Rethink the Use of Chronic Absenteeism as a School Accountability Measure

The research is clear that students significantly benefit from attending school regularly and that students who miss many days of school have worse academic and socioemotional outcomes.[40] Out of this research knowledge, advocates and policy makers developed the idea of a 10 percent threshold for absences, at which a student would be considered "chronically absent." Although chronic absenteeism is a useful indicator that schools or students need additional resources and support, it has limited utility as a policy tool. Indeed, chronic absenteeism might be a key example of Goodhart's law in action: as it has become a target that schools are focused on improving, it has ceased to be a good measure of school performance.

First, as a threshold measure, a school's chronic absence rate obscures any improvement in attendance that occurs below or above the threshold. For instance, in many Detroit schools, a third or more of students are missing more than 20 percent of enrolled school days. Schools may invest significant resources in improving attendance for those students, and they could even cut these students' absent days in half year over year. Yet because the students would still be at or above the 10 percent threshold, the school's chronic absence rate would not change, and they would still be penalized on their state school accountability score. The reverse is also true, where worrisome increases in absences below the 10 percent threshold might be ignored so long as students stayed under the cutoff. Not being able to demonstrate improvement on chronic absence even while improving attendance for many students not only leads to inappropriate penalties through accountability, but it can also erode relationships between practitioners and families, as we found in our research.

Second, as a binary measure, it masks variation within the categories of "chronically absent" and "not chronically absent." In particular, by pooling all students who miss 10 percent or more of school days into one category, the measure implies that those students are all similar in some way. As discussed in chapter 1, we have found that students who are categorized as "chronically absent" may have dramatically different absence patterns as well as reasons for their missed days. Some students have an "acute" pattern of absences, in which the majority of their absences occurred in groupings one to three times throughout a school year. Others have a "persistent" pattern of absences, where they miss similar amounts of school from week to week or month to month. Students with different absence patterns likely have very different needs for school attendance, and the chronic absence measure as currently operationalized does not convey anything about these patterns.

Relatedly, the chronic absence measure does not indicate *why* students are missing school, so it is difficult to act on. Unlike measures that come from standardized tests, which might allow a teacher to examine subscores on certain tested domains to identify where a student needs extra support, chronic absence gives no indication about the underlying causes of missed days. Yet students who miss 10 percent of school days because of a chronic illness, for instance, need significantly different support than students who miss 10 percent because of a persistent conflict between the school schedule and a parent's work schedule. Although they both may be chronically absent, it would be inappropriate to apply the same strategies to both cases.

Third, as we have documented, the threshold nature of the chronic absence measure can incentivize schools to focus on improving attendance for those students who are right around the cutoff and who have the best chance of missing fewer than 10 percent of days by the end of the year. While focusing on "bubble kids" may be a logical decision for schools to make given the accountability pressures, it risks leaving many students without adequate support to improve their attendance.[41]

Finally, the 10 percent cutoff itself is a somewhat arbitrary indicator of high numbers of absences. Much of the research that supports the idea that high numbers of absences are harmful to students uses linear measures (e.g., number or percentage of days absent or present) or alternative thresholds (e.g., eleven absences or more).[42] One major study found that the "harmful effects of absences are approximately linear," suggesting that there is not a cutoff at which accrued absences suddenly have a negative impact.[43] In other words, chronic absenteeism may be a useful—and easy to remember—proxy for student well-being and an indicator of needed supports, but it does not meaningfully distinguish between students whose attendance we should consider good or bad. While this threshold was chosen through a political process to support school accountability systems and encourage districts to pay attention to students who were missing high levels of school, we are now in a significantly different political context. Districts across the country are hyperaware of chronic absenteeism and many, like DPSCD, are paying close attention to it not only because of accountability pressures but also because of the knowledge that students are not able to benefit from improvement in other high-priority areas if they are not in school.

Given these major drawbacks to the chronic absenteeism measure, policy makers should consider removing it or reducing its weight in school accountability systems. States could continue to track absenteeism rates as a useful barometer of attendance issues and a measure that helps direct additional resources to schools and families. Still, they should limit policies that incentivize schools to focus their attention on improving their chronic absence rate rather than improving individual students' attendance over time. In addition, they may want to encourage districts to adopt alternative frameworks for thinking about student absences. See figure 6.1 for an example of how this kind of analysis could be organized: focusing on patterns of absences (e.g., acute vs. persistent absences) and the reasons for absences could guide practitioners to focus on those students whose barriers to attendance can be reasonably addressed with school and district resources as well as to partner with other agencies to support students outside that scope.

FIGURE 6.1 Framework for analyzing the barriers and patterns in student absences

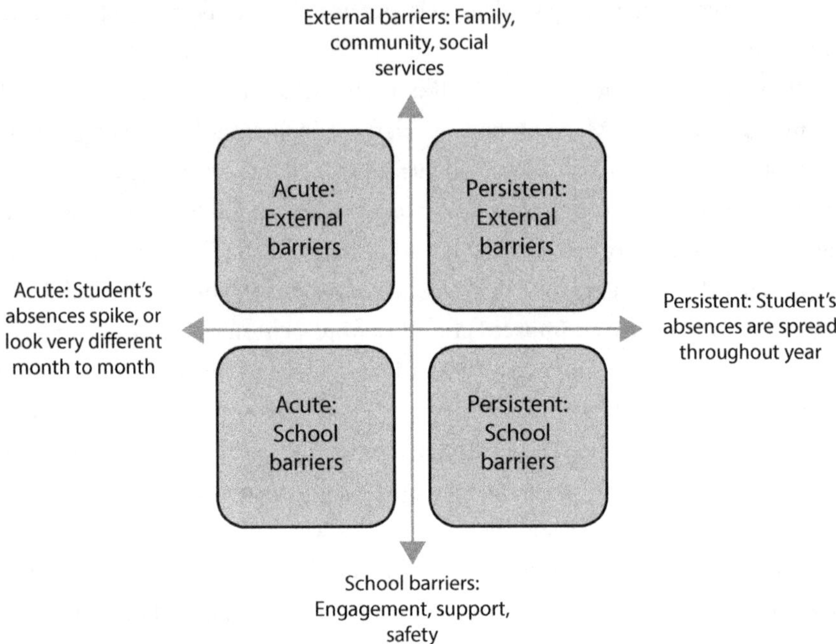

RECOMMENDATIONS FOR DISTRICT AND SCHOOL LEADERS

Though we believe that the responsibility for chronic absenteeism cannot fall on districts and schools alone, there are absolutely some things that educational leaders should do (and shouldn't do) to address attendance. Here, we share several recommendations for districts and schools, informed by our research in Detroit but relevant for district and school leaders in any high-absenteeism context who are seeking to build systems to improve attendance:

- Focus on effectively communicating with families about attendance in informative and supportive (but not punitive) ways; strengthening relationships between educators, students, and families; and creating an overall positive culture and climate.
- Work with families to better understand local barriers to attendance and either provide resources directly or connect them with available external resources and services.

- Avoid counterproductive practices, such as an overreliance on attendance incentives and punishments.
- Reconsider the role of attendance-specific staff and, to the extent that they are used, support them in becoming specialists on reducing absenteeism, such as by helping families navigate transportation problems, rather than generalists who must embody competing roles.

Address Factors Within Districts' Locus of Control, Such as Data Tracking and Communication

Schools have been tracking attendance data and communicating with students and families about attendance for over a century, and these activities can be seen as building blocks for school-based strategies to reduce chronic absenteeism.[44] It is important for schools and districts to be realistic about the purpose and potential impact of these efforts. Researchers have shown that nudging families through text messages or letters home can have a small positive impact on attendance, especially when the messages are positive, nonthreatening, concise, and specific to the student.[45] These types of tailored communications can be low cost and easy to implement with technology-enabled communication platforms, so they are worth the investment; but they should be treated as a starting point or necessary precondition for an attendance strategy, rather than a core intervention that will substantially improve attendance in a high-absenteeism context. Similarly, data-tracking systems can help schools and districts identify students in need of additional support for attendance. As we saw in Detroit, investing in high-quality and easy-to-use data systems can save educators a lot of time and help streamline their efforts. However, it is important to note these systems can be costly and take time to develop and implement. In Detroit, the district relied on philanthropic funding to create the sophisticated data system it uses now. Further, the data system will only be as effective as the interventions that follow, and districts should be wary about asking staff to devote so much time to data analysis that it draws their attention away from creating comprehensive strategies to address attendance barriers or working directly with families.[46] Further, data analysis that categorizes students into groups based on their attendance rate may be less productive than analysis that helps school and district staff document, aggregate, and see patterns within and between students' missed days and the reasons why they are missing. This kind of analysis could inform strategic development of interventions to reduce common barriers to attendance.

In addition to low-cost and easy-to-implement one-way communication, districts should consider intensive two-way engagement with families to identify and address student barriers to attendance. A 2021–22 pilot study in Connecticut, for example, found that a series of home visits by caseworkers with manageable caseloads was very effective at improving student attendance.[47] The challenge with these more intensive efforts is that they are costly, because they require a large amount of time and personnel. Thus, while this approach is worthwhile, it may be difficult for districts to implement at scale without substantially more funding or support from external agencies. Districts could explore the possibility of intensive casework with a subset of grades or schools to start, and they could advocate to the state for more funding to implement these evidence-based strategies. In addition, this sort of casework may be more feasible if districts already have a foundation of positive school-family relationships.

Focus on Building and Sustaining Positive Relationships with Students and Families

Strong relationships with students and families are another essential building block for school-based attendance strategies. Many of the success stories we heard about from attendance agents in Detroit had positive relationships at their core: attendance agents established a relationship with a family, which enabled them to address existing barriers to attendance and work with the family on an ongoing basis if new issues emerged. The importance of relationships in education generally is well established, and prior research suggests that strong school-family relationships require capacity building for educators and families alike.[48] Key elements of strong school-family relationships include authentic collaboration in planning and decision-making; trust between a school, families, and the community; family and community collaboration as a shared and embedded value; adequate funding, organizational systems, and routines to support collaboration; and equitable treatment and inclusivity for families of all backgrounds.[49]

It is important to be cautious when discussing the potential impact of improving school climate generally on attendance. While there is a well-established correlation between attendance and student perceptions of school climate, the causal direction of this relationship remains unclear.[50] In other words, it may be that schools have better climates because of their stronger attendance (e.g., allowing them to build stronger norms and rapport among students and staff), and not the other way around. Still, there is some evidence that strong relationships specifically can cause improved attendance. For example, a recent study found that among public schools in Illinois, those with stronger pre-pandemic family engagement (as measured by the "5 Essentials" survey) had smaller increases in chronic absenteeism postpandemic, even while controlling for prior school attendance and community and student demographic characteristics.[51] Positive school-family relationships in particular could lead to better attendance simply if students and parents feel a greater sense of belonging and connectedness to their schools; and schools may be able to substantially improve attendance if they are able to leverage those relationships to identify barriers to attendance and provide material support to families.[52] Further, educators are already focused on school climate broadly and school-family relationships specifically as a key part of school improvement.[53] Doubling down on these efforts is a much more productive approach than introducing new strategies and interventions, especially if they will have a null or negative impact on attendance. If districts do innovate around new attendance improvement strategies, they should start with small pilots first and carefully evaluate their effectiveness before scaling up.

Avoid Counterproductive Practices

While districts and schools may want to experiment with different strategies or initiatives, they should avoid practices that will likely be counterproductive. Counterproductive practices include ones that are ineffective, expensive, or unsustainable with limited impact, or actively harmful to students and families. Beyond simply "not working," these practices could negatively affect schools by straining organizational capacity and coherence and damaging school-family relationships.

Incentives for school attendance are one example of a potentially ineffective strategy. Common types of incentives are awards for perfect or improved attendance or rewards such as prizes or parties. As was the case in Detroit, educators turn to incentives because they are a familiar type of school-based strategy (since they are often used for academics or behavior as well) and because they are well within a school's capacity to implement. Yet there is almost no evidence base to support incentives as an effective attendance strategy.[54] In addition, there is reason to think that incentives can backfire, leading to worse attendance over time. For example, one study found no positive impact of awards on student attendance, and even found some students' attendance decreased after receiving an award, possibly because it signaled to students that their attendance was good enough.[55] Finally, we learned in Detroit that incentives have implementation costs: they require time and effort from school or district staff, which could potentially be spent on more productive strategies. Thus, while incentives for individual students (for example as part of an individualized plan) could make sense, schoolwide incentives may ultimately be counterproductive. Because school staff often feel that incentives are one of the only strategies within their control, districts should train staff on other strategies that are more likely to be productive. If schools do decide to implement incentives, they should have a clear rationale: they should be designed with a specific root cause in mind; the incentive should be selected intentionally to help address the root cause; they should be planned in a way that limits time and resource demands and minimizes potential backfiring; and they should be carefully evaluated for their effectiveness.[56]

Districts should also avoid threatening or carrying out court-based prosecution for truancy. First, even if districts rarely refer families for prosecution, the mere threat of prosecution can be counterproductive. We saw this firsthand in Detroit: attendance agents and other personnel often threatened families with truancy prosecution, which soured the relationship between families and their schools. Second, truancy prosecution is best understood as one of several ways that states essentially punish youth and parents because they live in poverty.[57] Some might argue that using the authority of the court is a way to ultimately connect families with resources that they need. Yet in theory this approach unnecessarily merges support with a punitive institution; and, in practice, there is evidence that such truancy diversion programs are ineffective.[58] Without modified state-level truancy policies, a greater investment in social services and resources from policy makers, and a stronger infrastructure for delivering those services and resources in response to chronic absenteeism referrals, districts are left somewhat reliant on truancy law as a channel to address chronic absenteeism. Still, in the meantime, rather than leaning heavily on truancy referrals, districts should focus on building supportive school-family relationships and helping families navigate available district and external resources that can reduce barriers to attendance.

Position Attendance-Specific Personnel as "Navigators"

Districts and schools do not necessarily need to hire personnel to be solely focused on attendance. Since absenteeism is an ecological problem, any major attendance initiative will require resources and functions across school district departments and external agencies. Concentrating responsibility for attendance in one or two people at a school has drawbacks because it leads to the blending and stacking of bureaucratic, school improvement, and casework duties that can be overwhelming and unproductive when assigned to a singular role. If there are specific tasks that need to be accomplished to support a comprehensive attendance strategy (e.g., data analysis), it may be more efficient to have a core group of staff working on a narrow set of tasks, rather than a generalist attendance agent who must master data analysis along with school improvement and caseworker functions. For instance, a core group of two to five district staff might be responsible for all the data analysis related to attendance, preserving the time of other staff to work on relationship building or schoolwide initiatives.

School districts could also consider developing staff into attendance "navigators" who are experts in one key issue area related to absenteeism. This kind of navigator role has been effective in other policy areas. For example, research on housing vouchers has shown that disadvantaged families are much more likely to access these housing benefits and move to "higher opportunity" neighborhoods when they have navigators supporting them.[59] Hospitals and other healthcare providers have also used navigators to help patients access necessary treatments and medications.[60] Finally, in some cases, navigators have helped increase students' access to educational opportunity—for example, by helping families choose higher-quality schools in complicated school choice systems.[61]

Attendance navigators could specialize in understanding the nature of a key barrier to attendance in the district and developing a toolbox of resources and contacts that would help families navigate through that barrier. For instance, a district could have a transportation attendance navigator who was a go-to resource on transportation issues. This person could develop expertise in the district's and city's transportation options, identify resources to support families with transportation needs, and begin to innovate alternative transportation solutions, such as a walking school bus or a backup carpool network. Other attendance navigators could focus on different major barriers to attendance, such as housing, health, and student engagement, and develop expertise accordingly. School staff could then call on these navigators to consult on students who were facing that barrier, or they could refer families directly to the attendance navigator to help. Depending on the size of the district, there may need to be more than one navigator focused on each key barrier.

Of course, schools and districts cannot come close to addressing all out-of-school issues on their own, and that is why policy makers and community leaders must play a central role in addressing chronic absenteeism. In the meantime, this kind of navigator role would help codify a commitment in principle to helping provide students and their families with the basic conditions that support regular attendance. Guided by that principle, districts should avoid investing time, resources, and money in practices that are unlikely to meaningfully address barriers to attendance. In addition, districts can continue focusing on effectively providing any resources that are already within their capacity. For example, districts often already provide some forms of transportation and health services, and they are required to provide additional resources to students who are experiencing homelessness.[62] Thus, to the extent that they can collect adequate data, they should start by evaluating the quality of the services and resources they already provide and explore opportunities to do so more effectively. Districts can also continue to partner with community-based organizations and external agencies that provide additional resources and services to students.

RECOMMENDATIONS FOR COMMUNITY-BASED ORGANIZATIONS AND COALITIONS

While community-based organizations and coalitions may not be able to marshal the level of new investment necessary to tackle chronic absenteeism, they can play a central role in advocating for these investments and coordinating with schools and districts. We offer three recommendations for community-based organizations and coalitions working on the issue of chronic absenteeism in their communities, all of which start with taking an ecological perspective on the issue and the possible solutions for solving it:

- Coordinate existing resources and work to identify needed resources for families in partnership with school districts.
- Work to improve other systems outside of schools that have an impact on attendance, such as city transportation systems or community development systems.
- Advocate for additional investments in the resources families need and in the systems that need improving to support attendance.

As we saw in Detroit, some members of the Coalition started with an ecological approach, but they turned their focus to influencing parent behavior and school-based efforts. Both were misaligned with the nature and magnitude of the issue. Thus, community organizations should maintain their focus on the complex and multifaceted causes of chronic absenteeism and map the existing assets in their community onto these causes to identify the barriers to attendance they are well positioned to address. From there, community leaders can coordinate existing resources that could help students; and they should be equally committed to coalition building and advocacy work, to help build the political will for the level of investment that is necessary to address the issue.

In many cases, community-based organizations have resources that they can provide to families and schools right now. Coordinating with schools can be challenging because it depends on district-level and principal leadership, including a clear vision for how to integrate community-based services and capacity for sustained engagement with community partners.[63] Thus, community leaders who have helpful resources for families should establish a commitment to collaboration and a shared ecological vision for addressing absenteeism with school leaders, and then create the necessary coordinating systems and routines to deliver available resources to families in formal partnership with districts and within their existing infrastructure for supporting students.

At the same time, community-based organizations should also work to address chronic absenteeism outside schools, using noneducational tools and resources. They should consider the various systems that create conditions for student attendance and work to improve those. For instance, if transportation is a major barrier to attendance, they could work with city and regional transportation authorities to pilot new systems for transporting youth to school, rather than working only with school districts to improve their transportation systems. Likewise, they could support initiatives to build social cohesion and belonging in neighborhoods, with the goal of generating the social network support that families rely on to raise their children. For instance, Detroit is in the process of implementing a Choice Neighborhoods Initiative grant from the US Department of Housing and Urban Development, with the goal of increasing mixed-income housing and creating a sustainable integrated neighborhood that supports all residents.[64] Community-based organizations could support these kinds of initiatives and work to ensure that their implementation leads to stronger communities that support children and families in accessing education.

Community-based organizations also have a central role to play in advocating for policy makers to make additional investments that are required to adequately address barriers to attendance. Community leaders, alongside students, families, and educators, have long played a central role in promoting more just and equitable policies in education and other sectors.[65] In addition, community-based coalitions and collective impact partnerships can be effective at organizing local resources and advocating for greater investments.[66] Thus, community leaders should embrace their potential role in articulating and organizing for policy changes, such as those recommended earlier, alongside their local educational leaders.

RETHINKING CHRONIC ABSENTEEISM

In May 2024, as the Coalition was beginning to consider how to move our work forward, Coalition leaders received an email from Grassroots Union asking us to weigh in on a chronic absenteeism parent guide put together by a local news outlet. In response to that request, Marvin Ashford wrote back a moving testament to what he and we have learned:

> Here is the key finding: This is a problem counted in school but it's not a school problem. It is a community problem rooted in poverty. It has learning effects. Does that make it a learning problem? Let's produce a learning guide. It has school culture effects, does that make it a school culture problem? Let's produce a school culture guide. It has teacher morale effects, does that make it a morale problem? Let's produce a morale building guide. It has social emotional effects, does that make it a psychology problem? All of these effects are real but isolating them as though they are not interconnected will only lead to marginal results and loss of belief the problem has a solution.
>
> Punishing parents (and by extension their families) will fail. It has failed. Because it locates the cause incompletely. Can parents contribute to the problem?

> Of course. But do you think 60,000 students are chronically absent because their parents don't care or are unaware? Really?
>
> [The Coalition] sees the challenge in an ecological (village) way. Every level of the village has a role to play. The student, their family, the church, businesses and other local institutions, the government and even our value system (we sneer at the poor). Seems like "trying to boil the ocean" as one commentator said in a meeting? No, it is being smart and seeing the problem in its complexity and doing the hard work of producing a "Community Guide." Not a parent guide as though this is a parent problem.
>
> Will we learn from our efforts or are we doomed to have every generation repeat the failed efforts of its predecessors (or ignore the successes)? Do we have the courage as a community to invent and implement community solutions? We are smart enough. Are we courageous enough?

The Coalition and DPSCD have rethought chronic absenteeism alongside us. Now we must continue working to reduce the great social and economic inequalities at the root of chronic absenteeism. We must tackle child poverty, address the misalignment between work and school schedules, and close the gaps in access to stable housing, reliable transportation, and robust health resources. We must continue to build on recent improvements in the learning and socioemotional environment of schools. And we must continue to learn more about how these expanded efforts can change how and why students attend school regularly, leading to greater learning, development, and opportunity in the long run.

Methodological Appendix

In this appendix, we provide additional details about the methods we used for the research that informs this book. The book combines findings from several of our research projects on the topic of chronic absenteeism in Detroit, including analyses of student attendance data; interviews with district and community leaders, attendance agents and other educators, parents, and students; surveys of parents; observations of educator trainings and meetings; and artifacts from the district and community organizations. This data collection and analysis took place from 2016 through 2023. Table A.1 provides an overview of the data collected in each of these prior studies. In the following sections, we describe how we collected and analyzed these different types of data. We also elaborate on our role as research partners and collaborators in the Coalition and in the Detroit Public Schools Community District (DPSCD).

STUDENT ATTENDANCE DATA

In most of our studies, we used anonymized student-level attendance data from longitudinal administrative datasets. We had three sources for the data: citywide data maintained by Michigan's Center for Educational Performance and Information (CEPI), data on students in DPSCD provided directly by the district, and data on a select number of charter schools in Detroit also provided directly by those districts. In the CEPI data, DPSCD data, and charter school data, we had access to the total number of days a student was present each school year and the total number of days they were enrolled that year, which we used to calculate average daily attendance (total days present divided by total days enrolled). In addition, the DPSCD data included daily attendance records, meaning an indicator of whether a student was present or absent on each school day they were enrolled. One other important aspect of the DPSCD data was that, for the 2020–21 school year, when Michigan temporarily adjusted its standards for counting attendance during the COVID-19 pandemic, the district continued to take attendance as

TABLE A.1 Data collected in prior research used in the book

Study	*Analysis of student attendance data*	*District and community interviews*	*Parent and student interviews*	*Survey participants*	*Hours of observations*	*Artifacts*
School climate and chronic absenteeism (2016)	Yes	—	—	—	—	—
Chronic absenteeism intervention strategy (2018)	Yes	12	—	—	30	—
Student exit, mobility, and attendance in Detroit (2019)	Yes	—	—	—	—	—
DPSCD attendance strategy study (2018–20)	Yes	70	—	295	27	80
Principals network evaluation (2022)	No	28	—	—	6	32
Attendance agents networked improvement community evaluation (2020–22)	Yes	28	—	—	25	44
Parent and student chronic absenteeism study (2020)	Yes	—	66	2,557	—	—
Cash assistance for chronic absenteeism (2020–21)	Yes	—	27	—	22	—
Homelessness study (2022)	Yes	—	20	—	—	—
4 Pillars study (2023)	No	39	—	74	20	10
Totals	*8 studies*	*177*	*113*	*2,926*	*130*	*166*

normal. Therefore, we had access to reliable attendance data for the district during that school year, whereas the state administrative data for that year are not comparable to those for other school years. With these data, we identified students as chronically absent if they were absent for 10 percent or more of school days (i.e., if their average daily attendance was 90 percent or lower). The data also included student demographic data (e.g., race/ethnicity, gender, grade level, special education status, "economically disadvantaged" status); enrollment data (i.e., the school and district where the student was enrolled); residential geocodes (indicating students' residential block but not their precise address); and other academic information (e.g., standardized test scores).

We used the student-level attendance data in multiple ways. We used these data to summarize the rates of attendance and chronic absenteeism in Detroit overall, as well as for different subgroups (e.g., different grade levels, different demographic groups). We summarized patterns in attendance and absenteeism, such as changes in attendance over time or differences in chronic absenteeism by neighborhood. We also combined the attendance data with other available datasets to identify associations between attendance and other school factors (e.g., ratings of school culture and climate) and contextual factors (e.g., residential blight, violent crime rates).

In addition to the student-level data for Detroit, we also conducted some analyses with citywide chronic absenteeism data collected by the US Department of Education's Office of Civil Rights. We used those data to compare Detroit with other major cities and combined those data with public datasets from other organizations (e.g., the Centers for Disease Control, the Federal Bureau of Investigation, the Census Bureau) to identify citywide factors associated with overall chronic absenteeism rates (e.g., asthma rates, crime rates, poverty rates).

DISTRICT AND COMMUNITY INTERVIEWS

Many of our studies also involved interviews with district leaders, community leaders, and attendance agents and other educators. We conducted interviews to learn about the attendance initiatives that district and community leaders were planning, and that attendance agents and other educators were implementing, to understand their perspectives on the nature of attendance issues and to receive updates and reflection on their efforts. We conducted semistructured interviews: we always prepared interview questions in advance, but we allowed ourselves the flexibility to follow up on participants' answers with additional questions during the interviews. Our interviews usually lasted about one hour. With permission from the participants, we recorded all interviews, then transcribed them (often using a secure paid service) and anonymized the transcripts. We used those transcripts for our analysis.

Though our specific analytic approach varied by study and research questions, we tended to follow a similar set of steps for analyzing interviews. We would load transcripts into Dedoose, a qualitative coding program. We would generate an initial "codebook," or a set of codes that we would apply to the data (e.g., specific sentences or whole paragraphs) in order to capture excerpts from the transcripts and organize them into topic-based categories. For example, in one study, we started with "parent" codes that included educator perceptions of the causes of absenteeism, their current initiatives to reduce absenteeism, and their experiences with training related to attendance and absenteeism. We then applied "child" codes to capture additional details of each excerpt. For example, under the parent codes for training experiences, we used child codes to indicate whether the excerpt included things like the topic of the training, the attendees at the training, or specific guidance provided to the trainees. We often applied additional codes (e.g., "grandchild" or "great-grandchild" codes) to further describe the content of the excerpts. We then read through excerpts and summarized emergent themes in analytic memos. Finally, based on the themes we articulated in those memos, we developed our key findings.

To complement our interviews with DPSCD attendance agents, we also conducted two districtwide surveys of attendance agents. The first survey took place in fall 2019, and the second in fall 2020. These surveys included questions about the practices that attendance agents prioritized, as well as their perceptions of chronic absenteeism's causes and any roadblocks to improving student attendance. Finally, we conducted surveys of staff in two schools that participated in an additional case study in the 2022–23 school year. While the answers to these survey questions were not as rich in detail as our interviews, they provided useful context for our interviews with attendance agents and other district personnel, and they provided districtwide data that helped to validate some of the prevailing themes in our interviews.

DISTRICT AND COMMUNITY OBSERVATIONS AND ARTIFACTS

In addition to interviews, we conducted observations of and collected artifacts from the district and community organizations. We observed district, school, and community-based organization meetings about attendance initiatives as well as attendance-related trainings for attendance agents and other educators. During these meetings and trainings, we collected additional data on how the district and community organizations were preparing for, developing, implementing, and adjusting attendance initiatives, as well as how they were making sense of their progress and the challenges they faced. With permission, we took "transcription-style" notes during these observations, writing (to the best of our ability) verbatim transcripts of meetings and training sessions. We also collected artifacts from meetings and training sessions, such as meeting agendas, handouts or resources used during the meetings or to be used in practice, and slide decks used for presentations. As we did with our interviews, we analyzed the transcription-style observation notes through multiple rounds of coding and analytic memos.

PARENT AND STUDENT INTERVIEWS

In multiple studies, we interviewed parents and students. While the specific interview protocol differed for each study, each included a set of questions focused on attendance. This included asking about the family's daily routine for getting to school; their mode of transportation; family members and friends they turn to for help with attendance; examples of times their children missed school; whether and how often they have dealt with specific barriers to attendance (e.g., transportation, health, safety, suspensions, childcare, relationships with teachers or students, housing, work, financial issues); and the kinds of interactions they have had with schools related to attendance. As for our district and community interviews, we recorded, transcribed, and anonymized these interviews, then analyzed them through multiple rounds of coding and analytic memos.

SURVEYS OF PARENTS

We conducted two surveys as part of our research. Both surveys were based on random samples of students, and their parents answered the surveys. The surveys were online, and we distributed them by text message and email. We relied on rosters provided by the districts for the surveys. The first survey sampled students in DPSCD. It was in the field in June and July 2021. We received a total of 776 responses, with a 9 percent response rate. The second survey sampled students in both DPSCD and participating Detroit charter schools (representing about 40 percent of charter school students in the city). It was in the field in January 2022. We received a total of 1,749 responses, with a 19 percent response rate. (Though these response rates are low, they are similar to other response rates from credible survey research in Detroit at that time. For example, the Detroit Metro Area Communities Study at the University of Michigan conducted a survey of Detroit residents from January 2021 through March 2021 and achieved a 10 percent response rate for new respondents.) We developed survey weights for our analyses, based on student demographics and school type.

The surveys included several questions related to attendance and factors that might affect student attendance. For example, we asked families detailed questions about their socioeconomic status; their transportation resources; their current housing situation and experiences with housing instability; whether their children have any chronic illnesses; the impact of the COVID-19 pandemic on their family and their children's attendance; their learning modality during the pandemic (e.g., online, in-person); the type of communication they received from their district; and their engagement with district technology hubs during the pandemic. In addition, in coordination with DPSCD and the charter school districts, we were able to link survey responses to student-level attendance data. This allowed us to analyze associations between the various items we collected on the surveys and students' attendance rates.

OUR POSITIONALITY AND SUBJECTIVITY

As research partners with the organizations and people in this study, our positionality and subjectivity are important dimensions of our methodological praxis. Sarah Winchell Lenhoff is a tenured faculty member at Wayne State University. She is a former middle school teacher in New York City Public Schools and has lived in Detroit since 2009. Her children attend school in DPSCD. Lenhoff became a formal partner with the Detroit public school district in 2016, its last year under state control, and then continued the partnership after DPSCD was created and Nikolai Vitti was appointed as superintendent. In 2017, Lenhoff also began a partnership with the Coalition, first as a participant observer, then as a formal member with the authority to direct the Coalition's research on absenteeism and contribute to decisions about the Coalition's work.

Jeremy Singer was a graduate student researcher on most of the studies in this book and is now a research faculty member at Wayne State University. He taught high school social studies in the Detroit Public Schools (during state emergency management, before the formation of DPSCD) and in the Education Achievement Authority, and he has lived in Detroit since 2014.

In the 2018–19 and 2019–20 school years, we partnered with DPSCD and the Coalition, with funding from the Skillman Foundation, to conduct a developmental evaluation of the district's attendance strategy, which was supported by the Coalition. Developmental evaluation is a research method that integrates continuous improvement processes into data collection and analysis throughout the entire research cycle. Lenhoff, Singer, and a team of researchers at Wayne State University met nearly monthly during the school year with leaders in the Coalition and DPSCD to review emerging findings, facilitate deep-dive discussions to make meaning from those findings, and generate ideas for improvement in district and Coalition practice. During this period, we facilitated fourteen developmental evaluation meetings. In addition, we presented research findings to DPSCD attendance agents in district professional development meetings several times. The funding the Coalition received to do its work, including the coaching provided to DPSCD, was separate from the research and evaluation funding we received from the Skillman Foundation.

In 2020, we were awarded a research-practice partnership grant from the Spencer Foundation. Members from our research team, the district, and the Coalition were principal investigators on that grant, and funds from the award supported functions in each organization to continue to partner, conduct research on absenteeism, and learn from our findings. This grant supported the development of a networked improvement community (NIC) among attendance agents. We helped facilitate twenty-five NIC meetings with thirty-three district attendance agents over two years and supported them in identifying the various factors that contributed to attendance problems, developing theories of change for their work, and designing small-scale interventions in their practice that they implemented and studied in order to adapt over time. We asked questions, gave guidance based on our prior research and knowledge about effective practices from other places, and provided feedback on the plan-do-study-act cycles that they created. The NIC was significantly disrupted by the COVID-19 pandemic, and most of these activities had to be adapted to that context.

The research we report in this book cannot be disentangled from our own personal and professional identities, roles, and relationships with our partners. This is true in all research, and especially when researchers partner with their participants to learn from the research in real time. Yet we built in several processes to guard against undue bias. First, during all meetings in which we played a facilitation role and formally observed the meeting for data collection, at least two research team members attended, so one person could take notes while another person participated in the discussion. Second, our team of graduate students, postdocs, and faculty colleagues participated in team meetings to design protocols and codebooks, and we developed coding procedures to ensure high levels of inter-rater reliability. Many of these colleagues were not active contributors to research partnership activities, giving them an important "arm's-length" perspective that helped strengthen our conclusions. In addition, the partnered research process itself helped to provide a check on our understanding and interpretation—allowing us to receive feedback along the way from DPSCD leaders and Coalition members—and we incorporated feedback and alternative perspectives gleaned from continuous improvement meetings in our final analyses. Finally, we used ethical research processes for working with human participants and sound qualitative and quantitative methodologies that strengthen the credibility of our research.

Of course, no purely objective analysis is possible. Data are not neutral and do not speak for themselves. In this book, we have done our best to give an accurate accounting of the story of Detroit's efforts to improve student attendance. We take responsibility for any errors that remain.

Notes

Introduction

1. Research participant names are pseudonyms.
2. Michigan school attendance data retrieved from MI School Data, https://mischooldata.org. Before 2017–18, students in Michigan were counted as absent only if they missed a full day of school. Since then, students have been counted as absent if they miss more than 50% of a school day. Therefore, it is somewhat difficult to compare attendance and chronic absenteeism rates over time.
3. Thomas J. Sugrue, *The Origins of the Urban Crisis: Race and Inequality in Postwar Detroit*, rev. ed. (Princeton, NJ: Princeton University Press, 2005).
4. Kevin Boyle, "The Ruins of Detroit: Exploring the Urban Crisis in the Motor City," *Michigan Historical Review* 27, no. 1 (2001): 109, https://doi.org/10.2307/20173897; John F. McDonald, "What Happened to and in Detroit?," *Urban Studies* 51, no. 16 (December 2014): 3309–29, https://doi.org/10.1177/0042098013519505.
5. Allen Law Group, *Review of Detroit Public Schools During State Management 1999–2016* (Detroit: Detroit Public Schools Community District, 2019), https://s3.documentcloud.org/documents/6549951/Review-of-Detroit-Public-Schools-During-State.pdf; Leanne Kang, *Dismantled: The Breakup of an Urban School System: Detroit, 1980–2016* (New York: Teachers College Press, 2020).
6. Allie Gross, "School Choice Gutted Detroit's Public Schools. The Rest of the Country Is Next," *Vice*, December 19, 2016, https://www.vice.com/en/article/a3j5va/school-choice-detroit-betsy-devos; Jeremy Singer, "Student Stratification Among a Combination of School Choice Policies in Detroit," *Journal of School Choice* 14, no. 1 (January 2, 2020): 122–53, https://doi.org/10.1080/15582159.2019.1689467.
7. Jeremy Singer et al., "Advancing an Ecological Approach to Chronic Absenteeism: Evidence from Detroit," *Teachers College Record* 23, no. 4 (2021): 36, https://doi.org/10.1177/016146812112300406; Sarah Winchell Lenhoff et al., "Beyond the Bus: Reconceptualizing School Transportation for Mobility Justice," *Harvard Educational Review* 92, no. 3 (2022): 336–60, https://doi.org/10.17763/1943-5045-92.3.336.
8. Samuel Speroni and Sarah Winchell Lenhoff, "School Transportation and Educational Equity," *Regulatory Review*, March 30, 2023, https://www.theregreview.org/2023/03/30/speroni-school-transportation-and-educational-equity/.
9. Sean F. Reardon, Joseph P. Robinson-Cimpian, and Ericka S. Weathers, "Patterns and Trends in Racial/Ethnic and Socioeconomic Academic Achievement Gaps," in *Handbook of Research in Education Finance and Policy*, 2nd ed., ed. Helen F. Ladd and Margaret E. Goertz (New York: Routledge, 2015), https://cepa.stanford.edu/content/patterns-and-trends-racialethnic-and-socioeconomic-academic-achievement-gaps-0.
10. Thomas S. Dee, "Higher Chronic Absenteeism Threatens Academic Recovery from the COVID-19 Pandemic," *Proceedings of the National Academy of Sciences* 121, no. 3 (January 16, 2024): e2312249121, https://doi.org/10.1073/pnas.2312249121.

11. Stacey Donato, Linda Rogers, and Jeff Raatz, Absenteeism and School Attendance, S. 282 (2024), https://iga.in.gov/legislative/2024/bills/senate/282/details; Nick Robertson, "Top Missouri Court Upholds Law Imposing Jail Time for Parents over Students' School Absences," *The Hill*, August 16, 2023, https://thehill.com/homenews/education/4154999-top-missouri-court-upholds-law-imposing-jail-time-for-parents-over-students-school-absences/.
12. Alec MacGillis, "Skipping School: America's Hidden Education Crisis," ProPublica, January 8, 2024, https://www.propublica.org/article/school-absenteeism-truancy-education-students; Jacey Fortin, "More Pandemic Fallout: The Chronically Absent Student," *New York Times*, April 20, 2022, https://www.nytimes.com/2022/04/20/us/school-absence-attendance-rate-covid.html; Jeremy Singer, "Attendance Practices in High-Absenteeism Districts" (EdWorkingPaper 24-932, Annenberg Institute at Brown University, Providence, RI, 2024), https://edworkingpapers.com/ai24-932.
13. Michigan school attendance data retrieved from MI School Data.
14. David F. Labaree, "The Winning Ways of a Losing Strategy: Educationalizing Social Problems in the United States," *Educational Theory* 58, no. 4 (November 2008): 447–60, https://doi.org/10.1111/j.1741-5446.2008.00299.x.
15. David F. Labaree, "Public Goods, Private Goods: The American Struggle over Educational Goals," *American Educational Research Journal* 34, no. 1 (1997): 39–81; Michael B. Katz, *Improving Poor People* (repr., Princeton, NJ: Princeton University Press, 1997); Harvey Kantor and Robert Lowe, "From New Deal to No Deal: No Child Left Behind and the Devolution of Responsibility for Equal Opportunity," *Harvard Educational Review* 76, no. 4 (December 1, 2006): 474–502, https://doi.org/10.17763/haer.76.4.yg7l5t01617h7628.
16. Donald J. Peurach et al., "From Mass Schooling to Education Systems: Changing Patterns in the Organization and Management of Instruction," *Review of Research in Education* 43, no. 1 (March 2019): 32–67, https://doi.org/10.3102/0091732X18821131; Jal Mehta, "How Paradigms Create Politics: The Transformation of American Educational Policy, 1980–2001," *American Educational Research Journal* 50, no. 2 (April 2013): 285–324, https://doi.org/10.3102/0002831212471417.
17. Jack Schneider, *Excellence for All: How a New Breed of Reformers Is Transforming America's Public Schools* (Nashville: Vanderbilt University Press, 2012); Mehta, "How Paradigms Create Politics."
18. Jillian M. Conry and Meredith P. Richards, "The Severity of State Truancy Policies and Chronic Absenteeism," *Journal of Education for Students Placed at Risk* 23, no. 1–2 (April 3, 2018): 187–203, https://doi.org/10.1080/10824669.2018.1439752; Michael Katz, *A History of Compulsory Education Laws* (Bloomington: Phi Delta Kappa Educational Foundation, 1976), https://files.eric.ed.gov/fulltext/ED119389.pdf.
19. Katz, *Compulsory Education Laws*.
20. Emily Rauscher, "Hidden Gains: Effects of Early U.S. Compulsory Schooling Laws on Attendance and Attainment by Social Background," *Educational Evaluation and Policy Analysis* 36, no. 4 (December 1, 2014): 501–18, https://doi.org/10.3102/0162373714527787; Titus J. Galama, Andrei Munteanu, and Kevin Thom, "Intergenerational Persistence in the Effects of Compulsory Schooling in the U.S." (CESR-Schaeffer Working Paper No. 2024_001, January 21, 2024), https://doi.org/10.2139/ssrn.4704151.
21. Judith Kafka, "Growing Up Together: Brooklyn's Truant School and the Carceral and Educational State, 1857–1924," *Journal of Urban History* 39, no. 5, published ahead of print, January 18, 2023, https://doi.org/10.1177/00961442221142053; David Tyack and Michael

Berkowitz, "The Man Nobody Liked: Toward a Social History of the Truant Officer, 1840–1940," *American Quarterly* 29, no. 1 (1977): 31–54, https://doi.org/10.2307/2712260.

22. Tyack and Berkowitz, "Man Nobody Liked," 36.
23. Ethan L. Hutt, "Measuring Missed School: The Historical Precedents for the Measurement and Use of Attendance Records to Evaluate Schools," *Journal of Education for Students Placed at Risk* 23, no. 1–2 (April 3, 2018): 5–8, https://doi.org/10.1080/10824669.2018.1438899; Katz, *Compulsory Education Laws*; Tyack and Berkowitz, "Man Nobody Liked."
24. Tyack and Berkowitz, "Man Nobody Liked," 34.
25. Conry and Richards, "Severity of State Truancy."
26. Conry and Richards, "Severity of State Truancy"; Kaitlin P. Anderson, "Academic, Attendance, and Behavioral Outcomes of a Suspension Reduction Policy: Lessons for School Leaders and Policy Makers," *Educational Administration Quarterly* 56, no. 3 (August 1, 2020): 435–71, https://doi.org/10.1177/0013161X19861138.
27. Clea A. McNeely et al., "Exploring an Unexamined Source of Racial Disparities in Juvenile Court Involvement: Unexcused Absenteeism Policies in U.S. Schools," *AERA Open* 7 (January 1, 2021): 23328584211003132, https://doi.org/10.1177/23328584211003132; Clea McNeely, Hedy Chang, and Kevin Gee, *Disparities in Unexcused Absences Across California Schools* (Stanford: Policy Analysis for California Education, 2023).
28. Peurach et al., "From Mass Schooling."
29. Though the 10% threshold for chronic absenteeism is now widely accepted, it is somewhat arbitrary given that additional absences above and below the cutoff are also consequential for student outcomes. In addition, definitions used in past research have varied slightly, due to differences in local definitions or data practices. See Shaun M. Dougherty, "How Measurement and Modeling of Attendance Matter to Assessing Dimensions of Inequality," *Journal of Education for Students Placed at Risk* 23, no. 1–2 (April 3, 2018): 9–23, https://doi.org/10.1080/10824669.2018.1438203; and Seth Gershenson, Alison Jacknowitz, and Andrew Brannegan, "Are Student Absences Worth the Worry in U.S. Primary Schools?," *Education Finance and Policy* 12, no. 2 (2017): 137–65.
30. Phyllis W. Jordan, "How Did Chronic Absenteeism Become a Thing?," *Education Next* (blog), May 12, 2017, https://www.educationnext.org/how-did-chronic-absenteeism-become-a-thing/.
31. Jordan, "How Did Chronic Absenteeism?"
32. Michael A. Gottfried, "Evaluating the Relationship Between Student Attendance and Achievement in Urban Elementary and Middle Schools: An Instrumental Variables Approach," *American Educational Research Journal* 47, no. 2 (June 1, 2010): 434–65, https://doi.org/10.3102/0002831209350494.
33. Jordan, "How Did Chronic Absenteeism?"
34. OCR used a slightly different definition of chronic absenteeism from the 10% threshold, instead capturing the percentage of students in each district who missed fifteen days or more of school.
35. "Chronic Absenteeism in the Nation's Schools," US Department of Education, 2016, https://www2.ed.gov/datastory/chronicabsenteeism.html.
36. Jordan, "How Did Chronic Absenteeism?"
37. Phyllis W. Jordan and Raegen Miller, *Who's In: Chronic Absenteeism Under the Every Student Succeeds Act* (FutureEd, 2017), https://www.future-ed.org/wp-content/uploads/2017/09/REPORT_Chronic_Absenteeism_final_v5.pdf.
38. James P. Spillane et al., "Striving for Coherence, Struggling with Incoherence: A Comparative Study of Six Educational Systems Organizing for Instruction," *Educational Evaluation*

and Policy Analysis 44, no. 4, published ahead of print, May 23, 2022, https://doi.org/10.3102/01623737221093382; Sarah Winchell Lenhoff and Jeremy Singer, "Promoting Ecological Approaches to Educational Issues: Evidence from a Partnership Around Chronic Absenteeism in Detroit," *Peabody Journal of Education* 97, no. 1 (January 1, 2022): 87–97, https://doi.org/10.1080/0161956X.2022.2026723.

39. Erica B. Edwards, Jeremy Singer, and Sarah Winchell Lenhoff, "Anti-Blackness and Attendance Policy Implementation: Evidence from a Midwestern School District," *Educational Researcher*, published ahead of print, March 29, 2023, https://doi.org/10.3102/0013189X221079853; Conry and Richards, "Severity of State Truancy."

Chapter 1

1. The data reported by the Department of Education were based on a slightly different definition of chronic absenteeism: missing fifteen days or more.
2. Jeremy Singer et al., "Advancing an Ecological Approach to Chronic Absenteeism: Evidence from Detroit," *Teachers College Record* 23, no. 4 (2021): 36, https://doi.org/10.1177/016146812112300406.
3. Comparing student attendance and chronic absenteeism rates over time in Michigan is complicated due to changes in the definition of an absence. Michigan originally identified students as chronically absent if they missed more than ten days in a school year, but the state changed that definition to missing 10% of all school days in 2017–18. In addition, beginning in 2017–18, students were considered absent if they missed 50% of the day or more, whereas previously students were only considered absent if they missed the entire day of school.

   From 1999 through 2005, the Detroit public school district was governed by a board appointed by the mayor and the state superintendent of instruction; and from 2009 through 2016, governance of the Detroit public school district was taken over by the State of Michigan. In addition, from 2011 through 2016, fifteen of Detroit's public schools were placed in a separate state-run district called the Education Achievement Authority (EAA). DPSCD was formed in 2016, through legislation that included a return to elected board governance and the reintegration of the EAA schools into the district. See Allen Law Group, *Review of Detroit Public Schools During State Management 1999–2016* (Detroit: Detroit Public Schools Community District, 2019), https://s3.documentcloud.org/documents/6549951/Review-of-Detroit-Public-Schools-During-State.pdf and Leanne Kang, *Dismantled: The Breakup of an Urban School System: Detroit, 1980–2016* (New York: Teachers College Press, 2020).
4. Singer et al., "Advancing an Ecological Approach." Population decline since the 1970s and racial segregation rates in the metro area reflect histories of divestment and discrimination that have ongoing implications for the financial, infrastructural, and institutional health of cities and their impact on residents. Poverty and unemployment rates capture the citywide socioeconomic context, and violent crime and residential vacancy rates reflect citywide safety issues. Community asthma rates reflect the likelihood that students will have to deal with this health issue that is well-documented as a contributor to absenteeism. Finally, average monthly temperatures capture the variation in climate that may affect students and their families. (We also looked at measures such as health insurance rates, residential mobility rates, average air quality, and average precipitation, but these were not correlated with citywide absenteeism rates.)
5. Singer et al. "Advancing an Ecological Approach."
6. Thomas J. Sugrue, *The Origins of the Urban Crisis: Race and Inequality in Postwar Detroit*, rev. ed. (Princeton, NJ: Princeton University Press, 2005).

7. Joshua Childs and Richard Lofton, "Masking Attendance: How Education Policy Distracts from the Wicked Problem(s) of Chronic Absenteeism," *Educational Policy* 35, no. 2 (March 1, 2021): 213–34, https://doi.org/10.1177/0895904820986771.
8. Singer et al., "Advancing an Ecological Approach"; Sarah Winchell Lenhoff and Jeremy Singer, "COVID-19, Online Learning, and Absenteeism in Detroit," *Journal of Education for Students Placed at Risk*, published ahead of print, January 18, 2024, https://doi.org/10.1080/10824669.2024.2304306.
9. Edith Abbot and Sophonisba P. Breckinridge, *Truancy and Non-attendance in the Chicago Schools: A Study of the Social Aspects of the Compulsory Education and Child Labor Legislation of Illinois* (Chicago: University of Chicago Press, 1917), https://www.loc.gov/item/17003577/.
10. David Tyack and Michael Berkowitz, "The Man Nobody Liked: Toward a Social History of the Truant Officer, 1840–1940," *American Quarterly* 29, no. 1 (1977): 31–54, https://doi.org/10.2307/2712260; Ethan L. Hutt, "Measuring Missed School: The Historical Precedents for the Measurement and Use of Attendance Records to Evaluate Schools," *Journal of Education for Students Placed at Risk* 23, no. 1–2 (April 3, 2018): 5–8, https://doi.org/10.1080/10824669.2018.1438899.
11. Edward M. Sosu et al., "Socioeconomic Status and School Absenteeism: A Systematic Review and Narrative Synthesis," *Review of Education* 9, no. 3 (October 2021): e3291, https://doi.org/10.1002/rev3.3291.
12. Erica B. Edwards, Jeremy Singer, and Sarah Winchell Lenhoff, "Anti-Blackness and Attendance Policy Implementation: Evidence from a Midwestern School District," *Educational Researcher*, published ahead of print, March 29, 2023, https://doi.org/10.3102/0013189X221079853.
13. Jeremy Singer, "School Choice, Socioeconomic Status, and Stratified Enrollment in Urban Districts: Evidence from Detroit," *Educational Evaluation and Policy Analysis*, published ahead of print, June 4, 2024, https://doi.org/10.3102/01623737241254783.
14. Kess Ballentine et al., "Exploring the Relationship Between Parental Work Schedules and Their Children's School Attendance" (slides prepared for presentation at the Association for Public Policy Analysis and Management conference, December 19, 2023), https://detroitpeer.org/wp-content/uploads/2023/11/APPAM-Ballentine-Lenhoff-11.6.23.pdf.
15. Singer et al., "Advancing an Ecological Approach."
16. Lenhoff and Singer, "COVID-19, Online Learning."
17. Richard O. Welsh, "School Hopscotch: A Comprehensive Review of K–12 Student Mobility in the United States," *Review of Educational Research* 87, no. 3 (June 2017): 475–511, https://doi.org/10.3102/0034654316672068.
18. Singer et al., "Advancing an Ecological Approach."
19. Singer, "School Choice, Socioeconomic Status."
20. Sarah Winchell Lenhoff et al., "Beyond the Bus: Reconceptualizing School Transportation for Mobility Justice," *Harvard Educational Review* 92, no. 3 (September 2022): 336–360, https://doi.org/10.17763/1943-5045-92.3.336; Sarah Winchell Lenhoff et al., "School Transportation Mode and Student Attendance Across Schools of Choice" (paper presented at the annual conference of the Association for Education Finance and Policy, Denver, 2023), https://detroitpeer.org/wp-content/uploads/2023/08/Transportation_Attendance_WorkingPaper.pdf.
21. Lenhoff et al., "Beyond the Bus."
22. Jeremy Singer and Sarah Winchell Lenhoff, *Attendance Throughout the Seasons in the Detroit Public Schools Community District* (Detroit: Detroit Education Research Partnership, 2020),

https://detroitpeer.org/wp-content/uploads/2022/09/6.-Attendance-Throughout-the-Seasons-ACCESSIBLE.pdf.

23. Singer et al., "Advancing an Ecological Approach."
24. Jeremy Singer, "The Effect of Suspensions on Student Attendance in a High-Absenteeism Urban District," *Urban Education*, published ahead of print, August 2, 2023, https://doi.org/10.1177/00420859231192084.
25. Sarah Winchell Lenhoff and Ben Pogodzinski, "School Organizational Effectiveness and Chronic Absenteeism: Implications for Accountability," *Journal of Education for Students Placed at Risk* 23, no. 1–2 (April 3, 2018): 153–69, https://doi.org/10.1080/10824669.2018.1434656.
26. Kimberly Stokes, Sarah Winchell Lenhoff, and Jeremy Singer, "Complicating the Role of Relationships in Reducing Student Absenteeism," *Children and Schools*, https://doi.org/10.1093/cs/cdae022.
27. David Heyne et al., "Differentiation Between School Attendance Problems: Why and How?," *Cognitive and Behavioral Practice* 26, no. 1 (February 1, 2019): 8–34, https://doi.org/10.1016/j.cbpra.2018.03.006.
28. Christopher A. Kearney, "School Absenteeism and School Refusal Behavior in Youth: A Contemporary Review," *Clinical Psychology Review* 28, no. 3 (March 1, 2008): 451–71, https://doi.org/10.1016/j.cpr.2007.07.012.
29. Lisa Dubay and Nikhil Holla, *Absenteeism in DC Public Schools Early Education Program: An Update for School Year 2013–14* (Washington, DC: Urban Institute, January 2015), https://eric.ed.gov/?id=ED559341.
30. Lenhoff and Singer, "COVID-19, Online Learning."

Chapter 2

1. Sarah Winchell Lenhoff, this book's first author, participated in Coalition meetings, first as an observer (2017–18), then as a research partner who led monthly continuous improvement sessions with the Coalition and DPSCD to share and learn from our research (2018–22). During this time, she also became a formal leader in the Coalition, directing the group's research agenda and contributing to decision-making.
2. Sarah Winchell Lenhoff and Jeremy Singer, "Promoting Ecological Approaches to Educational Issues: Evidence from a Partnership Around Chronic Absenteeism in Detroit," *Peabody Journal of Education* 97, no. 1 (January 1, 2022): 87–97, https://doi.org/10.1080/0161956X.2022.2026723.
3. "DPS Low Test Scores: Results, Analysis," *Michigan Chronicle* (blog), December 16, 2009, https://michiganchronicle.com/dps-low-test-scores-results-analysis/.
4. Mary L. Mason and Sarah Reckhow, "Rootless Reforms? State Takeovers and School Governance in Detroit and Memphis," *Peabody Journal of Education* 92, no. 1 (January 1, 2017): 64–75, https://doi.org/10.1080/0161956X.2016.1264813; Allen Law Group, *Review of Detroit Public Schools During State Management 1999–2016* (Detroit: Detroit Public Schools Community District, 2019), https://s3.documentcloud.org/documents/6549951/Review-of-Detroit-Public-Schools-During-State.pdf.
5. Sarah Winchell Lenhoff et al., "'Triage, Transition, and Transformation': Advocacy Discourse in Urban School Reform," *Education Policy Analysis Archives* 27, no. 32 (April 1, 2019): 1–35, https://doi.org/10.14507/epaa.27.4230; Allen Law Group, *Review of Detroit Public Schools*.
6. Lori Atherton, "Mapping Environmental Justice and Uplifting Community Survival in Southwest Detroit," *Stewards*, Spring/Summer 2023, https://seas.umich.edu/stewards/spring-2023/mapping-environmental-justice-and-uplifting-community-survival-southwest.

7. Lenhoff et al., "'Triage, Transition, and Transformation.'"
8. Allen Law Group, *Review of Detroit Public Schools*; Leanne Kang, *Dismantled: The Breakup of an Urban School System: Detroit, 1980–2016* (New York: Teachers College Press, 2020).
9. *Our Schools, Our Moment: Stepping Up So Detroit Kids Get the Education They Deserve* (Coalition for the Future of Detroit Schoolchildren, 2017), https://detroiteducationcoalition.org/wp-content/uploads/2017/12/CFDSreport2017-12-11.pdf.
10. Sarah Reckhow and Jeffrey W. Snyder, "The Expanding Role of Philanthropy in Education Politics," *Educational Researcher* 43, no. 4 (May 1, 2014): 186–95, https://doi.org/10.3102/0013189X14536607.
11. Dan Cohen, "Philanthropy to the Rescue? Detroit's Schools and Urban Policymaking Under Austerity," *Environment and Planning C: Politics and Space* 39, no. 7 (November 1, 2021): 1547–66, https://doi.org/10.1177/23996544211042636; Thomas C. Pedroni, "Urban Shrinkage as a Performance of Whiteness: Neoliberal Urban Restructuring, Education, and Racial Containment in the Post-industrial, Global Niche City," *Discourse: Studies in the Cultural Politics of Education* 32, no. 2 (May 1, 2011): 203–15, https://doi.org/10.1080/01596306.2011.562666; Jeremy Singer and T. Jameson Brewer, "How Does Teach for America Engage Its Alumni Politically? A Case Study in Detroit," *Education Policy Analysis Archives* 29, no. 21 (2021), https://doi.org/10.14507/epaa.29.5943.
12. Melissa Arnold Lyon, Shani S. Bretas, and Douglas D. Ready, "Design Philanthropy: Challenges and Opportunities in the Evolution of Philanthropic Giving," *Educational Policy* 37, no. 3 (May 1, 2023): 731–68, https://doi.org/10.1177/08959048211049426; Reckhow and Snyder, "Expanding Role of Philanthropy."
13. Oana Ciocanel et al., "Effectiveness of Positive Youth Development Interventions: A Meta-analysis of Randomized Controlled Trials," *Journal of Youth and Adolescence* 46, no. 3 (March 1, 2017): 483–504, https://doi.org/10.1007/s10964-016-0555-6.
14. "Accountability," Michigan Department of Education, https://www.michigan.gov/mde/services/school-performance-supports/accountability.
15. "Office for Civil Rights Releases New Civil Rights Data Collection Data," US Department of Education Newsroom, April 2018, https://www2.ed.gov/about/offices/list/ocr/newsroom.html#2018.
16. State School Aid Act of 1979, Pub. L. No. 94, § 388.1701 (1979), https://www.legislature.mi.gov/Laws/MCL?objectName=MCL-388-1701.
17. The citizens of the city of Detroit continue to pay the debt of the Detroit Public Schools (until that bill is satisfied, likely sometime between 2035 and 2045). However, as the newly created DPSCD, the district was now eligible to receive its full per-pupil funding without a large percentage going toward debt payments. Another part of the legislation required a new school board election and an appointed superintendent by June 30, 2017.
18. "3 Tiers of Intervention," Attendance Works, http://www.attendanceworks.org/tools/schools/3-tiers-of-intervention/; Christopher A. Kearney and Patricia A. Graczyk, "Multi-tiered Systems of Support for School Attendance and Its Problems: An Unlearning Perspective for Areas of High Chronic Absenteeism," *Frontiers in Education* 7 (September 20, 2022), https://doi.org/10.3389/feduc.2022.1020150.

Chapter 3

1. Detroit Public Schools Community District, *Blueprint 2020: Our Strategic Plan for Rebuilding Detroit's Public Schools* (Detroit: Detroit Public Schools Community District,

2020), 7, https://www.detroitk12.org/cms/lib/MI50000060/Centricity/Domain/4036/Blueprint_2020_Strategies_Only.pdf.

2. Detroit Public Schools Community District, *Attendance Plan* (Detroit: Detroit Public Schools Community District, 2018), 6, https://go.boarddocs.com/mi/detroit/Board.nsf/files/AZUMQ758BC5F/$file/Attendance%20Plan.pdf.
3. Jeremy Singer, "Attendance Practices in High-Absenteeism Districts" (EdWorkingPaper 24-932, Annenberg Institute at Brown University, Providence, RI, 2024), https://edworkingpapers.com/ai24-932.
4. Robert H. Horner and George Sugai, "School-Wide PBIS: An Example of Applied Behavior Analysis Implemented at a Scale of Social Importance," *Behavior Analysis in Practice* 8, no. 1 (May 1, 2015): 80–85, https://doi.org/10.1007/s40617-015-0045-4.
5. Detroit Public Schools Community District, *Attendance Plan*, 8.
6. David Tyack and Michael Berkowitz, "The Man Nobody Liked: Toward a Social History of the Truant Officer, 1840–1940," *American Quarterly* 29, no. 1 (1977): 31–54, https://doi.org/10.2307/2712260.
7. Tyack and Berkowitz.
8. "McKinney-Vento," National Center for Homeless Education, https://nche.ed.gov/legislation/mckinney-vento/.
9. Phyllis Jordan, *Attendance Playbook: Smart Strategies for Reducing Student Absenteeism Post-Pandemic* (FutureEd and Attendance Works, 2023), https://www.future-ed.org/wp-content/uploads/2023/05/Attendance-Playbook.5.23.pdf.
10. Hill M. Walker et al., "Integrated Approaches to Preventing Antisocial Behavior Patterns Among School-Age Children and Youth," *Journal of Emotional and Behavioral Disorders* 4, no. 4 (October 1996): 194–209, https://doi.org/10.1177/106342669600400401.
11. The Financial Transparency Dashboard on mischooldata.org reports the DPSCD revenue for 2019 as $734,583,628: "Financial Transparency Dashboard," MI School Data, https://www.mischooldata.org/financial-transparency-dashboard/.
12. Christopher A. Kearney and Patricia A. Graczyk, "Multi-tiered Systems of Support for School Attendance and Its Problems: An Unlearning Perspective for Areas of High Chronic Absenteeism," *Frontiers in Education* 7 (September 20, 2022), https://doi.org/10.3389/feduc.2022.1020150.
13. Tyack and Berkowitz, "Man Nobody Liked."

Chapter 4

1. Anthony S. Bryk et al., *Learning to Improve: How America's Schools Can Get Better at Getting Better* (Cambridge, MA: Harvard Education Press, 2015); James P. Spillane, *Standards Deviation: How Schools Misunderstand Education Policy* (Cambridge, MA: Harvard University Press, 2004).
2. Carly D. Robinson et al., "The Demotivating Effect (and Unintended Message) of Awards," *Organizational Behavior and Human Decision Processes* 163, published ahead of print, May 29, 2019, https://doi.org/10.1016/j.obhdp.2019.03.006; Rekha Balu and Stacy B. Ehrlich, "Making Sense out of Incentives: A Framework for Considering the Design, Use, and Implementation of Incentives to Improve Attendance," *Journal of Education for Students Placed at Risk* 23, no. 1–2 (April 3, 2018): 93–106, https://doi.org/10.1080/10824669.2018.1438898.
3. Joanne Chen, *Research Summary: Caseload Standards and Weighting Methodologies* (San Diego: Academy for Professional Excellence, 2019), https://theacademy.sdsu.edu/wp-content/uploads/2021/10/CWDS-Research-Summary_Caseload-Standards-and-Weighting.pdf.

4. Sarah Winchell Lenhoff et al., *Detroit Schools Severely Under-identify Students Experiencing Homelessness and Housing Instability* (Detroit: Detroit Partnership for Education Equity & Research, 2023), https://detroitpeer.org/wp-content/uploads/2023/06/HomelessIdentificationJuneFinal.pdf.
5. Chen, *Research Summary*.
6. David Gillborn and Deborah Youdell, *Rationing Education: Policy, Practice, Reform, and Equity* (Buckingham, UK: McGraw-Hill Education, 1999).
7. Jennifer Booher-Jennings, "Below the Bubble: 'Educational Triage' and the Texas Accountability System," *American Educational Research Journal* 42, no. 2 (January 2005): 231–68, https://doi.org/10.3102/00028312042002231.
8. Gillborn and Youdell, *Rationing Education*; Booher-Jennings, "Below the Bubble."
9. Sarah Winchell Lenhoff et al., "Beyond the Bus: Reconceptualizing School Transportation for Mobility Justice," *Harvard Educational Review* 92, no. 3 (2022): 336–60, https://doi.org/10.17763/1943-5045-92.3.336.
10. Gerard Robinson, "Hold Parents Responsible for Getting Their Children to School," American Enterprise Institute blog, July 15, 2016, https://www.aei.org/education/k-12-schooling/hold-parents-responsible-for-getting-their-children-to-school/.
11. Detroit Public Schools Community District, *Attendance Plan* (Detroit: Detroit Public Schools Community District, 2018), 7, https://go.boarddocs.com/mi/detroit/Board.nsf/files/AZUMQ758BC5F/$file/Attendance%20Plan.pdf.

Chapter 5

1. "Governor Whitmer Signs Executive Order Suspending Face-to-Face Learning at K–12 Schools for Remainder of School Year," press release, Office of Governor Gretchen Whitmer, April 2, 2024, https://www.michigan.gov/whitmer/news/press-releases/2020/04/02/suspending-face-to-face-learning-at-k-12-schools-for-remainder-of-school-year.
2. Mary M. Chapman, Julie Bosman, and John Eligon, "Coronavirus Sweeps Through Detroit, a City That Has Seen Crisis Before," *New York Times*, March 30, 2020, https://www.nytimes.com/2020/03/30/us/coronavirus-detroit.html.
3. Sarah Winchell Lenhoff and Jeremy Singer, "COVID-19, Online Learning, and Absenteeism in Detroit," *Journal of Education for Students Placed at Risk*, published ahead of print, January 18, 2024, https://doi.org/10.1080/10824669.2024.2304306.
4. Christine Ferretti, "Detroit Boosts Food Distribution Sites to Aid in Feeding City Families amid Pandemic," *Detroit News*, April 3, 2020, https://www.detroitnews.com/story/news/local/detroit-city/2020/04/03/detroit-boosts-food-distribution-sites-aid-families-amid-pandemic/2940886001/.
5. Detroit Public Schools Community District, *Continuity of Learning and COVID-19 Response Plan* (Detroit: Detroit Public Schools Community District, April 2020), https://www.detroitk12.org/cms/lib/MI50000060/Centricity/Domain/4/Continuity%20of%20Learning%20Plan_DPSCD_05.07.GSRPAddendum.pdf.
6. Thomas S. Dee, "Higher Chronic Absenteeism Threatens Academic Recovery from the COVID-19 Pandemic," *Proceedings of the National Academy of Sciences* 121, no. 3 (January 16, 2024): e2312249121, https://doi.org/10.1073/pnas.2312249121.
7. Statewide attendance data are not available for 2019–20 and 2020–21. Attendance data are incomplete for 2019–20 due to the abrupt end of regular attendance-taking in March 2020. In 2020–21, the state modified its attendance-taking requirements given that many students were participating in remote learning. More details on attendance requirements for 2020–21

can be found in Kyle L. Guerrant, "Return to Learn Law Details," memo, Michigan Department of Education, August 21, 2020, https://www.michigan.gov/-/media/Project/Websites/mde/Year/2020/08/21/Return_to_Learn_Details.pdf.

8. Jeremy Singer et al., "The Politics of School Reopening During COVID-19: A Multiple Case Study of Five Urban Districts in the 2020–21 School Year," *Educational Administration Quarterly* 59, no. 3 (August 2023): 542–93.
9. Singer et al., "The Politics of School Reopening."
10. Jeremy Singer, "School Reopening Decisions During the COVID-19 Pandemic: What Can We Learn from the Emerging Literature?" (EdWorkingPaper 22-617, Annenberg Institute at Brown University, August 2022), https://doi.org/10.26300/Z9W0-9Q22; Education Policy Innovation Collaborative, *Instructional Delivery Under Michigan Districts' Extended COVID-19 Learning Plans—May Update* (Michigan State University, 2021), https://epicedpolicy.org/wp-content/uploads/2021/05/EPIC_ECOL_report_May2021.pdf.
11. "Michigan Home Internet Options for the Economically Disadvantaged," Michigan Department of Education, https://www.michigan.gov/mde/services/academic-standards/instruction/michigan-home-internet-options-for-the-economically-disadvantaged.
12. Lenhoff and Singer, "COVID-19, Online Learning."
13. Ethan Bakuli, "Detroit School District Plans for Late January Return," Chalkbeat, January 11, 2022, https://www.chalkbeat.org/detroit/2022/1/11/22879163/covid-detroit-schools-michigan-omicron-virtual-learning-in-person/.
14. Ethan Bakuli, "Detroit District Credits Easing of COVID Quarantines for Decline in Chronic Absenteeism," Chalkbeat, July 12, 2023, https://www.chalkbeat.org/detroit/2023/7/12/23791935/detroit-public-schools-dpscd-chronic-absenteeism-covid-quarantine-decline/.
15. Sarah Cordes et al., *Choice in a Time of COVID: Immediate Enrollment Decisions in New York City and Detroit* (New Orleans: National Center for Research on Education Access and Choice, July 27, 2023), https://files.eric.ed.gov/fulltext/ED629590.pdf.
16. John Wisely, "'You're Giving Them Hope for the Future': Detroit Students Get Connected with New Laptops," *Detroit Free Press*, July 13, 2020, https://www.freep.com/story/news/education/2020/07/13/detroit-schools-computer-laptop-internet-digital-divide/5397603002/.
17. Eleanore Catolico, "New Hubs in the Detroit School District Will Help Families with Technology and Community Resources," Chalkbeat, November 17, 2020, https://www.chalkbeat.org/detroit/2020/11/17/21572641/new-hubs-in-the-detroit-school-district-will-help-families-with-technology-and-community-resources/.
18. "Get Support at Tech and Family Hubs!," Detroit Public Schools Community District, https://www.detroitk12.org/hubs#:~:text=DETROIT%20%E2%80%93%20November%2023%2C%202020%20%E2%80%93,online%20learning%20support%2C%20medical%20and.
19. Detroit Public Schools Community District, *DPSCD Reopening Plan: Fall 2021* (Detroit: Detroit Public Schools Community District, August 2021), https://www.detroitk12.org/cms/lib/MI50000060/Centricity/Domain/4/DPSCD%202021%20Fall%20Reopening%20Plan.pdf.
20. Enrollment data retrieved from MI School Data, https://mischooldata.org.
21. Hedy Chang, Robert Balfanz, and Vaughan Byrnes, "Pandemic Causes Alarming Increase in Chronic Absence and Reveals Need for Better Data," *Attendance Works* (blog), September 27, 2022, https://www.attendanceworks.org/pandemic-causes-alarming-increase-in

-chronic-absence-and-reveals-need-for-better-data/; Dee, "Higher Chronic Absenteeism"; Lenhoff and Singer, "COVID-19, Online Learning."

22. Malachi Barrett, "Detroit Bus Driver Shortage Still Causing Late Pickups, No-Show Service," BridgeDetroit, November 6, 2023, http://www.bridgedetroit.com/detroit-bus-driver-shortage-still-causing-late-pickups-no-show-service/; Isabel Lohman, "How Michigan Schools Are Trying to Attract 1,000 or More New Bus Drivers," Bridge Michigan, November 1, 2024, https://www.bridgemi.com/talent-education/how-michigan-schools-are-trying-attract-1000-or-more-new-bus-drivers; SaMya Overall, "Here's How the Detroit School District Is Addressing Students' Mental Health Needs," Chalkbeat, September 5, 2023, https://www.chalkbeat.org/detroit/2023/9/5/23860187/detroit-public-schools-community-district-mental-health-students-depression/; Lenhoff and Singer, "COVID-19, Online Learning."
23. Jeannie Oakes, Anna Maier, and Julia Daniel, *Community Schools: An Evidence-Based Strategy for Equitable School Improvement* (Boulder, CO: National Education Policy Center, 2017), https://nepc.colorado.edu/publication/equitable-community-schools; Megumi G. Hine, Steven B. Sheldon, and Yolanda Abel, "'Getting Things Done' in Community Schools: The Institutional Work of Community School Managers," *School Effectiveness and School Improvement* 35, no. 1, published ahead of print, December 13, 2023, https://doi.org/10.1080/09243453.2023.2293722; Jessica T. Shiller, "The Transformative Capacity of Baltimore's Community Schools: Limits and Possibilities in a Spatially Unjust Urban Context for Black Communities," *Education and Urban Society*, published ahead of print, March 3, 2024, https://doi.org/10.1177/00131245241233555.
24. Amy R. Anderson et al., "Check & Connect: The Importance of Relationships for Promoting Engagement with School," *Journal of School Psychology* 42, no. 2 (March 1, 2004): 95–113, https://doi.org/10.1016/j.jsp.2004.01.002.
25. Nora Reikosky, "Pipeline Philanthropy: Understanding Philanthropic Corporate Action in Education During the COVID-19 Era and Beyond," *Educational Policy* 38, no. 2, published ahead of print, April 18, 2023, https://doi.org/10.1177/08959048231163802.
26. Detroit Public Schools Community District, *Student's Rights, Responsibilities, and Code of Conduct 2023–2024* (Detroit: Detroit Public Schools Community District, 2023), https://go.boarddocs.com/mi/detroit/Board.nsf/files/CTFNYX61CC96/$file/23-24%20Student%20Code%20of%20Conduct%20FINAL%20DRAFT%20clean%20z.pdf.
27. Detroit Public Schools Community District, 21.
28. "Parent Toolbox / Family Resource Distribution Center," Detroit Public Schools Community District, https://www.detroitk12.org/Page/17004.
29. "Detroit Public Schools Community District Receives $4.5 Million to Launch 12 Health Hubs at Neighborhood High Schools," Detroit Public Schools Community District, July 31, 2023, https://www.detroitk12.org/site/default.aspx?PageType=3&DomainID=4&ModuleInstanceID=4585&ViewID=6446EE88-D30C-497E-9316-3F8874B3E108&RenderLoc=0&FlexDataID=81981&PageID=1.
30. Sarah Winchell Lenhoff et al., *Detroit Schools Severely Under-identify Students Experiencing Homelessness and Housing Instability* (Detroit: Detroit Partnership for Education Equity and Research, 2023), https://detroitpeer.org/wp-content/uploads/2023/06/HomelessIdentificationJuneFinal.pdf.
31. "Blueprint 2027," Detroit Public Schools Community District, https://www.detroitk12.org/Page/7733.

32. Ethan Bakuli, "School Attendance Agents Would Keep Their Jobs Under Latest DPSCD Budget Recommendations," Chalkbeat Detroit, May 4, 2023, https://detroit.chalkbeat.org/2023/5/4/23710694/detroit-public-schools-board-budget-attendance-agent-paraprofessional-culture-facilitator.
33. Ethan Bakuli, "Detroit Community Groups Play Critical Role in Fight Against Student Absenteeism," Chalkbeat, November 28, 2023, https://www.chalkbeat.org/detroit/2023/11/28/how-detroit-community-groups-are-helping-schools-chip-away-at-chronic-absenteeism/.

Chapter 6

1. Anna Aizer, Adriana Lleras-Muney, and Katherine Michelmore, "The Effects of the 2021 Child Tax Credit on Child Developmental Outcomes" (NBER Working Paper 32609, National Bureau of Economic Research, Cambridge, MA, June 2024), https://doi.org/10.3386/w32609; H. Luke Shaefer et al., "A Universal Child Allowance: A Plan to Reduce Poverty and Income Instability Among Children in the United States," *RSF* 4, no. 2 (2018): 22, https://doi.org/10.7758/rsf.2018.4.2.02; Robert Paul Hartley and Irwin Garfinkel, "Comparing Recent Income Proposals: Universal Basic Income, Negative Income Tax, and Child Allowance" (Poverty and Social Policy Brief, Columbia University Center on Poverty and Social Policy, February 13, 2020), https://www.povertycenter.columbia.edu/publication/2020/comparing-recent-income-maintenance-proposals.
2. Arohi Pathak and Kyle Ross, "The Top 12 Solutions to Cut Poverty in the United States," Center for American Progress, June 30, 2021, https://www.americanprogress.org/article/top-12-solutions-cut-poverty-united-states/.
3. Kathryn J. Edin, H. Luke Shaefer, and Timothy J. Nelson, *The Injustice of Place: Uncovering the Legacy of Poverty in America* (New York: Mariner Books, 2023); August Benzow et al., "Advancing Economic Development in Persistent-Poverty Communities: Executive Summary," Economic Innovation Group, https://eig.org/persistent-poverty-in-communities/.
4. Alisha Butler, Ariel Bierbaum, and Erin O'Keefe, "Leveraging Community Schools for Community Development: Lessons from Baltimore's 21st Century School Buildings Program," *Urban Education* 59, no. 8, published ahead of print, June 10, 2022, https://doi.org/10.1177/00420859221107615; Ariel H. Bierbaum and Jeffrey M. Vincent, "Putting Schools on the Map: Linking Transit-Oriented Development, Households with Children, and Schools," *Transportation Research Record* 2357, no. 1 (January 1, 2013): 77–85, https://doi.org/10.3141/2357-09.
5. Yonah Freemark, "No Single Policy Will Increase Housing Affordability. We Need a Comprehensive Strategy," Urban Institute, April 8, 2024, https://www.urban.org/urban-wire/no-single-policy-will-increase-housing-affordability-we-need-comprehensive-strategy.
6. Ryan Crowley et al., "Envisioning a Better U.S. Health Care System for All: Coverage and Cost of Care," *Annals of Internal Medicine* 172, no. 2_Supplement (January 21, 2020): S7–32, https://doi.org/10.7326/M19-2415.
7. Sandra Aguilar-Gomez et al., "This Is Air: The 'Non-health' Effects of Air Pollution" (NBER Working Paper 29848, National Bureau of Economic Research, Cambridge, MA, March 2022), https://doi.org/10.3386/w29848; Markus Amann et al., "Reducing Global Air Pollution: The Scope for Further Policy Interventions," *Philosophical Transactions of the Royal Society A: Mathematical, Physical and Engineering Sciences* 378, no. 2183 (September 28, 2020): 20190331, https://doi.org/10.1098/rsta.2019.0331.

8. Samuel Speroni and Sarah Winchell Lenhoff, "School Transportation and Educational Equity," *Regulatory Review*, March 30, 2023, https://www.theregreview.org/2023/03/30/speroni-school-transportation-and-educational-equity/.
9. Peter Bergman et al., "Creating Moves to Opportunity: Experimental Evidence on Barriers to Neighborhood Choice," *American Economic Review* 114, no. 5 (May 2024): 1281–337, https://doi.org/10.1257/aer.20200407.
10. "About: Pathways to Potential," Michigan Department of Health and Human Services, https://www.michigan.gov/mdhhs/doing-business/pathways-to-potential-test-page/about.
11. Chronic absenteeism data retrieved from MI School Data, https://mischooldata.org; "2023 Active Pathways to Potential Schools," Michigan Department of Health and Human Services, https://www.michigan.gov/mdhhs/-/media/Project/Websites/mdhhs/Doing-Business-with-MDHHS/Pathways-to-Potential/DHS_Pathways_Map_474252_7.pdf.
12. Bruce D. Baker, *Educational Inequality and School Finance: Why Money Matters for America's Students* (Cambridge, MA: Harvard Education Press, 2021).
13. Barbara Biasi, Julien M. Lafortune, and David Schönholzer, "What Works and for Whom? Effectiveness and Efficiency of School Capital Investments Across the U.S." (NBER Working Paper 32040, National Bureau of Economic Research, Cambridge, MA, January 2024), https://doi.org/10.3386/w32040; Danielle Sanderson Edwards, "Another One Rides the Bus: The Impact of School Transportation on Student Outcomes in Michigan," *Education Finance and Policy*, published ahead of print, July 13, 2022, https://doi.org/10.1162/edfp_a_00382; Jing Liu and Susanna Loeb, "Engaging Teachers: Measuring the Impact of Teachers on Student Attendance in Secondary School," *Journal of Human Resources* 56, no. 2 (March 2021): 343–79, https://doi.org/10.3368/jhr.56.2.1216-8430R3.
14. Christopher Saldaña et al., *Taking Equal Opportunity Rhetoric Seriously: Envisioning and Costing-Out a P–12 Public School System in North Carolina Where Every Child Thrives: A Working Document* (Boulder, CO: National Education Policy Center, April 25, 2024), https://nepc.colorado.edu/publication/rd-equal-opportunity.
15. Jack Schneider, *Beyond Test Scores: A Better Way to Measure School Quality* (Cambridge, MA: Harvard University Press, 2017), 239.
16. Caitlin Kearney et al., "Offer It and They Will Come? An Investigation of the Factors Associated with the Uptake of School-Sponsored Resources," *American Educational Research Journal* 61, no. 1 (February 2024): 145–76, https://doi.org/10.3102/00028312231209231.
17. A. Brooks Bowden et al., "An Economic Evaluation of the Costs and Benefits of Providing Comprehensive Supports to Students in Elementary School," *Prevention Science* 21, no. 8 (November 2020): 1126–35, https://doi.org/10.1007/s11121-020-01164-w; Lauren Covelli, John Engberg, and Isaac M. Opper, "Leading Indicators of Long-Term Success in Community Schools: Evidence from New York City" (EdWorkingPaper 22-669, Annenberg Institute at Brown University, Providence, RI, November 1, 2022), https://www.edworkingpapers.com/ai22-669.
18. Kearney et al., "Offer It?"
19. Megumi G. Hine, Steven B. Sheldon, and Yolanda Abel, "'Getting Things Done' in Community Schools: The Institutional Work of Community School Managers," *School Effectiveness and School Improvement* 35, no. 1, published ahead of print, December 13, 2023, https://doi.org/10.1080/09243453.2023.2293722; Jennifer Jellison Holme et al., "Community Schools as an Urban School Reform Strategy: Examining Partnerships, Governance, and Sustainability Through the Lens of the Full-Service Community Schools

Grant Program," *Educational Policy* 36, no. 3, published ahead of print, January 30, 2020, https://doi.org/10.1177/0895904820901479.

20. James P. Spillane et al., "Striving for Coherence, Struggling with Incoherence: A Comparative Study of Six Educational Systems Organizing for Instruction," *Educational Evaluation and Policy Analysis* 44, no. 4 (May 23, 2022): 567–92, https://doi.org/10.3102/01623737221093382.
21. Soledad De Gregorio et al., *Examining the Complex Social Safety Net for Low-Income Working Families: How Benefits and Resources Respond to Increases in Wages* (Los Angeles: USC Sol Price Center for Social Innovation, 2021), https://socialinnovation.usc.edu/wp-content/uploads/2021/10/Social-Safety-Net_Full-Report_FINAL_10.22.21.pdf.
22. Laura Tach and Kathryn Edin, "The Social Safety Net After Welfare Reform: Recent Developments and Consequences for Household Dynamics," *Annual Review of Sociology* 43, no. 1 (July 31, 2017): 541–61, https://doi.org/10.1146/annurev-soc-060116-053300.
23. Pamela Herd and Donald P. Moynihan, *Administrative Burden: Policymaking by Other Means* (New York: Russell Sage Foundation, 2018).
24. Covelli, Engberg, and Opper, "Leading Indicators"; Elaine Weiss and Paul Reville, *Broader, Bolder, Better: How Schools and Communities Help Students Overcome the Disadvantages of Poverty* (Cambridge, MA: Harvard Education Press, 2019).
25. Hine, Sheldon, and Abel, "'Getting Things Done'"; Kearney et al., "Offer It?"
26. Carolyn Sattin-Bajaj, "Student Transportation in Choice-Rich Districts: Implementation Challenges and Responses," *Education Finance and Policy* 18, no. 2 (Spring 2023): 351–64, https://doi.org/10.1162/edfp_a_00377.
27. Sarah Winchell Lenhoff et al., "Beyond the Bus: Reconceptualizing School Transportation for Mobility Justice," *Harvard Educational Review* 92, no. 3 (2022): 347, https://doi.org/10.17763/1943-5045-92.3.336.
28. Jennifer Erb-Downward et al., *A Stable Place to Live and Learn: Why Detroit Housing Policy Is Critical to the Success of City Schools* (Detroit: Detroit Partnership for Education Equity and Research, 2023), https://detroitpeer.org/wp-content/uploads/2023/08/StablePlace.pdf.
29. Kess Ballentine et al., "Exploring the Relationship Between Parental Work Schedules and Their Children's School Attendance" (slides prepared for presentation at the Association for Public Policy Analysis and Management conference, December 19, 2023), https://detroitpeer.org/wp-content/uploads/2023/11/APPAM-Ballentine-Lenhoff-11.6.23.pdf.
30. Weiss and Reville, *Broader, Bolder, Better*; Pedro A. Noguera and Lauren Wells, "The Politics of School Reform: A Broader and Bolder Approach for Newark," *Berkeley Review of Education* 2, no. 1 (2011): 5–25, https://doi.org/10.5070/B82110065; "Case Studies," Broader, Bolder Approach to Education, http://www.boldapproach.org/case-studies/.
31. Koby Levin, "How Michigan Punishes Its Poorest Families for Low School Attendance," Chalkbeat Detroit, May 24, 2023, https://detroit.chalkbeat.org/2023/5/24/23735005/student-attendance-michigan-schools-chronic-absenteeism-tanf-family-benefits.
32. Christopher A. Kearney, "School Absenteeism and School Refusal Behavior in Youth: A Contemporary Review," *Clinical Psychology Review* 28, no. 3 (March 1, 2008): 451–71, https://doi.org/10.1016/j.cpr.2007.07.012; Christopher Kearney and Melissa Spear, "School Refusal Behavior: School-Based Cognitive-Behavioral Interventions," in *Cognitive-Behavioral Interventions in Educational Settings: A Handbook for Practice*, 2nd ed., ed. Rosemary B. Mennuti, Ray W. Christner, and Arthur Freeman (New York: Routledge, 2012), 161–85.
33. Lawrence M. Berger and Kristen S. Slack, "The Contemporary U.S. Child Welfare System(s): Overview and Key Challenges," *ANNALS of the American Academy of Political*

and Social Science 692, no. 1 (November 1, 2020): 7–25, https://doi.org/10.1177/0002716220969362; Megan Feely et al., "The Social Welfare Policy Landscape and Child Protective Services: Opportunities for and Barriers to Creating Systems Synergy," *ANNALS of the American Academy of Political and Social Science* 692, no. 1 (November 1, 2020): 140–61, https://doi.org/10.1177/0002716220973566.

34. Kristen S. Slack and Lawrence M. Berger, "Who Is and Is Not Served by Child Protective Services Systems? Implications for a Prevention Infrastructure to Reduce Child Maltreatment," *ANNALS of the American Academy of Political and Social Science* 692, no. 1 (November 1, 2020): 182–202, https://doi.org/10.1177/0002716220980691.
35. Lauren Burr, Mark Ziegler-Thayer, and Jenny Scala, *Attendance Legislation in the United States* (American Institutes for Research, 2023), https://www.air.org/sites/default/files/2023-04/Attendance-Legislation-in-the-US-Jan-2023.pdf.
36. Jillian M. Conry and Meredith P. Richards, "The Severity of State Truancy Policies and Chronic Absenteeism," *Journal of Education for Students Placed at Risk* 23, no. 1–2 (April 3, 2018): 187–203, https://doi.org/10.1080/10824669.2018.1439752; Josh Weber, *Rethinking the Role of the Juvenile Justice System: Improving Youth's School Attendance and Educational Outcomes* (Justice Center, Council of State Governments, 2020), https://csgjusticecenter.org/wp-content/uploads/2020/09/CSG_RethinkingtheRoleoftheJuvenileJusticeSystem_15SEPT20.pdf.
37. Mark Lieberman, "Why Chronic Absenteeism Is a Budget Problem, Too," *Education Week*, May 13, 2024, https://www.edweek.org/leadership/why-chronic-absenteeism-is-a-budget-problem-too/2024/05.
38. Phyllis W. Jordan and Raegen Miller, *Who's In: Chronic Absenteeism Under the Every Student Succeeds Act* (FutureEd, 2017), https://www.future-ed.org/wp-content/uploads/2017/09/REPORT_Chronic_Absenteeism_final_v5.pdf.
39. Heinrich Mintrop and Gail L. Sunderman, "Predictable Failure of Federal Sanctions-Driven Accountability for School Improvement—and Why We May Retain It Anyway," *Educational Researcher* 38, no. 5 (June 1, 2009): 353–64, https://doi.org/10.3102/0013189X09339055.
40. Seth Gershenson, Alison Jacknowitz, and Andrew Brannegan, "Are Student Absences Worth the Worry in U.S. Primary Schools?," *Education Finance and Policy* 12, no. 2 (2017): 137–65; Michael A. Gottfried, "Evaluating the Relationship Between Student Attendance and Achievement in Urban Elementary and Middle Schools: An Instrumental Variables Approach," *American Educational Research Journal* 47, no. 2 (June 1, 2010): 434–65, https://doi.org/10.3102/0002831209350494.
41. Jennifer Booher-Jennings, "Below the Bubble: 'Educational Triage' and the Texas Accountability System," *American Educational Research Journal* 42, no. 2 (January 1, 2005): 231–68, https://doi.org/10.3102/00028312042002231.
42. Gershenson, Jacknowitz, and Brannegan, "Are Student Absences?"; Gottfried, "Evaluating the Relationship"; Michael A. Gottfried, "Chronic Absenteeism and Its Effects on Students' Academic and Socioemotional Outcomes," *Journal of Education for Students Placed at Risk* 19, no. 2 (2014): 53–75, https://doi.org/10.1080/10824669.2014.962696.
43. Gershenson, Jacknowitz, and Brannegan, "Are Student Absences?," 137.
44. David Tyack and Michael Berkowitz, "The Man Nobody Liked: Toward a Social History of the Truant Officer, 1840–1940," *American Quarterly* 29, no. 1 (1977): 31–54, https://doi.org/10.2307/2712260.
45. Peter Bergman and Eric W. Chan, "Leveraging Parents Through Low-Cost Technology: The Impact of High-Frequency Information on Student Achievement," *Journal of Human*

Resources 56, no. 1 (2021): 125–58, https://doi.org/10.3368/jhr.56.1.1118-9837R1; Zachary Himmelsbach et al., "Your Child Missed Learning the Alphabet Today: A Randomized Trial of Sending Teacher-Written Postcards Home to Reduce Absences," *Journal of Research on Educational Effectiveness* 15, no. 2 (April 3, 2022): 263–78, https://doi.org/10.1080/19345747.2021.1992812; Jessica Lasky-Fink et al., "Using Behavioral Insights to Improve School Administrative Communications: The Case of Truancy Notifications," *Educational Researcher* 50, no. 7 (October 1, 2021): 442–50, https://doi.org/10.3102/0013189X211000749; Carly D. Robinson et al., "Reducing Student Absenteeism in the Early Grades by Targeting Parental Beliefs," *American Educational Research Journal* 55, no. 6 (December 1, 2018): 1163–92, https://doi.org/10.3102/0002831218772274; Elise Swanson, *Results from Six Pilots in NCRERN's New York and Ohio Rural Research Network* (National Center for Rural Education Research Networks, 2022), https://ncrern.provingground.cepr.harvard.edu/sites/hwpi.harvard.edu/files/ncrern/files/ncrern_attendance_results.pdf?m=1667393939.

46. Yusuf Canbolat, "Early Warning for Whom? Regression Discontinuity Evidence from the Effect of Early Warning System on Student Absence," *Educational Evaluation and Policy Analysis*, published ahead of print, February 5, 2024, https://doi.org/10.3102/01623737231221503.
47. Steve E. Stemler et al., *An Evaluation of the Effectiveness of Home Visits for Re-engaging Students Who Were Chronically Absent in the Era of COVID-19* (Center for Connecticut Education Research Collaboration, December 31, 2022), https://portal.ct.gov/-/media/CCERC/Reports/CCERC-Exec-Summary-LEAP_FINAL.pdf.
48. Karen L. Mapp and Paul J. Kuttner, *Partners in Education: A Dual Capacity-Building Framework for Family–School Partnerships* (Austin, TX: SEDL, 2013), https://www2.ed.gov/documents/family-community/partners-education.pdf.
49. Felix Fernandez and Rachel Renbarger, "Increasing School District Capacity After COVID-19 Through Family and Community Collaboration: A Multiple Case Study Approach," *R&E Search for Evidence* (blog), June 28, 2024, https://researchforevidence.fhi360.org/increasing-school-district-capacity-covid-19-family-community-collaboration-multiple-case-study-approach.
50. Jing Liu and Monica Lee, "Beyond Chronic Absenteeism: The Dynamics and Disparities of Class Absences in Secondary School" (EdWorkingPaper 22-562, Annenberg Institute at Brown University, Providence, RI, 2022), https://edworkingpapers.org/sites/default/files/ai22-562.pdf; Daniel Hamlin, "Can a Positive School Climate Promote Student Attendance? Evidence from New York City," *American Educational Research Journal* 58, no. 2 (May 26, 2020): 315–42, https://doi.org/10.3102/0002831220924037; Sarah Winchell Lenhoff and Ben Pogodzinski, "School Organizational Effectiveness and Chronic Absenteeism: Implications for Accountability," *Journal of Education for Students Placed at Risk* 23, no. 1–2 (April 3, 2018): 153–69, https://doi.org/10.1080/10824669.2018.1434656.
51. Learning Heroes and TNTP, *Family Engagement Impact Study: Investigating the Relationship Between Pre-pandemic Family Engagement and Current Student and School Outcomes* (Learning Heroes and TNTP, 2024), https://bealearninghero.org/wp-content/uploads/2023/10/FACE-Impact-Study.pdf.
52. Stemler et al., *Evaluation of the Effectiveness*; Kimberly Stokes, Sarah Winchell Lenhoff, and Jeremy Singer, "Complicating the Role of Relationships in Reducing Student Absenteeism," *Child and Youth Services*, https://doi.org/10.1093/cs/cdae022.
53. Anthony S. Bryk, "Organizing Schools for Improvement," *Phi Delta Kappan* 91, no. 7 (April 1, 2010): 23–30, https://doi.org/10.1177/003172171009100705.

54. Rekha Balu and Stacy B. Ehrlich, "Making Sense Out of Incentives: A Framework for Considering the Design, Use, and Implementation of Incentives to Improve Attendance," *Journal of Education for Students Placed at Risk* 23, no. 1–2 (April 3, 2018): 93–106, https://doi.org/10.1080/10824669.2018.1438898.
55. Carly D. Robinson et al., "The Demotivating Effect (and Unintended Message) of Awards," *Organizational Behavior and Human Decision Processes* 163, published ahead of print, May 29, 2019, https://doi.org/10.1016/j.obhdp.2019.03.006.
56. Balu and Ehrlich, "Making Sense."
57. Kelley Fong, *Investigating Families: Motherhood in the Shadow of Child Protective Services* (Princeton, NJ: Princeton University Press, 2023); Ericka S. Weathers et al., "Absence Unexcused: A Systematic Review on Truancy," *Peabody Journal of Education* 96, no. 5 (October 20, 2021): 540–64, https://doi.org/10.1080/0161956X.2021.1991696.
58. Clea A. McNeely et al., "Long-Term Effects of Truancy Diversion on School Attendance: A Quasi-experimental Study with Linked Administrative Data," *Prevention Science* 20, no. 7 (October 1, 2019): 996–1008, https://doi.org/10.1007/s11121-019-01027-z.
59. Bergman et al., "Creating Moves to Opportunity"; Stefanie DeLuca, Lawrence F. Katz, and Sarah C. Oppenheimer, "'When Someone Cares About You, It's Priceless': Reducing Administrative Burdens and Boosting Housing Search Confidence to Increase Opportunity Moves for Voucher Holders," *RSF* 9, no. 5 (September 2023): 179–211, https://doi.org/10.7758/RSF.2023.9.5.08.
60. Nancy Carter et al., "Navigation Delivery Models and Roles of Navigators in Primary Care: A Scoping Literature Review," *BMC Health Services Research* 18, no. 1 (December 2018): 96, https://doi.org/10.1186/s12913-018-2889-0; Teri Browne et al., "Social Workers as Patient Navigators: A Review of the Literature," *Social Work Research* 39, no. 3 (September 1, 2015): 158–66, https://doi.org/10.1093/swr/svv017.
61. Jon Valant, "What Happens When Families Whose Schools Close Receive EdNavigator Support and OneApp Priority?" (policy brief, National Center for Research on Education Access and Choice, June 14, 2022), https://reachcentered.org/uploads/policybrief/REACH-EdNavigator-2022-06-14.pdf; Ashley Jochim, Georgia Heyward, and Betheny Gross, *Fulfilling the Promise of School Choice by Building More Effective Supports for Families* (Center for Reinventing Public Education, 2019), https://crpe.org/wp-content/uploads/crpe-fulfilling-promise-school-choice_0.pdf; Carolyn Sattin-Bajaj and Jennifer L. Jennings, "Homelessness and School Choice: Examining the School Choice Experiences of Families Living in Shelter," *Peabody Journal of Education* 97, no. 1 (January 1, 2022): 32–46, https://doi.org/10.1080/0161956X.2022.2026718.
62. Lenhoff et al., "Beyond the Bus"; Caryssa Lim et al., "School Attendance Following Receipt of Care from a School-Based Health Center," *Journal of Adolescent Health* 73, no. 6 (December 2023): 1125–31, https://doi.org/10.1016/j.jadohealth.2023.07.012; Sarah Winchell Lenhoff et al., *Detroit Schools Severely Under-identify Students Experiencing Homelessness and Housing Instability* (Detroit: Detroit Partnership for Education Equity and Research, 2023), https://detroitpeer.org/wp-content/uploads/2023/06/HomelessIdentificationJuneFinal.pdf.
63. Mavis G. Sanders and Adia Harvey, "Beyond the School Walls: A Case Study of Principal Leadership for School-Community Collaboration," *Teachers College Record* 104, no. 7 (2002): 1345–68, https://doi.org/10.1111/1467-9620.00206.
64. Sarah Winchell Lenhoff et al., "Community Development for Integrated Schools: The Detroit Choice Neighborhoods Initiative," in *Integration and Equity 2.0: New and*

Reinvigorating Approaches to School Integration (American Institutes for Research, 2023), 5.1-1–5.1-14.

65. Kysa Nygreen, "Reproducing or Challenging Power in the Questions We Ask and the Methods We Use: A Framework for Activist Research in Urban Education," *Urban Review* 38, no. 1 (March 2006): 1–26, https://doi.org/10.1007/s11256-006-0026-6; Jeannie Oakes, John Rogers, and Martin Lipton, *Learning Power: Organizing for Education and Justice*, John Dewey Lecture (New York: Teachers College Press, 2006).
66. Jeffrey R. Henig et al., *Putting Collective Impact in Context: A Review of the Literature on Local Cross-Sector Collaboration to Improve Education* (New York: Teachers College, Columbia University, 2015).

Acknowledgments

A project like this is not possible without a large, dedicated, brilliant team of scholars, educators, and community partners.

We want to thank our partners and friends in the Coalition—you know who you are. We have learned so much from you and with you, and we have grown as people and scholars because of your feedback, questions, support, and friendship. Our lives are forever changed because of you.

We want to thank our partners in the Detroit Public Schools Community District for inviting us to study chronic absenteeism and for allowing us to learn alongside you for nearly a decade. Approving research in a district that has faced so many challenges and so many doubters over the years is a brave and vulnerable thing to do, and we know it has often been uncomfortable. We hope that this book honors your hard work and commitment to the children of Detroit.

We want to thank our colleagues who contributed to the studies that we write about here, without whom this book would not have been possible. First, thank you to Ben Pogodzinski. Your vision and leadership helped to make a research partnership on chronic absenteeism possible, and we thank you for your innumerable contributions to this research. We also thank you for your friendship, which was steadfast through some of the most challenging times in our nation and in this work. We thank Erica Edwards for her brilliance and commitment to justice. Your expertise and passion made this work better, and we know we still have so much to learn from you. We thank Danica Brown, who joined us in the middle of the pandemic and became a leader and key contributor to this research. Your careful attention to detail made our work stronger.

We thank a team of research assistants and collaborators who contributed significantly to this work over the years, including Bianca Burch, Joi Claiborne, Walter Cook, Kate French, Sahar Khawaja, Bear Mahowald, Christina Stanojevich, and Kim Stokes.

We have also had the privilege to be supported informally by a community of scholars who contributed to our development and challenged us to do our best work, including Josh Childs, Tasmin Dhaliwal, Jennifer Erb-Downward, Josh Glazer, Michael Gottfried, Doug Harris, Ethan Hutt, Huriya Jabbar, Julie Marsh, Don Peurach, Linn Posey-Maddox, Katharine Strunk, Sheneka Williams, and Sarah Woulfin.

Thanks also to those who supported us at Wayne State University, especially Bill Hill and Julie Osburn.

Thank you to our families. Sarah thanks her parents, Becky and Dave Winchell, for their unwavering love and support. She also thanks her sister Jenny and brother-in-law Tim for always asking great questions, and for bringing little Sarah into the world with so much joy. We offer an additional shout-out to Jenny for inspiring our cover design. Sarah thanks the large, loving Lenhoff family, who made her their own and won't let go. Finally, she thanks her husband, Greg, and her children, Frances and Hazel, who have learned more about chronic absenteeism than they would ever want to know and, despite that, have been her loudest cheerleaders. Jeremy thanks his wife, Jenn; his parents, Marcie and David; and his sisters, Julie and Cara—as well as his friends and many extended family members—for all their support and encouragement, and for always taking interest in his research (and listening to him talk about it for a little bit longer than they probably anticipated).

We thank Punita Thurman, for championing an education-focused research center in Detroit and trusting us to build it. We also thank Terry Whitfield, for championing the Coalition and our work within it.

The research reported here was supported by the Spencer Foundation through Grant 202000154 and the Skillman Foundation through Grants 1806-2018000357, 1906-2018001501, 2006-2018002567, and 2107-2018003180 to Wayne State University. The parent surveys were supported in part by the Institute of Education Sciences, US Department of Education, through Grant R305C180025 to the Administrators of the Tulane Educational Fund. We also received funding from the Midwest Mobility from Poverty Network, community-based organizations affiliated with the Coalition, and Wayne State University. The opinions expressed are those of the authors and do not represent views of the Institute of Education Sciences, the US Department of Education, or any other funders, partners, or collaborators.

About the Authors

Sarah Winchell Lenhoff is the Leonard Kaplan Endowed Professor and an associate professor of educational leadership and policy studies at Wayne State University. She is the founding director of the Detroit Partnership for Education Equity & Research. She began her career as a New York City Public Schools teacher and earned her PhD in educational policy at Michigan State University. Before joining the faculty at Wayne State, she served as the director of research and policy at the Education Trust-Midwest. Her research examines how education and other social policies shape access to educational opportunity in urban public schools. In addition to attendance and chronic absenteeism, she has studied school choice, school improvement and reform, and the connection between neighborhoods and educational opportunity.

Jeremy Singer is an assistant research professor at Wayne State University and associate director of the Detroit Partnership for Education Equity & Research. Jeremy began his career in education and in Detroit as a teacher in the Detroit Public Schools. He completed his PhD in educational leadership and policy studies at Wayne State University and served as a postdoctoral research fellow with the Education Policy Innovation Collaborative at Michigan State University. As a researcher, he focuses broadly on the intersections between education policy and racial and socioeconomic inequality. In addition to attendance and chronic absenteeism, he has studied school choice, school improvement, and the relationship between housing and education.

Index